PARADIGM SHIFT IN HEALTH AND EDUCATION IN INDIA

PARADIGM SHIFT IN HEALTH AND EDUCATION IN INDIA

Edited by

K. Gangadharan

SERIALS PUBLICATIONS

NEW DELHI (INDIA)

First Published – 2009

ISBN: 978-81-8387-282-9

Published by

SERIALS PUBLICATIONS
4800/24, 1st Floor, Ansari Road
Darya Ganj, New Delhi-110002 (India)
Phone : 23245225. Fax : 91-11-23272135
E-mail: serials@satyam.net.in

CONTENTS

Section–II
EDUCATION

FOREWORD

This book is the outcome of a national conference entitled Policy Reforms in Education and Health and the Share of the Poor in India organized by the Department of Applied Economics, Kannur University on September 12th and 13th 2007. This is an edited compendium of 13 research papers contributed by eminent scholars in the area of health economics and education economics. The present volume is the opening of a window through which the reader can have glimpse of some of the facets of policies and programmes in the field of Health and education that implemented in India for the last 6 decades and also its impacts and loopholes which culminated in paradigm shift in the health and education development of India.

The subject of health and education is vast and complex. It is multidimensional and multidisciplinary. The expertise and experience of the contributor's are manifested in dealing with the subject authoritatively. The contributors of the papers have tried to analyze the causes for the educational and health deprivations of the people in India and suggested strategies and options for the educational and health empowerment. The volume gets enriched with the inclusion of papers like morbidity and healthcare, elementary and general education for the poor, paradigm shift in education and health etc. The book as a whole provides an excellent material for strengthening the informed decision making process and for formulating development policies and evolving suitable strategies for the health and education development of the vulnerable and deprived sections in India.

The volume is a valuable addition to the growing literature on the subject. I take this opportunity to congratulate Dr.K.Gangadharan in his sincere effort of publishing a fifth book and also for bringing this useful and timely publication in the area of health and education for the benefit of students, researchers, planners, administrators, policy makers and general public interested in the education and health development of India.

Mangattuparamba,
30.5.2008

DR. P. CHANDRAMOHAN
Vice-Chancellor
Kannur University

PREFACE

The post war models of development emphasized on accumulation of physical capital and expenditure on education and health was considered as a drain on accumulation of productive asset. But later the new classical growth models, endogenous growth models and others recognized investment in human capital and treated it as similar to investment in land, physical and financial capital.

The policy reform introduced since 1991 has proved the way for changing the economic climate of India. There has been a lot of debate about how much India's poor have shared in the economic growth particularly in during the economic reform period. Though overall rate of poverty has come down, there is considerable diversity in performance across the states. It is in India that has the world largest illiterate and HIV infected population. Based on life expectancy, access to education and standard of living their human development is ranked lower than that of many countries with comparable or even lower per capita income. It is also in India where the disparity in human development is very high across the states.

There is need to study together the issues relating in education and health. These two sectors are interrelated and educational development improves healthcare. Traditionally public sector has played an important role in financing educational and health services in India. But in recent years a paradigm shift occurred in the financing and prioritization of health and education sector of the country which created a severe threat to the health and education empowerment of the weaker and deprived sections of the society. The extent and pattern of public sector contribution to educational health services has changed very drastically and it adversely affected the human development of the country.

It is against this backdrop that the Department of Applied economics, Kannur University had organized a two day national conference on Policy Reforms in Education and Health and the share of the poor in India. Though more than 50 research papers were presented and extensively discussed in different thematic sessions, after a preliminary review only 14 papers were selected and substantially updated and revised in response to the insightful comments of the peer team. The present volume is an effort in this direction and a serious attempt is made to assess and analyze the extent and distributing pattern of public as well as private investment in education and health sector of the country. The book focuses on the issues and challenges of the education and health sector of the country and it also deals with the issues connected with the health and education empowerment of marginal and vulnerable section of Indian society. The book also reveals the real and possible impact of explicit policies in these sectors.

The book is divided into two sections. Section I deals with health and section II deals with education. The volume begins with an introductory section, an overview and a chapter on Health, Education and human development. Thus all the papers connected with health are arranged in this section and the papers related with education are arranged in the second section on Education.

The book is addressed to a wide audience including students, teachers, researchers, policy makers and general readers. Sincere and earnest effort has been made to provide data based analytical perspective in analyzing issues with latest development wherever possible. An extensive bibliography at the end of each chapter has also been included for those who wish to use the book as a starting point for further empirical research.

This book is an outcome of the collaborative effort of 13 scholars who have made significant research contribution on the health and education development of India. I am very much grateful to all of them for their valuable contribution to the volume. Special mention may be made of the Prof. (Dr.) M H Suryanarayana, Professor Indira Gandhi Institute Development Research, Mumbai, Prof. (Dr.) M. D. Ushadevi Professor, Centre for Human Resource Development, Institute for Social and Economic Change, Bangalore, Professor (Dr.) G. V. Joshi, Professor and Chairman, Department of Economics, Mangalore University, Mangalore, Prof. (Dr.) Harikumar, Professor, Department of Applied Economics ,CUSAT , Cochin. I take this opportunity to express my sincere gratitude to all of them. With deep sense of gratitude I express my sincere thanks to Dr. P. Chandramohan, Vice-Chancellor, Kannur University who practically guided us at every point of time to organize this conference, for imparting all sorts of academic ambience for the publication of this book and also for writing a valuable foreword to this volume. I also express my gratitude to all my colleagues including Johnson K.A, Shaharban, and Rejula Helan who made tireless efforts in organizing the National Conference. I thank Sri. K. P. Vipin Chandran, Doctoral Scholar of my department and faculty colleague who rendered immense help in bringing out this publication. I thank Serials Publications, New Delhi for their cooperation in bringing out this volume.

Mangattuparamba, K. GANGADHARAN
30.5.2008

LIST OF CONTRIBUTORS

K. Gangadharan, is Reader and Head, School of Development Studies, Department of Applied Economics, Kannur University, Kerala.

M. H. Suryanarayana, is Professor, Indira Gandhi Institute of Development Research (IGIDR), Gen. Vaidya Marg, Goregaon (East), Mumbai-400 065.

T. R. Dilip, is Lecturer, Centre for Development Studies, Ulloor, Trivandrum-695011.

V. Anbumani, is Professor, Department of Economics, Bharathiar University, Coimbatore, Tamilnadu.

M. Saravanakumar, is a Doctoral Scholar, Department of Economics, Bharathiar University, Coimbatore, Tamilnadu.

K. P. Vipin Chandran, is a Doctoral Scholar, Department of Applied Economics, Kannur University-670661, Kerala.

M. D. Usha Devi, is Professor & Head, Centre for Human Resource Development, Institute for Social & Economic Change (ISEC), Bangalore.

S. Harikumar, is Professor & Head, Department of Applied Economics, Cochin University of Science and Technology (CUSAT), Cochin, Kerala.

T. Remadevi, is Selection Grade Lecturer, Department of Economics. Government College, Attingal, Kollam, Kerala.

M. D. Devasia, is Selection Grade Lecturer, Post Graduate Department of Economics, Nirmalagiri College, Koothuparambu, Kannur, Kerala.

G.V. Joshi, is Professor & Chairman, Department of Economics, Mangalore University, Mangalore, Karnataka.

K. Mallikarjuna Reddy, is Head, Department of History, Sri Krishnadevaraya University, Anantapur, Andhra Pradesh.

T. K. Sebastian, is Lecturer, Post Graduate Department of Economics, Nirmalagiri College, Koothuparambu, Kannur, Kerala.

M. C. Rosa, is Lecturer, School of Pedagogical Sciences, Kannur University, Kerala.

Section–I

HEALTH

Chapter-1

INTRODUCTION AND OVERVIEW

K. Gangadharan

Health and education are two important aspects of human resource development. Good health care facilities and educational services are essential for creating a healthy citizens and a learned society that can effectively contribute to better human resource development and thereby social and economic development. With increased urbanization, industrialization and the changing environment, health and education related problems and issues are being emphasized and have become a great concern for the contemporary world.

The postwar models of development emphasized on a accumulation of physical capital and expenditure on health and education was considered as a drain on accumulation of productive assets. But later the new classical growth models, endogenous growth models and other recognized investment in human capital and treat it as similar to investment in land, physical and financial capital.

The policy reform introduced since 1991 has proved the way for changing the economic climate of India. There has been a lot of debate about how much of India's poor have shared in the economic growth particularly in during the economic reform period. Though overall rate of poverty has comedown there is considerable diversity in performance across the states.

It is India that has the world's largest illiterate and HIV infected population. Based on its life expectancy, access to education and standard living the Indian human development is ranked lower than that of many countries with comparable or lower GDP per capita. It is also in India; disparity in human development is very high across the states.

There is need to study together the issues relating to in education and health. These two sectors are interrelated and educational development improves healthcare. Traditionally public sector has played an important role in financing educational and health services in India. But in recent years this has changed. The extent and pattern of public sector contribution to education and health services has changed very drastically. In the changed environment it requires to be examined whether the share of public subsidies in these tow sectors are progressive or not. This is to find out whether beneficiaries in the lower socio-economic groups are proportionately higher. The present volume is an attempt in this direction to examine and analyze the extent and distributive pattern of investment, public as well as private in education and health sectors and to assess the real and possible impact of explicit policies in these sectors The volume also examine the hike in the morbidity load of the country especially in the era of health sector reform and especially in the era of expansion of private hospitals and also the threats of nutritional deprivation in India. The present volume is based on 13 papers contributed by eminent scholars in the filled of education and health that discuss the problems and challenges that emerged in the educational and health sector of the country as a paradigm shift in the new millennium.

The volume starts with a paper by **K. Gangadharan** on "Paradigm shift in Health and Education in India". This paper examined the education and health investment that the country made in the last 6 decades and the extent of improvement that gained in the area of human development through better health care and education. The paper also deals with the problems associated with the health and education development in India and also examined the impacts caused due to the shortage of investment in the basic social sector segments of the country. The paper reveals that for proper human development along with economic development, social sectors must be linked with the engine of economic growth and in this regard a paradigm shift occurred in the health and educational development of India.. Social services provide a better chance of self expression and for community recreation. Social services are the tools of human resource development and all development in the ultimate sense should culminate in human resources improvement and thereby human development. There is urgent need to fill in the gaps in the health and education sectors in India as they have a lasting effect on the quality of life of the people of the country. The paper suggests that policy makers, planners, administrators and politicians should realize that augmenting the quality of population through better education and better health care will provide a sound edifice for rapid and sustained economic development.

The paper "Nutrition and health Transition: Lessons from Kerala" by **K. Gangadharan** made an attempt to correlate the nutritional deprivation that occurred Kerala recently and the consequent hike in morbidity in Kerala especially among children. The study is fully based on the recent three NFHS data which provides details of nutritional deprivation that occurred in India for the last one decade. The paper reveals that compared to Kerala, our neighbour state Tamilnadu has improved their position better with regard to the proportion of total anemic children, stunted, and wasted and underweight children. In the case of maternal mortality also Tamilnadu has improved their potion compared to their position in 1990's.

M. H. Suryanarayana in his paper "Morbidity and healthcare in Kerala: A distributional profile and implications" examined the pattern and intensity of morbidity both acute and chronic and also the distributive pattern of morbidity among different segments of the society in Kerala. The study ponders the basic reasons behind the hike in morbidity in Kerala when the country has initiated a series of economic reform measures. As regards the morbidity in the State of Kerala, despite its remarkable achievements in levels of human development why morbidity is high in Kerala? What would be the welfare implications of such high levels of morbidity in Kerala in the wake of economic reform and privatization of health care? The implications of these new reforms measure would depend upon the incidence of illness across socio-economic characteristics and their relative access to health care facilities. This paper examined these issues pertaining to the health sector in Kerala in a larger comparative perspective in the Indian context.

The chapter by **T. R. Dillip** on "Consolidation of Private Hospitals in Kerala: Policy Implications" examined the threat to equity in the inpatient care facilities in the eve of expansion of private hospitals in Kerala. The study is an attempt to understand the characteristics of private hospitals and equity in accessing them, using secondary data available for the period 1986-2004. The study reveals that private hospitals did not expand in numbers but a strong consolidation by large hospitals. Public policy favoring increased private sector participation in medical education coupled with opening of super specialty hospitals has lead to a situation where small hospitals or nursing homes loosing their significance and a large number them have been phased out. Annual Hospitalization rates showed a rise in demand for hospitalization care facilities across this time period. Rich-poor divide in potential to seek care from private hospitals highest during 1995-96, but declined marginally in 2004. The paper concludes that overall economic marginalization and over-whelming dominance of the private sector across time has resulted in low social groups getting more and more restricted access to private hospitals.

The chapter on "Policy Reforms and Health Sector in India" by **V. Anbumanai and M. Saravanakumar** examined the impacts of economic reforms on the health sector of India. According to them health sector reforms are part of economic reforms and health sector reforms have been implemented in an effort to improve health services management and supervision. These reforms are intended to decentralize health systems, reduce bureaucracy, and increase cost-effectiveness and efficiency by reorganizing services, streamlining management, and allocating resources to better meet local needs. The paper reveals that alternate ways of financing health care should receive policy attention in a major way. Clearly there is scope of formulating demand side financing mechanisms so as to provide access to poor. Private sector should be seen as a national asset and alternate service delivery systems e.g. social franchising should be considered. It is also critical to work with private sector in terms of certification and accreditation systems. Thus, within available resources we can move towards achieving the optimum in health services for all Indians, given the resolve to rethink prevailing paradigms and take some hard steps.

K. P. Vipinchandran in his paper "Malnourished Indian Children: The Post Reform Scenario" examined the nutritional deprivation in India that worsened recently especially in the eve of economic reforms. The 1990s witnessed widespread economic reforms and liberalization in India. The background of his paper is that much of the discussions on the effects of economic reforms in India have been centered on the sequential movement in the poverty and inequality magnitudes. General under nutrition, characterized by under-weight among children is more prevalent amongst rural children, scheduled castes and tribes, and amongst children with illiterate mothers. After India became independent in 1947, several steps were taken for the improvement of the health situation and well-being of its citizens. But still child malnutrition is a major problem in India. According to NFHS-3 (2005-06), 46 per cent of India's children under the age of three are underweight. The major responsible factors underlying these are household food insecurity, inadequate preventive and curative health care services, and poor perception of health care. The present challenges of communicable diseases and maternal and child survival reveal the weaknesses of the health system. The paper reveals the differences in the levels of undernourishment that vary widely across Indian states. The states like Punjab, Kerala, Jammu Kashmir, and Tamilnadu report the lowest proportions of underweight children (27 to 33%); whereas Chhattisgarh,

Bihar, Jharkhand, and Madhya Pradesh report the highest levels of underweight children (52 to 60%). Economic growth and continuation of existing programmes will not be sufficient to overcome the problem of child malnutrition in particular.

M. D. Usha Devi's chapter on "Elementary education for the vulnerable and marginalized children: The current strategies and the ground realities" discusses the goals, intensions, ground realities and the need for a different policy frame work to address the issues pertaining to the educational of marginalized and deprived sections of Indian society. Within the framework of Millennium Development Goals and Education for All, one of the major concerns is to achieve universal primary education by 2015 along with improvements in education in the developing countries including India. The paper reveals that over the years, there have been substantial investments for improving infrastructure facilities, physical, material and human resources in education sector. Capacities of schools, teachers and educational functionaries have also seen considerable augmentation as a result of concerted efforts by the state and the union governments through enhanced resource support. In order to address issues relating to education of the marginalized population segments, a wide array of alternative and innovative education programmes have been on the anvil across the states in India to impart elementary education.

Under the national flagship programme of Sarva Shiksha Abhiyan Mission, the education of the marginalized groups has received further impetus. The mission mode approach to elementary education indeed has been able to raise educational awareness in communities and mobilize enrolment of children in schools, even from the marginalized sections. However, the flipside of the national and state efforts in the field of elementary education suggests that problems continue to persist in India albeit in different forms. The paper categorically reveals that while the mainstream schools continue to experience the problem of low retention, irregular attendance and poor quality of educational outcomes, the alternative and innovative educational interventions aimed at educating the

6-14 age group boys and girls from the marginalized sections riddled with problems of huge shortfalls in enrolment, low retention and poor quality of teaching learning.

The chapter by **S. Harikumar and T. Ramadevi** presents the need for internationalization of higher education to meet the needs of fast moving global economy by capturing the benefits of technological progress. The paper highlights the need for revamping technical education in the Kerala perspectives since Kerala has been identified as a state suffering from high educated unemployment. The paper provides a detailed analysis of the influence of globalization, knowledge revolution and information technology on education. The paper reveals that the globalization of the economy has led to globalization of higher education. The higher education institutions everywhere are subject to global trends. The impact of new communication technology, accountability of academic intuitions to government, an increasingly international and mobile academic profession, global research network etc. are the features of global higher education. Globalization has brought about a shift from manufacturing economies to knowledge economies as a result of which the knowledge content of production has grown. In knowledge based production the sale of ideas has a higher premium than goods. Education, no doubt, enhances human capacity and choices to improve the knowledge content of production.

The paper reveals that the impact of globalization, knowledge economy and IT Revolution on education and employment lead to the conclusion that the state cannot afford to set up its target for enrolments on the basis of manpower requirement within the state. The products of our educational system are for the global market. There is in essence an internationalization of human capital. In a growth led employment approach the prospects for generating employment depends on the growth rate and composition of the GNP. The experience of Kerala in general, has shown that the output growth in different sectors has not been able to absorb the backlog of the unemployed because of lower and more declining employment output elasticity .So the state has to find economically feasible alternatives for the productive employment of the products of education. Education that helps to make workers more flexible and adaptable to new technologies is now considered a valuable way of contributing to manpower development just as much as education that prepares them for specific jobs. The Information Age records one of the master narratives of our times and the market prefers only those graduates who have practical application of knowledge. In Kerala the system of education fails to meet the global challenges. Technology, particularly substantially knowledge based technologies such as IT will thrive only in the ambiance of excellence in higher learning, and scientific research. Kerala educational system does not appear to be adequate in this regard. The failure to diversify and modernize our system of education, comes at a time when the state's economy is getting integrated with the global economy which is becoming increasingly knowledge-driven. In that sense the paper reveals the need for the reorientation of the educational system in Kerala towards the emerging demands of the economy.

Devassia M. D. in his paper "Pricing Higher Education: How to bridge equity and affordability" made an attempt to suggest a pricing method for higher education sector of the state. The paper is arranged in IV sections. Section I gives an introduction that narrates the context and relevance of the issue and a note on database and methodology. Section II analyses the important concepts like equity, quality, affordability, cost and pricing in the very context of Kerala economy. Section III is devoted to derive an appropriate pricing method to resolve the crisis and section IV gives a brief summary of the findings. The paper reveals the stark reality about Kerala in the sense that although, more than 90% of the population is literate, youth enrollment in higher education is abysmally low in Kerala. Manpower planning has not received the due attention. Opening of Self-financing colleges is suggested as a remedy for resource crunch government to finance for Higher Education to provide adequate facilities and maintenance of quality. But it is alleged that, the cost of education in such institutions will be unaffordable to poor students and that will result in the simple eviction of them however meritorious they may be. Consequently, a lot of State's energy and scarce finance has been drained so far on this issue through arbitration, litigation, campaign, street war and struggle. The present paper an attempt is made to suggest a pricing method for higher education sector of the State, so as to bridge equity, quality, cost and affordability in the provision of higher education.

G. V. Joshi's chapter on "Taking general higher education to the poor and the role of the state" reveals the strong demographic dividend that India possesses due to the hike in the working age group in the population of the country. He postulates that if this dividend is reaped there is every possibility of India joining the group of developed countries by 2020. First the percentage of people in the working age group would be higher in India than most of the developed countries over the next 30-50 years. This is because India's population growth has come down significantly in recent years where as it is used to be much higher in earlier periods.

The paper reveals that even China will experience labour shortage in the next decades because of the belated effect of the strict one child norm imposed much earlier. So, India may be more favorably placed in terms of its age composition of the population. Our dependency ratio is falling whereas in industrialized countries and even in China it is rising. The presence of a skilled young population in an environment where investment is expanding and industrial would is ageing could be a major advantage. It is important to realize however that we can only reap this demographic dividend if we invest on human resource development and skill productive employment for our relatively young working population. Growth without jobs can neither be inclusive nor can it bridge divides. All avenues for increasing employment opportunities including these that can be provided by micro and small enterprises need to be explored. The paper warns that if we fail to do so, the demographic dividend turns into a demographic nightmare. The paper reveals that it is Deemed Universities, Foreign Universities, autonomous colleges, fully self-financed colleges, fully self-financed courses and minority colleges- all of these have discriminatory standards that nullify our dreams of general higher education. Any withdrawal of the state from this field would amount to denying general higher education to the poor. Only the state funded and the state controlled colleges and Universities could at least provide avenues of general higher education to the poor. The Universities in India should not go to the market just for the sake of making profits or in the name of privatization. It is obvious that a regulator or an authority of any kind, a university included, cannot and should not be held by a few shareholders seeking profits. Instead it must continue to be held by public at large via the structure of government. The ills, if any rising out of such an ownership structure of lack of autonomy or financial allocation must be handled head on and not via such alternatives that may lead us all to poverty of money and knowledge. In the name of reforms the state should not withdraw from the higher general education. For carrying our reforms to successful conclusion it will have to change its methods of support to higher general education. The paper concludes by categorically stating that the task of taking General Higher Education to the doorsteps of the poor calls for greater involvement of the state which in term would necessitate greater financial commitment and careful planning of the Central and State Government's. This financial commitment and planning may have to be periodically monitored and reviewed to ensure the optimum utilization of financial resources as also to guarantee quality of higher education in the interest of the poor in India.

The chapter by **K. Mallikarjuna Reddy** "Riddles of Higher Education Policy- A Reminder" reveals the wide inequality in the educational status among the rural and urban. The urban elites as a group are able to attain all the benefits of higher education, at the same time the rural deprived sections are totally alienated from the attainments of fruits of higher and general education. The paper reveals that the European system of higher education was introduced to India by the British in 1857 with the establishment of Universities for European education in Bombay, Calcutta and Madras. Although modeled after the University of London, these Universities were not meant to be institutions for the advancement of knowledge or full-fledged centers of higher learning. The British government had established them with two limited objectives; To introduce the Indian elite to European culture and thus to colonize the country culturally; To produce of cadre of Indians equipped to serve the British administration in India and to practice the professions of law, medicine and teaching as required by the British.

These twin aims set the tone of Indian higher education in the later half of the nineteenth century. Today the colonizers agenda seems very shocking but more shocking is its insidious impact on our country held view of higher education. Although higher education project in India began with the echoes of most inspiring sentiments, it was essentially anchored in the exclusionist, elitist idea of education of the colonial rulers. As a consequences, this idea ended up in splitting our country into two radically different worlds, one that is India in which the urban elites got the themselves entrenched and enjoyed all the privileges of modern state and the other, that is Bharat consisted largely of rural population, was kept away from any benefits that are associated with higher education in India. English as a medium of instruction for higher learning brought about this split. The mastery of English language is implicit in current discourse of higher education in the country and an authentic alternative model of higher education in the country cannot but subscribe to the breaking of the English language monopoly at the centers of our higher learning and replace English with the major vernacular language of the country. The paper concludes by highlighting the need for reinterpreting the idea of higher education at the earliest.

T. K. Sebastian in his paper "Education–An invisible capital: Evidences from migrated cultivators in Malabar", The two way relationship between the economic standard and education suggests that, as in the case of nations, families may enter either into virtuous cycle of high economic standard and large gains in education, or a vicious cycle of low economic standards and low rates of education. In the first case, the level of economic standard and education are mutually reinforcing each other leading towards an upward spiral of development. In the second case, if persists long, the households may fall into a poverty trap. The existence and persistence of these cycles depend on the strength of the linkages between the two variables. Households may also find themselves into a lopsided state, with relatively good economic potentials in physical terms but poor education or vice versa. Financially weak could not afford to avail the modern job oriented education, which, in turn, block the economic attainments.The relative educational immobility observed among the sons/daughters of low educated ancestors support the above hypothesis. Supporting evidence is the sons/daughters of CL are facing the problem of relative immobility in occupation. These education -economic standard linkages are connected to the household inability to free the children at school going age to go to school, due to the high subsistence value of the time for the household concerned.

M. C. Rosa's chapter on "Dalit education for the upliftment of society" argues for providing better educational access and facilities for dalits. She reveals that in India scheduled castes are a stigmatized lot and on this account they suffer from a number of disabilities. Some of their disabilities are untouchability, segregation, low economic status, politically less powerful, low level of education and little chances of modernization. Though legally sand constitutionally they are no longer untouchables, in practice many of them still bear that stigma. Education is the strong instrument for eradicating all these inequalities. For the proper development of the society the downtrodden should be brought to the mainstream of society. The term Dalit has been used to include all those people of different communities among the scheduled caste who were traditionally subjected to individual discrimination on grounds of untouchability and categorized as untouchables, downtrodden, exterior caste, depressed classes or dalits. Educational dropouts among the dalits is too much and it is mainly due to financial problem, domestic work including the care of infants, prolonged illness of the child, negative attitude of teachers, lack of interest in studies and alcoholism and drug abuse etc. Poverty is also suggested as an important reason for high dropouts among dalits in primary and high school level of education. She also provides some suggestions for the betterment and empowerment of dalits in the educational sphere.

CHAPTER-2

PARADIGM SHIFT IN HEALTH AND EDUCATION

K. Gangadharan

Human Capital formation plays a vital role in economic development. The knowledge and skills that individuals acquire and the institutional framework in which these gets deployed together determine an economy's capacity to prosper. This is all the more relevant in the knowledge economy, in which the prime determinant of value is the knowledge wielded by workers (Dash, 2007). The classical economist Adam smith considered the high potential, abilities and ambience on the part of individuals as a sort of capital. Irving Fisher moves a step ahead and treats capital as all-inclusive. Schultz considered human beings as part and parcel of the wealth of nations. Investment in people can enlarge the range of choice available to them. Unless societies recognize that their real wealth is their people, an excessive obsession with the creation of material wealth can obscure the ultimate objective of enriching human lives (Human Development Report 1994).

Economic growth without improving the quality of life of the people is meaningless. The every existence of pure drinking water, provision of education, provision of sanitation and housing provision and accessibility for health care service etc. are the very basis on which the quality of life and progress of human development of a country depends. It is also proved that many advanced countries experienced that investment in health and education accelerate growth in terms of Gross Domestic Product. Though this is the case, the investment pattern that followed in India since the inception of the planning era reveals that education and health has not received much attention and is neglected though the economists and social scientists argue for heavy investment in social sectors. The health and Education sector in India has undergone a paradigm shift since the reform era which culminated in a fall in the Human Development. The paper reveals that for proper human development along with economic development, social sectors especially education and health must be linked with the engine of economic growth and in this regard a paradigm shift occurred in the health and educational development of India.

HEALTH

Good health is not only an outcome of increase in income but is also a determinant of the latter. Apart from governing, the core of human well being, health itself promotes development via increase in productivity and hence income, which is known as health income linkages. The improvement in the health status of people is essential to sustain economic and social development.

The majority of the people living in India have yet to reach the utopian ideal of the health for all, despite many decades of planning and implementation programmes. Successive governments in India have over the past five decades, proposed and implemented many schemes for the provision of safe water, sanitation, and nutrition and vaccination coverage. Yet millions do not have access to these basic needs. The recent NFHS data (NFHS III 2005-06) reveals that 48% of Indian children are anemic and 40% of children are under weight. Vaccination coverage is inadequate and only 43.5% children below five years were undergone for all the basic vaccinations. Table 1 clearly reveals the differentials in health status across the country, and it reveals that the conditions of health is very deplorable in poor performing states like Orissa, Bihar, Rajasthan, Uttarpradesh and Madhyapradesh and also

West Bengal and many North Eastern States including Assam and Tripura. Even after 6 decades of planned development health status of these states are very poor in terms of the basic indicators of health.

DEMAND AND SUPPLY OF HEALTH SERVICES

Despite substantial improvement in key health indicators since independence the burden of disease in India attributable to preventable, communicable diseases remains extremely high. Recent estimates shows that India comprises 19% of disease burden globally measured using Disability Adjusted Life years[1] (WHO 1999). It is generally agreed that in order to continue the downward trend in mortality and morbidity indicators, in particular for women and children, rapid improvements in access to good quality essential health services such as immunization and emergency obstetric care is required particularly in the BIMARU[2] States.

Ensuring that sick individuals receive the care they need depends on two broad factors: First the availability of health services (i.e. supply) and secondly the health seeking behavior (i.e. demand). The extent and way in which supply and demand interact or do not will determine to a significant degree the extent to which the burden of disease reduces.

The amount of health service supplied in a country is influenced partly its level of wealth, but also the priority given to it. Compared with countries of broadly equivalent income levels[3], India has similar number of doctors (both in the public and private sectors) but relatively low number of nursing staff (Table 2).

Table 2
Supply of Health Professionals India International Comparisons

Country	*Doctors per 1,00,000 Population*	*Nurses per 1,00,000 Population*
India	45	112
Pakistan	57	34
Bosnia Herzegovina	143	452
Zimbabwe	14	129
Tonga	44	315

Table 1
Differentials in Health Status among Major States

	IMR	*Under five Mortality*	*Percentage of under Weight* Children*	*Percentage of stunted children*	*Diabetic (Per one lakh women)*	*Asthma*	*Diabetic (Per one lakh men)*	*Asthma*	*All basic vaccination*
India	57	74.3	42.5	48	881	1696	1051	1627	43.5
Punjab	41.7	52.0	24.9	36.7	849	945	802	802	60.1
Rajasthan	65.3	85.4	39.9	43.7	282	1565	362	1739	26.5
M.P	69.5	94.2	60.0	50.0	558	1283	555	1102	40.3
Uttarpradesh	72.7	96.4	42.4	56.8	383	1089	456	1225	23.0
Bihar	61.7	84.8	55.9	55.6	1024	1696	940	981	32.8
Orissa	64.7	90.6	40.7	45.0	556	2533	1179	1592	51.8
West Bengal	48.9	59.6	38.7	44.6	1641	3304	2323	4365	64.3
Meghalaya	44.6	70.5	48.8	55.1	910	1618	641	746	32.9
Assam	66.1	85.0	36.4	46.5	402	1411	601	1105	31.4
Tripura	51.5	59.2	39.6	35.7	1656	5924	2392	5086	49.7
Maharashtra	37.5	46.7	37.0	46.3	479	1714	906	1855	58.8
Gujarath	49.7	60.9	44.6	51.7	968	1530	524	1844	45.2
Andhra	53.5	63.2	32.5	42.7	838	2151	2116	2189	46.0
Karnataka	43.2	54.7	37.6	43.7	681	1259	973	691	55.0
Kerala	15.3	16.3	22.9	24.5	2549	4037	3078	2984	75.3
Tamil Nadu	30.4	35.5	29.8	30.9	2188	1126	1351	687	80.9

*Includes children who are below -3 standard deviation from the International Reference Population Median.

Source: NFHS-3.

Table 3
Total Government Allopathic Hospitals including CHCS and Bed Ratio to population

States and UTs	*Total No. of Govt. Hospital*	*Total No. of Govt. Hospital Beds*	*Population served per Govt. Hospitals*	*Population served per Govt. Hospital Bed*
Andhra Pradesh	521	35021	154376	2297
Arunachal Pradesh	66	2053	17500	562
Assam	100	3000	280500	9350
Bihar	101	3030	869406	28980
Chattigarh	138	5565	159500	3955
Goa	20	2639	74650	566
Gujarat	503	35056	108974	1564
Hariyana	133	71187	170444	3185
Himachal Pradesh	141	7786	45106	817
Jammu division	36	1700		
Kashmir division	40	1595		
Jharkand	47	1410	602191	20073
Karnataka	723	413.4	76744	1343
Kerala	189	25839	177614	1299
MadhyaPradesh	324	17702	186373	3411
Maharashtra	1170	76447	86560	1325
Manipur	28	670	91464	3822
Meghalaya	30	2157	80367	1118
Mizoram	20	1169	47150	807
Nagaland	48	2060	43938	1024
Orissa	406	13146	96190	2971
Punjab	160	8773	158350	2824
Rajasthan	510	32080	120176	1910
Sikkim	7	730	82714	793
TamilNadu	424	43567	153917	1498
Tripura	26	2231	129808	1513
U.P	294	8820	601241	20041
Uttaranchal	36	1080	247917	8264
W.Bengal	642	58516	131924	1447
A.N. Island	8	897	48125	424
Chandigarh	7	2200	138428	
Dadra & Nagar Haveli	2	105	121000	23.5
Daman & Diu	4	192	42500	585
Delhi	165	20368	144076	743
Lakshwadeep	5	160	1300	406
Pondicherry	15	3173	68467	2336
Total	7029	469559	156088	2336

Source: Govt. of India (2005) Health Information. India, Ministry of Health and Family Welfare, New Delhi.

Table 4
Percentage Deliveries Attended by a Health Personnel

State	*Deliveries Attended by a Health Personnel*
India	46.6
Delhi	64.1
Hariyana	48.9
Himachal Pradesh	47.8
Jammu & Kashmir	56.5
Punjab	68.2
Rajasthan	41.0
Uttranchal	38.5
Chattisgarh	41.6
M.P	32.7
Uttarpradesh	27.2
Bihar	29.3
Jharkhad	27.8
Orissa	44.0
West Bengal	47.6
Arunachal Pradesh	30.2
Assam	31.0
Manipur	59.0
Meghalaya	31.1
Mizoram	65.4
Nagaland	24.7
Sikkim	53.7
Tripura	48.8
Goa	94.0
Gujarath	63.0
Maharashtra	68.7
A.P.	74.9
Karnataka	69.7
Kerala	99.1
Tamil Nadu	90.6

Source: NFHS-3, 2005-06

Table 3 shows the supply of health services in terms of the density of Government Hospitals including primary health centers/across The Indian States. Table 4 presents the percentage of births/deliveries attended by health personnel. Among the major states Himachal Pradesh, Rajasthan, West Bengal, etc. have largest density of Govt Hospitals (Table 3) but it reveals that they are having relatively low level of birth attended by a health professionals (Table 4), one of the most important strategies needed for the reduction of maternal and infant mortality. The available data revealed that in West Bengal only 47.6% and Rajasthan 41.6% and H.P only 47.8% of births were attended by health professionals.

DEMAND FOR HEALTH SERVICE IN INDIA

The data revealed by the Table 3. And Table 4 suggests that simply establishing a health facility in a particular location does not guarantee that the service provided will be used. Distance to a facility, the cost of consultation with a doctor, availability and cost of alternative providers and perceptions of service quality are just some of the factors that will influence the way in which demand (patents) and supply (health professionals) do or do not interact (Government of India, 2005). The most reliable quantitative analysis of the usage of health services at the all India level is available from the National Sample Survey (NSS) as well as from the National Council of Applied Economic Research. The usage of private health facilities increased significantly from an already high level as observed between the 42nd and 52nd round (1995-96) of the NSSO.

The evaluation of the India's Xth Five Year Plan (2002-2007) and the ongoing consultation in the preparation of reproductive and child health programme for the Ist phase of XIth Five year Plan provides a unique opportunity to assess the health and population outcome achieved and the failures and loopholes associated with the programme.

By all evidence available, the public funded part of India's Health and Family Welfare Sector is in a crisis. Over crowded and dirty hospitals, non-functioning primary health services, absent staff, lack of dignity and privacy for clients, wasted investments, in fructuous expenditures, corruption are all found in the system. It is estimated that over 80% of the recurring expenditure goes for salaries (especially in states like Kerala) and a very meager percentage has been allocated to medicines and supplies which itself makes public health centers as scarecrow (Gangadharan, 2005). The basic issues of the health centers is that there will be equipment but no acumen to operate it and even if equipments are available t is not properly maintained. Routine services are in disarray and the contract or adhoc mode of implementation now prevails is adversely affecting the routine functioning still further. In the population (Family Welfare) sub sector, rates of population growth are not dropping fast enough in the most populous states. In states where reductions have taken place, the drop has been fuelled mostly by Government drives for female sterilization. Vertical disease centers progremmes are showing limited results at best and killer diseases like material and tuberculosis are resurgent. The spread of AIDS/HIV is a major threat. The declining female to male ratio is a potential disruption to social order. The management systems, namely the secretaries and directorates, are fragmented, over whelmed with routine personnel and procurement matters and lack both the capacity and the will to think and act strategically (Govt. of India, 2005).

Table 5
Pattern of Investment in Health (including Family Welfare) in different Five Year Plans in India

Period and Plan	*Percentage on health out of total plan investment outlay*	*Percentage on family welfare out of Total Plan Investment outlay*	*Total for Health & Family Welfare*
First Five Year Plan (1951-56)	3.3	0.1	3.4
Second Five Year Plan (1956-61)	3.0	0.1	3.1
Third Five Year Plan (1961-66)	2.6	0.3	2.9
Annual Plan (1966-1969)	2.1	1.1	3.2
Fourth Five Year Plan (1969-1974)	2.1	1.8	3.9
Fifth Plan (1974-79)	1.9	1.2	3.1
Annual Plan (1979-80)	1.8	1.0	2.8
Sixth Plan (1980-85)	1.8	1.3	3.1
Seventh Plan (1985-90)	1.7	1.4	3.1
Annual Plan (1990-91)	1.6	1.3	2.9
Annual Plan (1991-92)	1.7	1.5	3.2
Eight Plan (1992-97)	2.3	1.7	4.0
Ninth Plan (1997-2002)	2.09	1.83	3.97
Tenth Plan (outlays) (2002-2007)	1.6	1.3	2.9

Source: Health Information of India, Ministry of Health & Family Welfare.

FINANCIAL CONSTRAINTS AND LIMITED FUNDING

An important issue faced by the health sector in India especially the family welfare segment is the acute shortage of funds. The allocation of funds for health and family welfare from the First Plan to the Xth plan (Table 5.) reveals the negligible proportion earmarked for the health sector and even after 6 decades of planned development there was no much improvement in the allocation to this sector and actually it declined from 3.3% in the First Plan to 2.09% in the Tenth Five year Plan.

The major constraint in family welfare programme has been the accumulating of arrears payable to the state overtime. The National Family Welfare Programme, which is a centrally sponsored programme is usually financed for both plan and non-plan activities by the Central Govt. Since State Governments have responsibilities for the implementation of the programme, shortfalls in the central funding has resulted in accumulation of substantial arrears payable to the States. These large arrears are bound to have adverse impact on programme delivery.

Thus the shortfall in public spending provides an opportunity for the private sector to occupy the space and later began to control the entire expenditure in the sector.

The share of private expenditure in total health expenditure increased steadily and the recent estimate (National Accounts Statistics 2001[4], WHO 2002, shows that it fetched to record level of around 83%. This reveals the domination of private sector in the health care environment of India and the vanishing role government in the overall health care expenditure of the country. (Table 6) when compared to other developing and developed countries the position of India is very bleak with regard to the Govt. expenditure on health as a percentage of total expenditure on health.The figure 83% represents the out of pocket expenses incurred by household and included expenditures incurred while seeking services from both public and private sectors[5].

Thus to revamp and revitalize public health care delivery system top item on the agenda would be to restore credibility to the public sector primary health service operating at the urban, rural, tribal and remote areas. For ensuring credibility of the system, enough funds along with the supply properly trained manpower and very committed monitoring and follow up action at the national level must also be ensured to work the system meaningfully to cater the health needs of the deprived, marginalized and vulnerable millions.

Table 6
Public and Private Expenditure on Health in Selected Countries

Countries	*Total Expenditure as Health as percentage of GDP*	*Pvt. Expenditure on Health as % of total expenditure of Health*	*Govt. expenditure on health as % of total expenditure of health*
Australia	8.3	27.6	72.4
Bangladesh	3.8	63.6	36.4
Brazil	8.3	59.2	40.8
Canada	9.1	28.0	72.0
China	5.3	63.4	36.6
France	9.5	24.0	76.0
Germany	10.6	24.9	75.1
India	4.9	82.2	17.8
Iran	5.5	53.7	46.3
Italy	8.1	26.3	73.7
Jappan	7.8	23.3	76.7
Mexico	5.4	53.6	46.4
Nigeria	2.2	79.2	20.8
Pakisthan	4.1	77.1	22.9
Philipines	3.4	54.3	45.7
Russia	5.3	27.5	72.5
South Africa	8.8	57.8	42.2
Thailand	3.7	42.6	57.4
U.K	7.3	19	81
USA	13	55.7	44.3
Uganda	3.9	62	38.0
Tanzania	5.9	53	47.0
Zambia	5.6	37.9	62.1

Source: WHO, The World Health Report (Geneva, WHO, 2002)

EDUCATION

Like health, education is also an important segment of social development and investment in education is essential for better human development. Alfred Marshal treated investment in education as national investment (John Vaizey, 1968) and its benefits should percolates to all sections and all communities. Educational advancement has been considered as the pre condition for agricultural and industrial development. A study made by Schultz, Harbison and Mayer (1964), Kendrick, Simon Kuznets and other reveals that investment in education is more productive than investment in physical capital The success story of all advanced countries lies in the outmost significance given to educational planning and development and this has been well proven in the case of Countries like U.S., Japan, Soviet Union etc. and the East Asian economic miracle was the outcome of successive and sustained public investment in Education.

In 1960 Pakistan and Korea had similar level of income, whereas by 1985 Korea's GDP percapita was nearly three times of Pakistan. Investment in education has important egalitarian effect on equity and alleviation of poverty (Dash, 2007) Education has important links with other aspects of human resource development such as health and fertility (Cochrane 1979). The strong link between education and life expectancy, disease and nutrition has been reinforced by Cochrane, O Hara and Leslie (Cochrane et al 1980). Studies held in India revealed that education play a significant role in bringing about a socio economic change. A study of 14 most populated States in India during the period 1961-81 has shown that one additional year of education of the workforce was associated with a 15 per cent increase in income output (Loh Jacqueline 1995). Spending on education therefore is not simply a consumption activity, but it is an investment in human capital.

The investment in education and the development of the education sector in India is a matter of concern even after 6 decades of planned development of this country. Though the average literary rate was estimated at 65% in 2001 census, there are wide sex, regional and community differences in the literary rates in India (Table 7). Similarly the educational attainment, accessibility, dropout rates etc. are also very high among the backward States and back ward communities in India. Table 8 reveals the dropout rates in classes 1-X, the accessibility of schools within the premises for children in the upper primary level and number of schools per thousand population etc in different states in India and it reveals the severity of inequality and differentials that exists among different states and also the deteriorated profile of education in these states which directly affects the quality of human development.

Table 7
Literacy in Major States in India 2001 (in percentage)

States	*General Literacy*			*Literacy among Scheduled Caste and Schedule Tribes*	
States	*Male*	*Female*	*Persons*	*Persons*	*Persons*
Andhra Pradesh	70.85	51.17	61.11	31.59	17.16
Arunachal Pradesh	64.07	44.24	54.74	–	34.45
Assam	71.93	56.03	64.28	53.94	49.16
Bihar	60.32	33.57	47.53	19.49	26.78
Goa	88.88	75.51	82.32	–	42.91
Gujarat	76.46	55.61	66.43	61.07	36.45
Haryana	79.25	56.31	68.59	39.22	–
Himachal Pradesh	84.57	67.08	75.91	53.20	47.09
Jammu & Kashmir	65.75	41.82	54.46	–	–
Karnataka	76.29	57.45	67.04	38.06	36.01
Kerala	94.20	87.86	90.92	79.66	57.22
Madhyapradesh	76.50	50.55	64.08	35.08	21.54
Maharashtra	86.27	67.51	77.27	56.46	36.79
Manipur	77.87	59.70	68.87	–	–
Meghalaya	66.14	60.41	63.31	–	–
Mizoram	90.69	86.13	88.49	–	–
Nagaland	71.77	61.92	67.11	–	60.59
Orissa	75.95	50.97	63.61	36.78	22.31
Punjab	75.63	63.55	69.55	41.09	–
Rajasthan	76.46	44.34	61.03	26.29	19.44
Sikkim	76.73	61.46	69.68	–	59.01
Tamil Nadu	82.33	64.55	73.47	46.74	27.89
Tripura	81.47	65.41	73.66	–	40.37
Uttarpradesh	70.23	42.97	57.36	26.85	35.70
West Bangal	77.58	60.22	69.22	42.21	27.78
All India	75.64	54.03	65.20	37.41	29.60

Source: National Human Development Report 2002 Figure of 2001.

Availability of financial resources is vital for any

Table 8
Dropout Rates in Class I-X, Number of Schools Per Thousand Population and Accessibility Schools within Premises among Major States in India

	Dropout rates in classes I-X in 1998-99			*Population with U.P Schools**		*Number of Schools per 1000 population in 1997-98*		
States	*Boys*	*Girls*	*Children*	*Within Habitation*	*Up to 1.0 km*	*Total up to 10 km*	*Primary*	*Upper Primary*
Andhra Pradesh	76.52	78.65	77.44	42.99	13.70	56.69	5.34	1.56
Arunachal Pradesh	76.09	78.67	77.20	33.13	6.80	39.93	8.21	4.64
Assam	76.55	75.32	76.00	22.40	26.69	49.09	8.62	3.58
Bihar	81.44	87.26	83.47	27.13	29.39	56.52	3.97	1.92
Gujarat	70.12	74.96	72.29	76.79	6.70	83.49	2.86	6.12
Haryana	45.24	55.98	50.04	64.70	10.24	74.94	4.06	1.24
Himachal Pradesh	42.21	43.20	42.67	17.33	19.82	37.15	10.03	2.19
Jammu &	61.47	70.24	65.10	38.41	20.16	58.57	7.89	4.93
Kashmir	67.21	68.91	68.02	60.86	10.45	71.31	3.82	6.61
Karnataka	30.02	19.16	24.70	50.54	16..97	67.51	2.20	1.54
Kerala	60.37	75.22	66.73	31.36	11.45	42.18	8.18	3.76
Madhya Pradesh	55.02	64.22	59.33	61.08	7.82	68..90	3.97	3.68
Maharashtra	76.35	76.74	76.54	37.25	25.60	62.85	8.69	4.02
Manipal	62.12	63.74	62.89	25.57	21.21	46.78	13.38	6.05
Meghalaya	73.85	71.10	72.56	77.58	3.01	80.58	11.17	11.11
Mizoram	63.84	60.98	62.59	47.76	5.32	63.08	6.80	4.56

Contd...

States	Dropout rates in classes I-X in 1998-99			Population with U.P Schools*			Number of Schools per 1000 population in 1997-98	
	Boys	Girls	Children	Within Habitation	Up to 1.0 km	Total up to 10 km	Primary	Upper Primary
Nagaland	52.42	62.05	52.27	34.21	18.25	52.46	9.66	4.99
Orissa	39.99	44.35	42.02	45.41	17.67	63.08	4.84	1.65
Punjab	77.63	82.74	79.29	46.96	8.74	55.70	4.88	3.88
Rajasthan	89.38	89.00	89.21	26.38	16.88	43.26	6.72	3.05
Sikkim	57.22	58.35	58.01	35.36	32.44	67.80	4.91	1.43
Tamil Nadu	79.94	83.95	81.78	24.92	28.38	53.30	4.14	1.77
Uttar Pradesh	55.13	72.68	61.25	21.69	22.16	43.85	4.21	1.71
West Bangal	78.50	88.03	82.73	14.16	40.92	55.08	5.28	0.54
All India	65.44	70.22	67.44	37.02	19.89	56.91	5.04	2.75

*Figures as on 1993.

Source: National Human Development Report 2001.

development programme in the field of education. The Central Govt., State Governments and households are the main sources of finance for education. The ability of the state governments to finance education depends on their revenue raising ability and the transfer of resources through the Finance and Planning Commission. As total expenditure On education is low, expenditure by the Central and State Government was only 3.56% of the GDP in 1995-96 which rise to 4.33% in 2000-01 and again declined. to 3.97% in 2002-03 (Table 9). The recent data reveals that this has again declined to 3.54% in 2004-05.

Table 9
Public Expenditure on Education in India

Year	*Percentage of Expenditure on Education to Expenditure on all Sectors (including Centre and State)*	*Percentage of Education Expenditure to GDP*
1951-52	7.92	0.64
1955-56	10.65	1.15
1960-61	11.99	1.48
1965-66	9.82	1.69
1970-71	10.16	2.11
1980-81	10.67	2.98
1990-91	13.37	3.84
1995-96	13.34	3.56
1999-2000	14.60	4.25
2000-01	14.42	4.33
2001-02	12.89	3.82
2002-03	12.74	3.97

Source: Govt. of India, Ministry of Human Resource Development, Selected Educational Statistics 2002-03, New Delhi.

The plan expenditure for the last 6 decades reveals that top most priority has been given to elementary education, but the allotment remain the same for 9th and 10th plan period. The proportion allocated for Higher Education has shown a steady increase during 2nd, 3rd, 4th and 5th Plan period, but thereafter it declined steadily and the 10th plan allocated only 9.5% on higher education. The expenditure pattern of education in India reveals that expenditure composition is skewed towards secondary and tertiary education.

Table 10
Percentage of Plan Expenditure on different segment of Education

Sector	*1st* Plan	*IInd* Plan	*IIIrd* Plan	*IVth* Plan	*Vth* Plan	*VIth* Plan	*VIIth* Plan	*XIIIth* Plan	*IXth* Plan	*Xth* Plan
Elementary education.	58	35	34	50	52	32	37	48	65.7	65.6
Secondary education.	5	19	8	–	–	20	24	24	10.5	9.9
Adult education	–	–	2	2	6	6	5	24	2.9	2.9
Higher education	8	18	15	25	28	21	16	10	10.3	9.5
Others	15	10	12	13	9	11	3	3	1.6	1.4
Technical	14	18	21	10	9	10	14	10	9.5	10.7
Total	100	100	100	100	100	100	100	100	100	100

Source: Gopalji and Soman Bhatt, Statistical data on Indian Economy..., New Delhi.

As a country moving towards a knowledge economy allocation of more funds to the education sector is most inevitable to develop its human capital base. Since public sector is starving of funds, for social sector investment private sector must be encouraged to invest heavily in the higher education segment of the economy when productivity is high and instant.

HUMAN DEVELOPMENT

The need for increasing investment in human capital formation is of crucial importance at the present level of development and the postponement of this will invite severe threat for the knowledge economy of the country.

UNDP's global Human Development Report for 2005 ranks India at 127 out of 177 countries of the world in terms of a composite Human Development Index. Compared to 2000 in 2003 the HDI has fallen from 124 to 127 at the same time gender development index improved from 105 to 98. During this period some India's neighbors (Table 11) not only improved their HDI and GDI values but also improved their relative ranks. The progress of social development has varied across states. While Kerala stood apart from the rest and achieved high level of human development comparable to the rich developed countries, whereas the so called BIMARU States (viz. Bihar, Madhyapradesh, Rajasthan and Uttar Pradesh) performed very badly (Table 12).

Table 11

India's Global Position on Human and Gender Development

	Human Development Index (HDI)		*HDI Rank*		*Gender Development Index*		*GDI Rank*	
Country	*2000*	*2003*	*2000*	*2003*	*2000*	*2003*	*2000*	*2003*
Norway	0.942	0.963	1	9	0.941	0.960	3	1
Australia	0.939	0.955	5	3	0.956	0.954	1	2
Sri Lanka	0.741	0.751	89	93	0.737	0.747	70	66
China	0.726	0.755	96	85	0.724	0.754	77	64
Indonesia	0.684	0.697	110	110	0.678	0.691	91	87
India	0.577	0.602	124	127	0.560	0.586	105	98
Pakistan	0.499	0.527	138	135	0.468	0.508	120	107
Bangladesh	0.478	0.520	145	139	0.468	0.514	121	105
Nepal	0.490	0.526	142	136	0.470	0.511	119	106
Mozambique	0.322	0.379	170	168	0.307	0.365	144	133
.....	0.277	0.281	172	177	0.263	0.271	146	140

Source: UNDP Human Development Report 2002 and 2005.

Table 12

Human Development Index for Selected States

States	*HDI Value 2001*	*2001 Rank*
Andhra Pradesh	0.416	10
Assam	0.386	14
Bihar	0.367	15
Gujarat	0.479	6
Haryana	0.509	5
Karnataka	0.478	7
Kerala	0.638	1
Madhya Pradesh	0.394	12
Maharashtra	0.523	4
Orissa	0.404	11
Panjab	0.537	2
Rajasthan	0.424	9
Tamil Nadu	0.531	3
Uttar Pradesh	0.388	13
West Bangal	0.472	8

Source: Human Development Report-India.

For proper human development along with economic

development, social sectors must be linked with economic growth. Social services provide a better chance of self expression and for community recreation. Myrdal is of the view that vicious circle of poverty can be turned into virtuous circle where meeting social needs is cumulatively raising the levels of production (Chopra 1992). Social services are the tools of human resource development and all development in the ultimate sense should culminate in human resources and thereby human development. We are therefore required to emphasis simultaneously economic development and social development. We need to fill in the gaps in the health and education sectors in India as they have a lasting effect on the quality of life of the people of the country. The policy makers, planners, administrators and politicians should realize that augmenting the quality of population through better education and better health care will provide a sound edifice for rapid and sustained economic development.

NOTES

1. This includes 23.9% of all DALY, lost due to communicable diseases and 14.9% due to non communicable diseases.
2. BIMARU includes Bihar, Chattisgarh, Jharkhand, Mandhya Pradesh,Orissa , Rajasthan, Uttar Pradesh and Uttaranchal.
3. Based on purchasing power parity dollars, which adjust for price differentials between countries and as reported in the World Fact Book 2001, India at PPP $2200 percapita has the same level of income as Tonga. Other countries with similar level includes Pakistan (2000) Bosnia & Herzegovina (1700) and Zimbabwe (2500).
4. National Account Statistics 2001, Central Statistical Organization, Ministry of Statistics and Programme Implementation, Govt. of India, July 2001.
5. Out of pocket health expenditure by households includes; Buying services from a purely private allopathic (Western Indian) practitioner (doctor, nurse, pharmacist or Para medical) working in a private clinic or corporate hospital.User charges at government facilities includes buying medicines and or diagnostic services from open market when these are not available at government facility or illegal payments to government doctors in a public health facility.

REFERENCES

Chopra R. M. (1992), Impact of Social Services on Economic initiative, Anmol Publications New Delhi.

Dash L.N. (2007), Economics of Infrastructure Growth and Development, Regal Publishers, New Delhi.

Economic Survey, 2004-05.

Gangadharan (2005), Utilization of Health Services in Urban Kerala. A Socio Economic Study, Serials Publications, New Delhi.

Gopalji and Bhakti S. (2005), Statistical Data on Indian Economy, Taxman Allied Services, New Delhi.

Government of India (2003), National Human Development Report 2002 Planning Commission, Govt. of India, New Delhi.

Govt. of India (2003), National Human Development Report 2001.

Govt. of India (2007), NFHS-3: Indian Institute of Population Studies, Mumbai.

Harbison F. and Myres (1964), Education, Manpower and Economic Growth, McGraw Hill, New York.

Jacqueline Loh (1995), Education and Economic Growth in India An Aggregate Production Function Approach, Ministry of Human Resources Development, New Delhi.

John Vaizey (1968), What some Economist said about Education, Readings in the Economics of Education, UNENCO, Paris.

Schultz J. W. (1961), Education and Economic Growth in N.B. Henry (ed) Social Forces Influencing American Education, University of Chicago Press, Chicago.

Susan H. Cochrane (1979), Fertility and Education what Do We really Know? John Hopkins University Press, Baltimore.

Susan H. Cochrane, Donald O. Hora and John Leslie (1980), The Effects of Education on Health, World Bank Staff Working Paper No. 405, World Bank, Washington.

The Govt of India (2005), Selected Educational Statistics 2002-03 Ministry of Human Resource Development, New Delhi.

UNDP, Human Development Report (Various Issues).

WHO (2002), The World Health Report, WHO, Geneva.

Chapter-3

NUTRITION AND HEALTH TRANSITION: LESSONS FROM KERALA

K. Gangadharan

INTRODUCTION

Health is considered as a fundamental human right and a worldwide social goal. It is essential for the satisfaction of basic human needs and to improve the quality of life. The development of any nation depends on the health of its people. The World Health Organization has defined health as "a complete state of physical, mental and social wellbeing, and not merely the absence of illness or disease". Among the several non-economic indicators of human welfare and national development, the health status of a nation's population requires prominent position. It is a fundamental factor affecting the quantity and quality of the population and thereby their productivity.

Conventional emphasis in public policy for economic growth and development has generally been on physical capital accumulation and technological progress for productivity improvements. There was little by way of recognition of the importance and role of human capital in promoting growth and poverty reduction. This is not to state that governments had little concern for these dual dimensions of human capital. In fact, the emphasis on health was largely based on welfare considerations rather than the perspective of human capital as a factor of production. Good health would enhance growth by:

(i) Reducing productivity losses due to illness.
(ii) Permitting utilization of resources which otherwise would have remained in accessible or unutilized.
(iii) Promoting school enrollment of children and enabling them to learn.
(iv) Saving on resources required for treatment of illness (World Bank 1993).

WHAT IS UNDER NUTRITION?

The term under nutrition is defined as the outcome of insufficient food intake (hunger) and repeated infectious diseases. Under nutrition includes being underweight for one age too short for one's age (stunted) dangerously thin (wasted) and deficient in vitamins and minerals (micronutrient and nutrition). When individuals are under nourished they can no longer maintain natural bodily capacities such a growth, resisting infections and recovery from disease, learning and physical work, pregnancy and lactation in women. Poor feeding of infants and young children, especially the lack of optimal breast feeding and responsible complementary feeding along with such illness as diarrhea, pneumonia, malaria and HIV/AIDS are major cause of under nutrition.

Nutritional deficiencies and poor health of children are major public health concerns in developing countries, where they present both a cause and a reflection of poverty. After the Independence the elected Governments in India has undertaken a lot of steps for the improvement of the health and well being of the population especially the health of the children. But still malnutrition is a severe problem in India, according to NFHS-3, 46 per cent of the India's children under the age of three are suffering from underweight and 79% of them are categorized anemic. This malnutrition is a severe hurdle in the way of proper health care development at the global level and the developing countries are the greatest victims of this nutritional deprivation.

It is hypothesized that severe malnutrition is attributable to inadequate diet, while moderate to mild malnutrition could be due to environmental factors (Seckler 1982) Empirical nutrition studies show that increase in food energy intake would reduce malnutrition once the other variables are controlled. Table 1 provides the nutritional status of children at the global level and it indicates the pathetic condition of India with 47% of underweight children. Similarly in the case of stunting and wasting also India dominates over all other developing countries.

Table 1
Nutrition Status of Under Five–A Global View

	% of under five suffering from		
Region	*Under Weight*	*Stunting*	*Wasting*
Latin America	6	14	2
& Caribbean	24	35	8
Africa	28	30	9
Asia	47	45	16
India	48	45	10
Bangladesh	19	40	3
Bhutan	45	36	20
Maldives	48	51	10
Nepal	40	36	14
Pakistan	33	20	13
Sri Lanka	22-27	28-32	7-9
All Developing Countries			

Source: UNICEF (2006), 'State of the World's Children'.

INDIA AND SOUTH ASIA–SOUTH ASIAN ENIGMA

South Asia has the dubious distinction of having the highest prevalence of malnutrition in children-higher than even Sub-Saharan Africa which in many ways is lesser developed than South Asia. Ramalingaswami, et al (1996) refers to this as the 'South Asian Enigma'. 'The South Asian Enigma' can be explained by three key differences between south Asia and Sub-Saharan Africa. Firstly, low birth weight is the single largest predictor of under nutrition; and over 30% Indian babies are born with low birth weights, compared to approximately 16% is Sub-Saharan Africa. Secondly, women in South Asia tend to have lower status and less decision-making power than women in Sub-Saharan Africa. This limits women's ability to access the resources needed for their children's health and nutrition, and has been shown to be strongly associated with low birth weight, as well as poor child feeding behaviours in the first twelve months of life. Thirdly, hygiene and sanitation standards in South Asia are well below those in Africa, and have a major role to play in causing the infections that lead to under nutrition in the first two years of life. (Table 2).

Table 2
Child Deprivation in India and South Asia (2004)

Country	*Bangladesh*	*Bhutan*	*India*	*Nepal*	*Paksitan*	*Sri Lanka*
Immunization(% of children under 3 years who have not received the stated vaccine)						
BCG	5	8	27	15	20	1
DTP3	15	11	36	20	35	3
MCV	23	13	44	27	33	4
Polio	15	10	30	20	35	3
Child under-nutrition (% of children with the stated condition)						
Underweighted	48	19	47	48	38	29
Stunting	43	40	46	51	37	14
Wasting	13	3	16	10	13	14
Infant and child mortality (per 1,000 live births)						
Infant mortality rate	56	67	62	59	80	12
Under- 5 mortality rate	77	80	85	76	101	14

Source: UNICEF (2006), 'State of the World's Children.

India is compared with other countries; the comparison is usually made the China or the United States. Yet there is a great to learn from looking around us within South Asia, especially in matters of child nutrition and health. Far from being 'backward' in comparison with India, other South Asia countries are generally doing better than India is this field. It may come as a alarm to learn that India has the lowest child immunization rate in South Asia. For instance, the proportion of children who have not bad a BCG vaccine in India is twice as high as in Nepal, more than five times as high as in Bangladesh, and almost 30 times as high as in Sri Lanka. Turning to child under nutrition, India emerges with a poor picture with only Nepal doing worse and despite its sophisticated medical system and vast army of doctors; India has not been able to achieve higher rates of child survival than any of its neighbors except Pakistan. Almost any 'summary index' of these child development indicators would place India at the bottom of this list of countries.

It is significant to note that the contrast between India and other South Asian countries would be even sharper if we were to focus on deprived regions or communities in each country, instead of national averages. This is a serious problem throughout the country but with large disparities between states and groups. Bihar, Madhya Pradesh, Uttar Pradesh, and Rajasthan account for more than 43 per cent of all underweight children. Furthermore, inequalities in nutritional status worsened in the 1990s, between income groups, urban and rural dwellers, castes and genders. Under-nutrition is concentrated in a relatively small number of districts and 10 per cent of villages and districts account for almost 30 per cent of all under weight children; a quarter of districts and villages account for more than half of all underweight children.

The present study takes up the issues pertaining to health sector in Kerala in a larger comparative perspective in the Indian Context. It would focus on the changes that occurred in the nutritional status over the time period and also on the incidence of morbidity across socio economic dimensions and their implications for economic policy.

NUTRITION AND ITS DETERMINANTS

Nutrition is an integral part of the health and well being of all individuals. Good nutrition is determined by the consumption of an adequate diet and also a person's ability to resist disease and infections that interface with digestive and absorption process of the biological system. On the one hand, good nutrition enables us to lead a socially and economically active life whereas malnutrition has an adverse impact on morbidity. It hinders physical growth; lead to functional impairment, disability diminishes productivity and reduces resistance to diseases.

The important determinants of Nutritional status are educational facilities for all the members of the society and also facilities for continuing informal education. Similarly the living environment like good sanitation, safe drinking water, proper facility for travel and communication, electrification, proper health care facilities, family income, members in the family, proper spacing among children, housing set up, occupation of the household members etc influence a lot in the nutritional enrichment of the society. Chart 1 provides how poverty and illiteracy are connected with nutritional deprivation:

WHY STUDY KERALA?

Chart 1
Ecology of Malnutrition

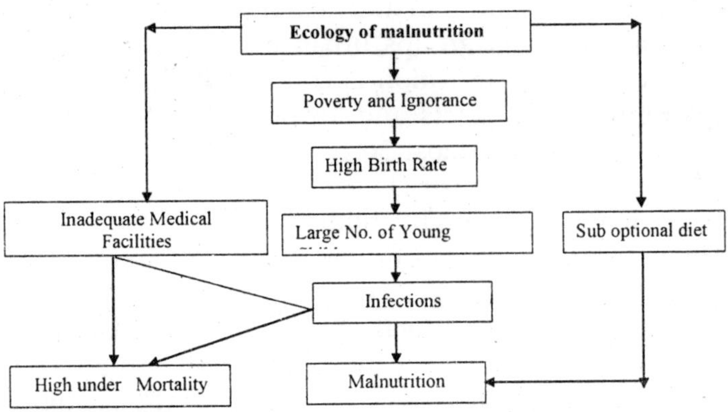

The state of Kerala is located in the Southern tip of India. It is a narrow strip of land flanked by Arabian Sea on the west, and Western Ghats mountain ranges on the East. With over 30 million living in an area of 38,863 Km², Kerala's, density of population stands at 950/Km².

Kerala has been recognized as a state with better health care indices which is even comparable with most advanced nations of the world. This achievement has been stated as the culmination of great stress on social development, better social justice (Ratcliff 1978) or a combination of greater stress on education and improved health delivery system (Nair, 1974). Table 3 provides a summary of key health indices of Kerala in comparison with India and some other countries. These figures indicate the advancement the State has gained in many spheres of health. The gains are all the more impressive since the income of the State falls below the national average.

Table 3
Kerala's Health Indicators in Comparison to India and to some other Countries

					Health Expenditure (as % of GDP)	
Countries/ State	*IMR*	*Under 5 Mortality rate*	*Life Expectancy*	*TFR*	*Total*	*Govt. (%)*
Kerala	14	19	73.5	1.8	6.2	1.4 (22)*
India	60	87	62	3.0	6.1	1.3(21)
China	27	37	71	1.8	5.8	2.0(34)
Sri Lanka	11	15	71	2.0	3.7	1.8(49)
US	7	8	77	2.1	14.6	6.6(45)
Canada	5	6	80	1.5	9.6	6.7(70)

Source: World Health Report 2005 except for Kerala which was taken from SRS for the year 2005*.

The state of Kerala within India has received international attention and acclaim for its conscious policy intervention for high levels of human development. Contrary to the previous apprehension about the sustainability of the Kerala model, recent evidence seems to show that high levels of human development have also been instrumental in registering sustained economic growth. However the recent trends related to morbidity, nutrition etc. reveals that Kerala is passing through a stage of health care transition in which the advancement gained in health care in the initial stages of development in 1960's and 1970's and 1980's is now eroding fastly due to the hike in the morbidity load on the one side and gaining momentum of the nutritional deprivation among the under five children. The Human Development Report 2005 for Kerala and NFHS 3 report also shows trends in this direction.

NUTRITIONAL DEFICIENCY AND CALORIE CONSUMPTION

Clearly India is eating less. People are increasingly becoming poor and marginalized which directly tells upon their food intake and so the nutrition their bodies receive. Moreover what the Indians and eating is also bad. Its nutritional deficiency adversely affects the health and working potential of all.

Table 4
State wise Population with Calorie Intake Less than 90% of Recommended Norms

(in percentage)

	Urban		*Rural*	
State	*1983*	*1999-2000*	*1983*	*1999-2000*
Andhra Pradesh	53.8	50.8	39.3	51.0
Assam	49.9	46.6	48.8	61.5
Bihar	44.4	43.5	39.6	45.9
Gujarat	52.1	51.3	46.7	53.6
Haryana	43.5	46.2	27.5	30.2
Karnataka	48.8	51.2	42.3	54
Kerala	55.9	52.5	61.2	61.6
Madhya Pradesh	44.6	49.1	33.7	50.7
Maharashtra	57.1	52.7	44.4	52.4
Orissa	35.7	31	46.2	42.1
Punjab	48.1	44.6	24.1	31
Rajasthan	42.6	34.5	28.8	24.3
Tamil Nadu	65.6	55	62.9	65.2
Uttar Pradesh	52.1	46.5	31	32.9
West Bengal	53.1	49	53.6	47.8

Source: C.P. Chandra Shekhar & Jayanthi Gosh, 2003, The calorie consumption puzzle in Business line, February 11.

What is shocking is that, the state like Kerala also witnessed a slight improvement in increasing the population of people with caloric intake less than 90% of the recommended norms. Still in Kerala around 52% of the people are getting less than 90% of the recommended calorie intake which reveals the extend of nutritional deprivation and vagaries of malnutrition in Kerala. The class wise calorie consumption (Table 5) also reveals that the BPL Categories and poverty line categories in Kerala have respectively obtained only 1100 and 1389 calories per day (rural) instead of the basic minimum of 2738.6 calories recommended by the ICMR. In this case it is pitiable to note that Kerala records the rock per day for the rural poor.

Table 5
Class wise Calorie Consumption 1999-2000
(in kilo-calories/day)

States	*Rural*		
	B.P.L (Below Poverty Line)	*Poverty Line*	*A.P.L (Above Poverty Line)*
Andhra Pradesh	1406	1662	2095
Assam	1585	1767	2136
Bihar	1769	1977	2401
Gujarat	1468	1684	2065
Haryana	1523	1745	2539
Himachal Pradesh	1982	1942	2495
Karnataka	1442	1646	2151
Kerala	1100	1389	2073
Madhya Pradesh	1649	1888	2305
Maharashtra	1584	1780	2145
Orissa	1792	2117	2421
Punjab	1506	1712	2440
Rajasthan	1755	2003	2532
Tamil Nadu	1307	1543	1960
Uttar Pradesh	1839	1990	2548
West Bengal	1664	1935	2296

MATERNAL AND CHILD HEALTH

Though the state of Kerala has witnessed rapid strides in the health sector, the recent NFHS data related to child health, nutritional standards among women and children reveals that Kerala is now in the reverse trend in the health care advancement or in other words Kerala now finds it very difficult to sustain the tempo of advancement that gained in the health sector for the last three decades and it is passing through a health transition in all its spheres. The data related to overweight of women steadily increased over 14 % during the short span of 1998-99 to 2005-06. Similarly though infant mortality reduced to considerable extent in Kerala compared to all India level (see Table 1), they are celebrating their each birthday with acute health problems. The proportion of children in the age group of 6 to 35 months with anaemia actually increased from 43.9 in 1998-99 (NFHS I) to 55.7% in 2005-2006 (See Table 6). Similarly anaemia among the women also increased from 22.7% to 32.3% over the same period (see Table 6). The problem of anameia has been also severe among the pregnant women and the same has increased from 20.3% in 1998-99 to 33.1% in 2005-06. The children's nutritional status at the Inter State level (Table 7) reveals that though the states of Kerala is for better compared to other Indian states, the reduction in nutritional problem like underweight, wasting and stunting over the time period is far speedier and better in other Indian states compared to Kerala.

Table 6
Child Immunization, Vitamin Supplementation and Treatment of Childhood Diseases, Child Feeding Practices and Nutritional Status of Children-Variation over time period in Kerala

	NFHS-I	*NFHS-II*	*NFHS-III 2005-06*		
Particulars	*All*	*1998-99*	*All*	*Urban*	*Rural*
Fully immunized children in *percentage (in the age group 12-23 months)*	*54.7*	*79.7*	*75.3*	*87.5*	*69.4*
Children who have received BCG (%) in the age group of 12-23 months	*86.1*	*96.2*	*69.3*	*100*	*94.6*
Children who have received 3 doses of polio vaccine in %	75.2	88.4	83.1	91.7	78.9
Children who have received 3 doses of DPT vaccine in %	73.2	88	84	93.1	79.6
Children who have received Measles vaccine in %	60.5	84.6	82.1	–	76.9
Children with diarrhoea In the last two weeks who received ORS in %	16.6	47.9	34.6	–	34.4
Children within the last two weeks taken to a health facility in %	71.4	82.1	67.4	–	75
Children with acute respiratory infection of fever in the last two weeks taken to health facility	NA	NA	81.4	85.7	79.8

Full dose means BCG, Measles and 3 doses each of polio and DPT

Source: NFHS-I, NFHS-II and NFHS-III.

Table 7
Nutritional Status and Anemia among Children and Adults Variation over Time Period in Kerala

	NFHS-I	*NFHS-II All*	*NFHS-III 2005-06*		
Particulars	*All*	*1998-99*	*All*	*Urban*	*Rural*
Women whose Body Mass Index is below normal in %	NA	18.7	12.5	9.1	14.3
Women whose Body Mass Index is below normal in %	NA	–	11.9	11.2	12.3
Women who are over weight or obese in %	NA	20.6	34	40.1	30.9
Men who are over weight or obese in %	NA	–	24.3	28	21.9
Children in the age of 6 to 35 months who are anemic in %	NA	43.9	55.7	51.3	57.9
Married women in the age of 15 to 49 who are anemic in %	–	22.7	32.3	32.3	32.4
Pregnant women in the age of 15 to 49 who are anemic in %	–	20.3	33.1	27.7	35.8
Children under 3 years who are stunted in %	25.2	21.9	21.1	21.3	21.1
Children under 3 years who are wasted in %	12.8	11.1	16.1	10.1	19.1
Children under 3 years who are underweight in %	27	26.9	28.8	22.5	31.9

Source: NFHS-I, NFHS-II and NFHS-III.

The population of children who are having under weight and wasted also recorded a hike in the last two NFHS reports (Table 6) indicating that over the time period the health status of the children in Kerala deteriorated heavily. This transition in the child health may be due to the change in the dietary habit of mothers and the involvement of mothers in the active labour force. Even during pregnancy period the employed women are not able to eat properly due to the stress and strain of the work in which they are indulged and the nature of food consumption also changed a lot. A sort of fast food culture has also emerged in urban Kerala which culminated in breeding diseases like diabetics, blood pressure and hike in cholesterol even among youngsters. The urbanization and migration to

Figure 1
Children in the Age Group of 6 to 35 months who are Anemic (in per cent age)

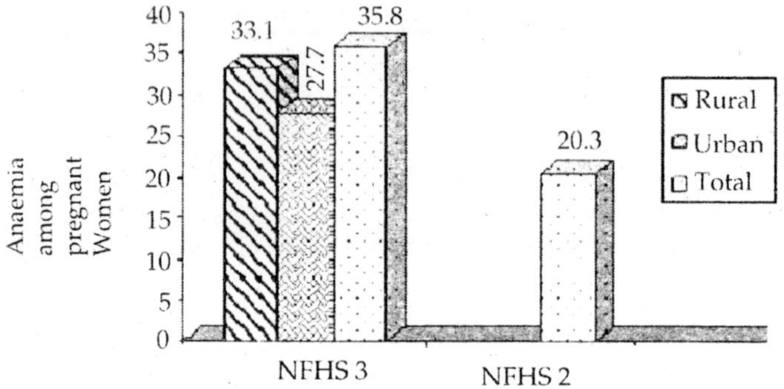

Figure 2
Pregnant Women who are Anemic (in per cent age)

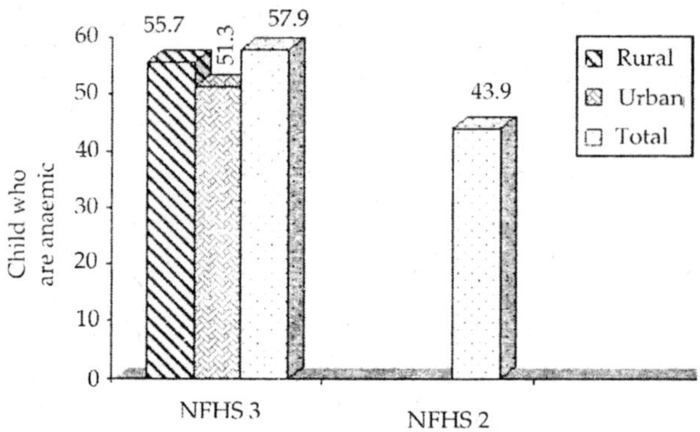

Figure 3
Percentage of Stunted, Wasted and Under Weighted Children from NFHS I to NFHS III

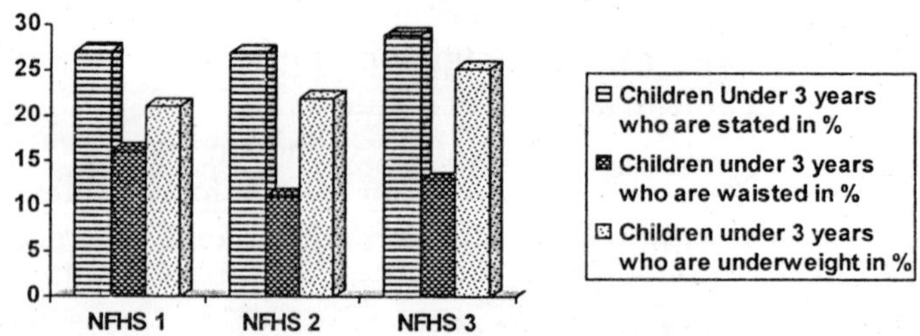

urban centres in Kerala is also accounts for the change in dietary style and health transition of the people.

MORBIDITY PROFILE AND HEALTH TRANSITION

The urban community as a whole including the kids going to K.G. School is experiencing a hectic life cycle from to morning to evening. Faty foods and lack of any sort of exercise or body movement on the part of urban dwellers and overall negligence of environmental hygiene caused for the morbidity hike in Kerala. (Table 7). Incidence of morbidity is higher in Kerala than India as a whole. (Table 12 and 13) for the population as a whole. It is 25.11% for Kerala as against 9.11% for All India. For both men and women It is higher, though marginally in the rural sector than in the urban in Kerala and the reverse at the all India level. Similarly though life expectancy has improved a lot in Kerala (Table 8) compared to other Indian States the 60+ categories are experiencing a bitter life due to hike in morbidity among them. (Table 9). Arthrities, blood pressure, asthma, pain in joints, mental illness, Hypertension, Urinary complaints, Cardiological, paralysis etc. are the important ailments faced by the 60+ categories. The better and advanced health care facilities provided by the high-tech private hospitals in Kerala are one important factor responsible for hike in life expectancy in Kerala. Though they are morbid due to chronic illness, the advancement of modern medical care facility and regular and continuous treatment enabled , majority of them to succeed better in extending their life and this can be noticed as an important health care transition that occord recently in Kerala.

In the case of treatment also majority of the aged prefers allopathic care from private (409/1000) followed by Govt.(288/1000). Moreover 32 out of 1000 prefers self treatment and on the other extreme 38 out of 1000 prefers no treatment at all (Table 10). The ranking of states in terms of life expectancy at birth has always put Kerala on the top. However in terms of absolute improvement in life expectancy at birth between 1970 and the 1990's Kerala ranked in the 9th position among the states in India indicating the deteriorating quality of life of the people.

Table 8
Children's Nutritional Status:Inter-state Trends

	Percentage of Children							
	Stunting		*Wasting*		*Underweight*		*Children age 6-35 months who are Anemic*	
States	*NFHS-2 1998-1999*	*NFHS-3 2005-2006*	*NFHS-2 1998-1999*	*NFHS-3 2005-2006*	*NFHS-2 1998-1999*	*NFHS-3 2005-2006*	*NFHS-2 1998-1999*	*NFHS-3 2005-2006*
Andhra Pradesh	39	34	9	13	38	37	72.3	79
Assam	50	35	13	13	36	40	63.2	76.7
Bihar	55	42	20	28	54	58	81.1	87.6
Chattisgarth	58	45	19	18	61	52	87.7	81
Delhi	37	35	13	16	35	33	69	63.2
Goa	18	21	13	12	29	29	53.4	49.3
Gujarat	44	42	16	17	45	47	74.5	80.1
Haryana	50	36	5	17	35	42	83.9	82.5
Himachal Pradesh	41	27	17	19	44	36	69.9	58.8
Jharkhad	49	41	25	31	54	59	82.4	77.7
Jammu & Kashmir	39	28	12	15	35	29	71.1	68.1
Karnataka	37	38	20	18	44	41	70.6	82.7
Kerala	22	21	11	16	27	29	43.9	55.7
Madhya Pradesh	49	40	20	33	54	60	71.3	82.6
Manipur	31	25	8	8	28	24	45.2	52.8
Meghalaya	45	42	13	28	38	46	67.6	68.7
Mizoram	35	30	10	9	28	22	57.2	51.7
Maharashtra	40	38	21	15	50	40	76	71.9
Nagaland	33	30	10	15	24	30	43.7	na
Orissa	44	38	24	19	54	44	72.3	74.2
Punjab	39	28	7	9	29	27	80	80.2
Rajasthan	52	34	12	20	51	44	82.3	79.6
Sikkim	32	29	5	13	21	23	76.5	56.9
Tamilnadu	29	25	20	22	37	33	69	72.5
Tripura	40	30	13	20	43	39	61.8	67.9
Uttaranchal	47	32	8	16	42	38	77.4	61.5
West Bengal	42	33	14	19	49	44	78.3	69.4
INDIA	46	38	16	19	47	46	74.2	79.2

Table 9
Life Expectancy at Birth by Sex in India (1996-2002)(Average for Four Years)

	Life Expectancy			
States in India	*1996-2000*		*1998-2002*	
	Male	*Female*	*Male*	*Female*
India	61	62.7	61.6	63.3
Andhra Pradesh	61.7	64.3	62	64.6
Arunachal Pradesh	–	–	–	–
Assam	57.4	57.7	57.7	58.1
Bihar	60.9	59.1	61.4	59.5+
Goa	–	–	–	–
Gujarat	62.1	64	62.4	64.4
Haryana	64.4	65.1	64.7	65.4
Himachal Pradesh	65.4	66	65.7	66.3
Jammu & Kashmir	–	–	–	–
Karnataka	62.5	65.8	62.8	66.2
Kerala	70.7	76.7	70.8	75.9
Madhya Pradesh	56.6	56.3	57	56.7
Maharashtra	64.7	67.2	65	67.4
Manipur	–	–	–	-
Meghalaya	–	–	–	–
Mizoram	–	–	–	–
Nagaland	–	–	–	–
Orissa	57.8	58	58.4	58.5
Punjab	67.1	69.2	67.4	69.5
Rajasthan	60.1	61.1	60.5	61.6
Sikkim	–	–	–	–
Tamil Nadu	63.9	65.9	64.2	66.3
Uttar Pradesh	59.1	57.9	59.4	58.5
West Bengal	63	64.5	63.3	64.8

Table 10
Morbidity Prevalence among the 60+ Categories in Kerala

	Age Group					
Type of Ailment	*60-70*	*70-80*	*80-90*	*Above 90*	*Total*	*Per 1000*
Diabetics	566	331	92	11	1000	155
Hypertension	537	346	104	13	1000	214
Arthritis	512	347	122	19	1000	273
Asthma	520	347	117	16	1000	88
Abdominal problems	555	320	108	17	1000	39
Urinary Complaints	525	334	123	18	1000	14
Liver Problems	556	315	112	17	1000	5
Skin diseases	577	303	105	15	1000	11

Contd...

	Age Group					
Type of Ailment	*60-70*	*70-80*	*80-90*	*Above 90*	*Total*	*Per 1000*
T.B	589	313	91	7	1000	5
Brain Disease	531	335	119	15	1000	6
Cardiological	558	337	95	10	1000	38
Cancer	559	338	95	8	1000	4
Psychological Problem	553	330	104	13	1000	5
Paralysis	273	343	277	107	1000	4
Others	561	311	109	19	1000	139

Source: Report on Survey of Aged in Kerala 2003-04.

FERTILITY, MORTALITY AND MORBIDITY

With regard to total fertility rate in Kerala, it can be seen that it is declining from the 1960s. Total Fertility Rate (TFR) which was 5.6 per woman in the 1950s declined to 3.7 in the 1970s and reached to 1.8, which is below the replacement level in the 1990s. The fertility rate declined in both rural and urban areas and there is virtually no difference between the two. By contrast in India, the TFR was 6.3 in the 1950s and declined to 3.3 in the 1990s. Though Kerala and India had a difference of 0.7 children during 1950s, the difference has widened to 1.5 children 1990s indicating a faster decline in Kerala than in India as a whole.

Figure 4
TFR Overtime in India and Kerala

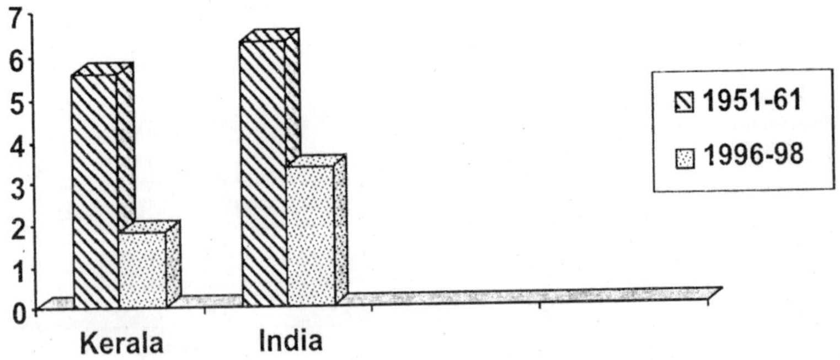

Figure 5
IMR Overtime in India and Kerala

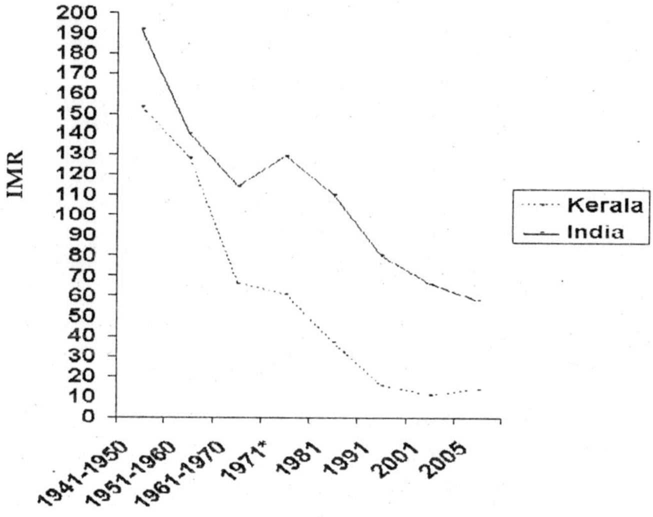

Among the numerous indicators available to measure health status of a population, the most dominant among them one are mortality, fertility and morbidity. It can be seen that (Table 11) IMR in Kerala declined steadily for the last 6 decades and now records the lowest rate of 14 per thousand live births.

At the beginning of the century the IMR of the state was very high and did not differ much from the all India average. While in Kerala the IMR declined steadily throughout this century to the present level of 14 per thousand live birth. It can be seen that (Table 12) IMR also began to increase recently and it was 11 for the year 2001 now in 2005. This has reached to 15 indicating a sort of transition which is a signal to the health status of Kerala.

The Crude Birth Rate (CBR) which remained at 17.7/1000 in 1992 has declined to the present level of 15.3 per thousand population and the Crude Death Rate remained the same at the rate of 6.4 for the same period. A unique feature of Kerala's population profile is that, unlike in the rest of India, the gender ratio favours women (1058:1000). The Projection of birth rate

Table 11
Age and Method of Treatment (in per 1000)

Age Group	*Self Treatment*	*No Treatment*	*Allopathy (Govt.)*	*Allopathy (Pvt.)*	*Ayurveda (Govt.)*	*Ayurveda (Pvt.)*	*Homeo (Govt)*	*Homeo (Pvt.)*	*Others (Govt)*	*Others Pvt.*	*All*
60-70	34	39	294	409	93	83	10	9	14	15	1000
70-80	28	36	285	413	98	94	10	8	13	15	1000
80-90	28	38	273	404	108	104	8	8	14	15	1000
Above 90	30	45	262	401	105	116	7	6	12	16	1000
Total	32	38	288	409	97	89	10	9	13	15	1000

and death for Kerala for the next 10 years revealed that constant birth rate will reduce to 13.47 per thousand population and death rate will come down to 7.04 per thousand Population. This indicates that the demographic transition in Kerala is moving in such a way that natural growth rate will be declined from 9.75 in 1996-2001 to 6.42 in 2011-2016.

Table 12
Infant Mortality Rate of Kerala and India

Year	*Kerala(K)*	*India(I)*	*K as % of I*
1941-1950	153	192	80
1951-1960	128	140	91
1961-1970	66	114	58
1971*	61	129	47
1981	37	110	34
1991	16	80	20
2001	11	66	17
2005	14	58	24

Source: 1. Kannan. KP. Thankappan K. R. *et al* 1991. Health and Development in Rural Kerala KSSP, p. 06.
2. Registrar General of India, Sample Registration SystemFrom 1971 onwards SRS started providing vitals statistics data.

MORBIDITY INDICATORS

Though mortality and fertility has declined sharply for the last few decades in Kerala, the available data related to morbidity is surprising in nature. The morbidity data available from different studies reveals that Kerala surpasses all other Indian states with regard to the prevalence of chronic and acute illness (Sharief 1995, Gangadharan 2005, Gangadharan 2006, Gangadharan 2007, KSSP 2006). Among the chronic illness diabetes, heart diseases, mental, asthma, blood pressure, cancer etc. arc having highest prevalence. The Table 10 reveals pattern of morbidity prevalence among the 60+ categories and Table 13 shows the nature and pattern different acute and chronic illness reported in the public health centres in Kerala (Govt. of Kerala 2005) and Table 14 and 15 shows the incidence of morbidity by gender and sex and incidence of morbidity by sector respectively.

Table 13
Number of Attack and Death Due to Major Principal Diseases during 2006-2007

	Attack		*Death*	
Name of Diseases	*2006*	*2007*	*2006*	*2007*
Acute Diarrhoeal Diseases	475434	344603	4	5
Diptheria	1	3	0	1
Acute Polimyelitis	0	0	0	0
Tetanus–Others	10	4	1	3
Neonatal Tetanus	0	0	0	0
Whooping Cough	156	116	0	1
Measles	2766	2076	0	0
Chickenpox	13739	13776	6	5
Acute Respiratory infection	7929133	5611490	165	110
Pneumonia	25908	11047	62	54
Enteric Fever	6385	3129	2	2
Dengue Fever	1087	387	2	2
Viral Hepatitis-A	6515	4683	7	2
Viral Hepatitis-B	624	348	1	9
Weils Disease (Leptospirosis)	1708	648	59	58
Japanese Encephalitis	0	0	0	0
Meningococal Meningitis	22	7	2	0
Rabies (Hydrophobia)	23	11	23	11
Syphilis	38	33	0	0
Gonococal Infection	318	6	0	0
Pulmonary Tuberculosis	13601	8781	232	73
All Other Diseases (including communicable and non communicable diseases	22605338	26241325	5424	4326
Total	31082806	32242533	5990	4667

Source: Directorate of Health Services, Thiruvananthapuram.

Table 14
Incidence of Morbidity by Gender and Sex-Kerala and All India (2004)

	All Kerala			*All India*		
Gender	*Rural*	*Urban*	*Combined*	*Rural*	*Urban*	*Combined*
Male	24.28	23.56	24.06	8.36	9.11	8.56
Female	26.66	24.51	26.10	9.30	10.86	9.69
Total	25.53	24.06	25.15	8.82	9.95	9.11

The data reveals that infectious and parasitic diseases contribute a significant share of total illness in the population and incidence of morbidity is higher in Kerala than India as a whole.

In spite of many short falls in the nutritional intake and health care spending, the state has been successful in managing the mortality, and fertility and Gender equality to a great extent compared to other Indian States. The secret behind this management lies in the Costrica's development path followed by the successive Governments in Kerala. The domination of adult literacy and universalisation of primary education acted as the lubricant force in creating better health awareness among the people.

Table 15
Incidence of Morbidity by Sector: Kerala and All India (2004)

Per cent

	Kerala			*India*		
MPCE Decile Group	*Rural*	*Urban*	*Combined*	*Rural*	*Urban*	*Combined*
1	22.4	17.10	20.60	6.10	7.80	6.20
2	19.7	19.40	20.00	6.30	8.50	6.50
3	22.6	18.80	23.10	6.60	8.20	7.30
4	27.10	23.20	24.90	7.7	8.5	8.00
5	21.30	21.50	21.90	8.0	9.5	8.7
6	23.80	21.50	24.80	8.8	9.9	9.10

Table 16
Consumption of Pattern of Poverty Line Class. 1999-2000
(Percentage Adjusted Norms)

	Rural			*Urban*		
State	*Calories*	*Proteins*	*Fats*	*Calories*	*Proteins*	*Fats*
Arunachal Pradesh	69.3	109.8	48.3	85.3	100.4	62.4
Assam	73.6	100.9	46.6	70.4	99.8	40.2
Bihar	82.4	111.6	46.8	93.0	115.0	48.9
Gurajat	70.2	116.2	89.0	77	713.6	107.1
Hariyana	72.7	124.1	73.9	69.4	123.0	76.1
H.P	80.9	126.3	73.8	–	–	–
Karnataka	68.6	110.6	65.7	87.7	106.3	69.6
Kerala	57.9	100.9	63.4	76.3	109	72.6
Madhyapradesh	78.7	114.7	52.3	93.4	119.7	74.7
Maharashtra	74.2	116.4	65.6	84.4	115.9	88.7
Orisa	88.2	94.9	29.2	116.7	100.0	34.9
Punjab	71.3	126.0	80.1	75.7	124.3	82.6

Contd...

	Rural			Urban		
State	Calories	Proteins	Fats	Calories	Proteins	Fats
Rajsthan	83.5	135.2	76.9	94.6	123.7	95.2
Tamil Nadu	64.3	97.7	55.7	77.3	100.5	69.3
Uttarpradesh	82.9	123.9	52.1	85.5	124.2	66.6
West Bengal	80.6	101.7	59.4	84.3	104.0	54.6
All India	77.8	111.3	53.1	91.0	111.6	77.9

Source: (Computed from Government of India (2001)).

The enrollment of children in the age group of 6-11 in the lowest annual income groups (less than 20,000 per annuam) household is 96.9% (HDR, 2007) whereas at the all India level this was only 60.6%. A unique feature of the educational system in Kerala is the high enrollment of girls in schools and college education. The gross enrollment ratio for females in Kerala is 96.7% and literacy rate among the female is 94.2% compared to 87.9% among men. Female literacy has been treated as a very important determinant for affecting decline in mortality (Cald Well, 1986). This indomitant linkage is responsible for fall in Infant mortality Rate (IMR) and rise in female literacy in Kerala.

Table 17
Percapita Cereal Consumption of Poverty Line Class (Kgs Per Month)

State	Kerala		Urban	
	1993-94	1999-2000	1993-94	1999-2000
A.P	11.40	10.95	11.25	10.62
Assam	12.98	12.11	10.96	10.33
Bihar	15.11	13.32	12.74	12.79
Gujarat	9.87	9.88	8.97	8.07
Haryana	11.33	9.79	9.98	7.91
Himachal Pradesh	12.37	11.48	11.89	9.80
Karnataka	11.84	10.18	10.69	9.71
Kerala	9.21	8.18	9.24	8.67
M.P.	14.11	12.48	12.08	11.28
Maharashtra	11.25	20.89	9.80	9.46
Orissa	16.96	15.44	14.20	17.18
Punjab	9.09	9.24	8.10	8.37
Rajasthan	13.71	12.84	11.80	11.61
Tamil Nadu	10.86	9.79	10.32	9.14
Uttar Pradesh	13.82	12.89	11.4	20.34
West Bengal	14.57	13.03	11.92	10.97
All India	13.19	12.27	20.89	10.75

Source: Govt. of India (1995) and (2001).

REFERENCES

Caldwell J. C. (1986), Routes to Low Mortality in Poor Countries, *Population and Development Review*, Vol. 12.

Govt. of India (2001), Preliminary Tables–Kerala, Director of Census Operations, New Delhi.

Gangadharan K. (2005), Life After Sixty. Problems of Ageing and Ill Health, *Kerala Calling*, Vol. 25.

Gangadharan K. (2006), Deteriorating Health of Mothers and Children. A Study on Urban Kerala, *Asian Economic Review*, Vol. 48, No. 2.

Gangadharan K. (2006), Emerging Issues in Urban Health Care with Special Reference to Kerala, *India Journal of Social Development*, Vol. 6, No. 1.

Gangadharan K. (2007), Changing Health Profile of Kerala, *Economic Affairs*, April-June.

Gangadharan K. (2007), Health for all in Kerala, *Kerala Calling*, June.

Govt. of India (1995), Nutritional Intake in India 1994-95. National Sample Survey Organization, Ministry of Statistics and Programme Implementation, New Delhi.

Govt. of India (2001), Nutritional Intake in India (1999-2000), National Sample Survey Organization, Ministry of Statistics and Programme Implementation.

Govt. of India (2004), Health Information of India, Ministry of Health and Family Welfare, New Delhi.

Govt. of Kerala (2005), Economic Review, State Planning Board, Thiruvananthapuram.

Govt. of India (2006), National Family Health Survey, NRHS-3, Fact Sheet, India, International Institute for Population Science, Mumbai.

Govt. of Kerala (2005), Report on Survey of Aged in Kerala, Dept. of Economic and Statistics, Thiruvananthapuram.

Govt. of Kerala (2006), Human Development Report 2005, Centre for Development Studies, State Planning Board, Thiruvananthapuram.

Keralas Sastra Sahithya Parishad (2006), How Kerala Thinks and Acts in Sastra Sahitya Parishath, TVM.

Nair, P. R. G (1974), Decline in Birth Rate in Kerala. An Explanatory Hypothesis about the Relationship between Demographic

Variables, Health Service and Education, *Economic ad Political Weekly*, Vol. 9.

Panicker P. G. K. and Soman C. R. (1984), Health Status of Kerala Economic Backwardness and Health Development, Centre for Development Studies, Thiruvananthapuram.

Ratcliffe, J. (1978), Social Justice and Demographic Transition. Lessons from India's Kerala State, *International Journal of Health Services*, Vol. 8.

Ramalingaswamy, V. Jonsson U. and Rhode J. (1996), The Asian Enigma, The Progress of Nations, UNICEF.

Seckler D. (1982), Small but Health; A Basic Hypothesis in the Theory Management and Policy in Nutrition in P.V. Sukhatme (ed), Newer Concepts and their Implication for Policy, Pune, Maharashtra, Association for Cultivation of Science.

Sharief (1995), Health Transition in India. Differentials and Determinantes of Morbidity in India by Disaggregated Analysis Working Paper No. 57, NCAER, New Delhi.

Soman C. R. (1992), Nutrition and Health Development Lessons From Kerala, *Proceedings of the Nutrition Society*, Vol. 51.

World Bank (1993), World Development Report 1993. Investing in Health, Oxford University Press, New York.

CHAPTER-4

MORBIDITY AND HEALTH CARE IN KERALA: A DISTRIBUTIONAL PROFILE AND IMPLICATIONS

M. H. Suryanarayana

INTRODUCTION

Conventional emphasis in public policy for economic growth and development has generally been on physical capital accumulation and technological progress for productivity improvements. There was little by way of recognition of the importance and role of human capital in promoting growth and poverty reduction. This is not to state that governments had little concern for these dual dimensions of human capital. In fact, the emphasis on education and health, two major ingredients of human capital, was largely based on welfare considerations rather than the perspective of 'human capital as a factor of production'. Both education and health are important from the economic growth perspective too. While education has a role with respect to productivity, levels as well as rate of growth, health would contribute to growth from several perspectives as shown below. Good health would enhance growth by:

(a) Reducing productivity losses due to illness.
(b) Permitting utilization of resources which otherwise would have remained inaccessible or unutilized.
(c) Promoting school enrollment of children and enabling them to learn.
(d) Saving on resources required for treatment of illness (World Bank 1993).

The World Development Report 2000 has even gone to the extent revising its concept of deprivation with reference to the multiple dimensions involving both income and non-income aspects. The Millennium Development Goals adopted by the UN member countries too acknowledge this fact and seek to reduce incidence of deprivation in some major dimensions like education and health.

India has miles to go in terms of comprehensive policies with respect to education and health, the latter in particular. It is precisely at this juncture that the country has initiated a series of economic reform measures in terms of revising the scope for public health centers, cost recovery and privatization (Purohit and Siddiqui, 1995; Bhat 2000), which is likely to have considerable costs from a welfare perspective. This naturally would raise the question regarding the most appropriate cost-effective strategy for improving health in India? As a special case study, one may consider the unique experience of Kerala for the following reasons: As regards the health sector, levels of morbidity in the State of Kerala, despite its remarkable achievements in human development (including life expectancy), are quite high. There is a hypothesis that high levels of morbidity along with low rates of mortality could be due to a poor health status associated with low levels of income and hence, inadequate nutrition (Panikar and Soman, 1984). A moot question would be to ask whether the hypothesis is valid any longer given the recent evidence that Kerala has caught up and has even done better than most of states in terms of growth and levels of living during the post-1973 scenario. If so, it would be worthwhile to examine the levels of living in Kerala as well as different parts of Kerala vis-à-vis that of all-

India, morbidity rates, their causes, type and extent of institutional facilities available for their treatment. This would provide some clues to address the question on the welfare implications of such high levels of morbidity in Kerala in the wake of economic reform and privatization of health care.

To be specific, this paper takes up the issues pertaining to the health sector in Kerala in a larger comparative perspective in the Indian context. It would focus on the incidence of morbidity across socio-economic dimensions and their implications for economic policy. The rest of the paper is organized as follows: Section 2 provides the motivation for taking up a study of Kerala. Section 3 provides a macro profile of morbidity, health care facilities and utilization in Kerala, rest of the states and India as a whole. Section 4 socio-economic dimensions, occupational and regional profile of morbidity in Kerala. The final section sums up the paper.

WHY STUDY KERALA?

The State of Kerala within India has received international attention and acclaim for its conscious policy intervention for high levels of human development. Contrary to the previous apprehension about the sustainability of the Kerala model, recent evidence seems to show that high levels of human development have also been instrumental in registering sustained economic growth. However, there are doubts regarding the quality and type of education as well as status of health in Kerala and also the soundness of the recent growth experience. As regards health, one feature that stands out is the high level of morbidity co-existing with low levels of mortality and high life expectancy in Kerala. The Human Development Report 2005 for Kerala highlights the fact that morbidity estimate was 71 per 1000 persons for acute illness and 83 per 1000 persons for chronic illness in the year 1973-74; it corroborates this point with additional evidence from several studies (Centre for Development Studies, 2006; p.29). Of course, these estimates have been interpreted from different perspectives. There have been different types of explanations for this paradox, which are as follows:

(1) Panikar and Soman (1984) explain the paradox of low mortality but high morbidity in terms of a lopsided health strategy, which emphasized curative medicine to reduce death rates and not sustained improvement in health status through nutrition, housing, water supply, sanitation and medicine. (p. 100). In other words, it is a case of "averting death without improving life". As per their assessment, one salient feature of the morbidity profile of Kerala is that diseases of poverty coexist with those of affluence. Panikar and Soman (1984) also point out that morbidity estimates for Kerala could be over-estimates because of high levels of education and public awareness of rights and access to health services involving higher-than-normal utilization of such services.

(2) Another hypothesis seeks to explain high levels of morbidity in terms of better reporting in a state with higher levels of education and awareness.

(3) Human Development Report 2005 adduces increase in life expectancy as one of the reasons for high levels of morbidity in Kerala (Centre for Development Studies, 2006).

(4) Chen and Schaik (1986) explain the paradox with reference to lopsided emphasis on social development overlooking the importance of income growth. The explanation runs as follows: (a) Curative medical care combined with a literate and articulate society will go a long way in curbing mortality rates; (b) Incidence of morbidity depends on risk factors governing exposure to disease like housing, water supply and sanitation which in turn depend upon income; and (c) Nutritional status depends upon food consumption, which in turn is a function of income and economic access. As a result of Kerala's lopsided emphasis, fertility and mortality declined without corresponding improvements in health and nutritional status.

(5) There are studies (Kannan *et al.*, 1991), which authenticate the high estimates of morbidity for Kerala on two grounds: (i) Infections account for a majority of morbidity; and (ii) incidence of illness is more for the poor than the rich.

(6) The findings of National Family Health Survey II (1998-99) provide evidence of high prevalence of illness like asthma and Tb in Kerala: Incidence of asthma was 5.08 per cent in rural Kerala, 3.90 per cent in urban Kerala and 4.81 per cent in Kerala as a whole while the corresponding estimates for all-India were 2.64, 1.97 and 2.47 respectively (IIPS and ORC Macro, 2000; pp. 200-202).

The set of issues and explanations listed above, if valid, have indeed serious policy implications. As point out by the *Human Development Report 2005: Kerala,* the findings call for an emphasis on (i) 'better nutrition, environmental sanitation and preventive health care'; (ii) enhanced role for the public sector and (iii) greater regulation of the private sector from a welfare perspective (Centre for Development Studies, 2006; p. 163).[1] However, recent evidence on Kerala's growth experience casts doubts on the hypothesis regarding poverty as the cause of morbidity.

(1) Income does not seem to be a severe constraint any longer. Due to high levels of human development and hence, emigration and income remittances, Kerala has caught up with the rest of the country and has even excelled the rest in terms of levels living during the post-1973 scenario. Average consumer expenditure levels, which were less than that of all-India prior to 1973, have exceeded and even grown faster than that of all-India average.

(2) Estimates of measures of nutritional intake like energy, protein and fat show general improvement for all poorer decile groups in rural and urban Kerala (Suryanarayana, 2003). Available information for the recent year 2004-05 shows that estimates of nutritional intake (calorie, protein and fat) per consumer unit are high in both rural and urban sectors (Table 1).

Table 1
Measures of Nutritional Status Across States: 2004-2005

	Rural								Urban							
	% expenditure on		*per capita per day intake of*			*per consumer unit per day intake of*			*% expenditure on*		*per capita per day intake of*			*per consumer unit per day intake of*		
State	*Food*	*Cereals*	*Calorie (Kcal)*	*Protein (gm)*	*Fat (gm)*	*Calorie (Kcal)*	*Protein (gm)*	*Fat (gm)*	*Food*	*Cereals*	*Calorie (Kcal)*	*Protein (gm)*	*Fat (gm)*	*Calorie (Kcal)*	*Protein (gm)*	*Fat (gm)*
Andhra Pradesh	55.2	19.4	1995	49.8	33.5	2475	61.8	41.6	41.6	12.2	2000	50.9	43.2	2449	62.4	52.9
Assam	66	24.8	2067	52.7	26.7	2515	64.1	32.4	49.5	13.6	2143	55.9	36.8	2593	67.6	44.5
Bihar	64.8	27.1	2049	57.8	28.4	2560	72.3	35.5	51.1	17.2	2190	62.2	40.4	2683	76.1	49.5
Chhatisgarh	56.2	27.2	1942	47.4	19.9	2424	59.2	24.8	39	12.1	2087	53.9	37.2	2550	65.9	45.4
Gujrat	58	13.3	1923	53.3	50.9	2380	65.9	63	44.9	8	1991	57.3	63.5	2436	70.1	77.7
Haryana	48.6	8.6	2226	69.6	55.4	2738	85.6	68.1	41.4	6.9	2033	60.5	54.4	2487	74	66.6
Jharkhand	61.9	27.2	1961	51.2	22.8	2440	63.8	28.4	46.9	13.4	2458	69.5	53.8	3013	85.2	65.9
Karnataka	55.7	16.5	1845	48.8	33.9	2276	60.2	41.8	43.2	11.1	1944	52.2	43.3	2385	64	53.1
Kerala	45	11	2014	55.4	40.8	2549	70.1	51.6	40	8.4	1996	56.7	44.9	2534	72	57.1
Madhya Pradesh	52.9	18.1	1929	58.8	35.1	2386	72.7	43.4	38.9	9.8	1954	58.2	43.4	2397	71.4	53.2
Maharashtra	51.7	14.5	1933	55.7	41.5	2405	69.3	51.6	40.4	8.4	1847	52.1	50.1	2261	63.8	61.3
Orissa	61.6	28.3	2023	48.3	17.8	2512	59.9	22.1	49.9	16.8	2139	55.2	28.3	2596	67	34.4
Punjab	49.2	8.8	2240	66.7	58.7	2763	82.3	72.5	37.6	6.4	2150	63.4	61	2614	77	74.2
Rajasthan	54.8	14.5	2180	69.6	50.9	2714	86.7	63.3	41.6	9.6	2116	64	56.4	2586	78.2	69
Tamilnadu	52.4	15.5	1842	44.9	29.6	2294	55.9	36.9	42.7	10.3	1935	49.2	41.1	2394	60.8	50.8
Uttar Pradesh	53.6	17.6	2200	65.9	37.5	2743	82.1	46.8	45	11.4	2124	65.1	46.1	2598	79.7	56.4
West Bengal	58.7	23.4	2070	52	26.5	2545	64	32.6	43.4	11.3	2011	55.1	39.1	2467	67.6	48
All	55	18	2047	57	35.5	2540	70.8	44	42.5	10.1	2020	57	47.5	2475	69.9	58.2
Upper quartile			2070	58.8	41.5	2560	72.7	51.6			2139	62.2	53.8	2596	76.1	65.9

Source: GoI (2007a; p. 44).

(3) Since 1997, Kerala's domestic growth performance too has caught up with that of major growing states like Maharashtra and is toady one of the fastest growing Indian states (Ahluwalia, 2000; Kannan, 2005).

(4) Other correlates of standard of living also corroborate the relative high status of Kerala in terms of standard of living.

  (a) One major factor, which is a good measure of standard of living and has a positive influence on health status is the type of dwelling. About 73 percent of rural households in all-Kerala lived in pucca structures as against the estimate of 48 per cent for rural all-India. The corresponding estimates for urban households were 84.7 per cent for all-Kerala and 84.2 per cent for all-India. The percentage numbers of households living in kutcha structures were meager for all-Kerala (7.2 per cent for rural and 2.4 per cent for urban) when compared with those for all-India (18.8 per cent for rural and 4.3 per cent for urban) (Government of India (GoI), 2006; p. 36).

  (b) Though Kerala is comparable to all-India with reference to percentage number of households depending upon safe sources for drinking water, it comes out poorly in terms of awareness and hygiene. Only 3.9 per cent of the rural households in all-Kerala (as against 19.9 per cent for rural all-India) and 32.9 per cent of the urban households in urban Kerala (as against 37.5 for urban all-India) treated water before drinking (GoI, 2006; pp. 37-38).

  (c) Still morbidity has increased between July 1995-June 1996 and January–June 2004 from 11.8 to 25.5 per cent in rural Kerala and from 8.8 to 24 per cent in urban Kerala.[2]

The set of issues and different perspectives presented above would naturally give rise to several questions on the incidence of morbidity across income groups in different parts as well as Kerala as a whole, morbidity profiles and the role of medical institutions. A clear perspective would call for a verification of the level of health status, morbidity rate across income groups, their causes and policy imperatives in Kerala.

DATA BASE

The current study is based on the NSS findings from its 60th round survey during January-June 2004 of morbidity and utilization of health services. The findings are based on published report (Report no 507) as well as tabulation of unit record data.

The survey was based on a two-stage stratified sample design: census villages in the rural and blocks in the urban areas constituted the first stage units and households were the second stage units in both the sectors. The survey was carried out during two sub-rounds of three months each between January and June 2004.

The NSS definition of illness includes (i) disabilities related to visual, hearing, speech, loco motor and mental faculties; (ii) physical damages involving cuts, wounds, hemorrhage, fractures and burns due to accidents; and (iii) spontaneous abortion, natural or accidental". The details are ascertained in terms of probing questions to the extent possible the individual members of the sampled household. The enquiry regarding morbidity was with reference to the 15 days preceding the date of enquiry. As regards hospitalization, the preceding 365 days was the relevant reference period.

Generally, studies refer to either the State as a whole or isolated regions or localities. This paper seeks to provide profiles of northern and southern parts of Kerala and examine their features. For this purpose, special tabulations of the NSS unit record data from the 60th round survey on 'Morbidity and Health Care' are carried out for the two NSS regions in Kerala. They are (i) Northern region (consisting of the districts of Kannur, Kasaragod, Kozhikode, Malappuram, Palakkad and Wayanad) and (ii) Southern region (consisting of the districts of Alappuzha, Ernakulam, Idukki, Kollam, Kottayam, Pathanamthitta, Thiruvananthapuram and Thrissur). Statistical details about sample size by region and sector, extent of response and representativeness are as follows (Tables 4):

(1) In keeping with the population weights, the rural samples were larger than the urban ones in both North and South Kerala; (Table 2);

Table 2
NSS Sample Size for 60th Round (January–June 2004)

(No of households)

Region/State	*Sector*	
	Rural	*Urban*
Northern Kerala	870	360
Southern Kerala	969	630
All-Kerala	1839	990
All-India	47302	26566

Source: Tabulated from NSS Unit record data (60th Round).

(2) Extent of (rural and urban) household response and capability was higher in all-Kerala than in all-India, and higher in the North than in the South within Kerala (Table 3).

Table 3
Response to Survey: Kerala Vs. All-India

Response	*Rural*				*Urban*			
Response Code	*North Kerala*	*South Kerala*	*All-Kerala*	*All-India*	*North Kerala*	*South Kerala*	*All-Kerala*	*All-India*
Co-operative & capable	95.98	86.38	90.92	76.02	93.33	90.16	91.31	79.61
Co-operative & incapable	3.68	12.18	8.16	21.68	5.83	7.94	7.17	17.62
Busy	–	0.52	0.27	1.34	–	0.95	0.61	1.49
Reluctant	0.34	0.72	0.54	0.76	0.83	0.63	0.71	1.09
Others	–	0.21	0.11	0.20	–	0.32	0.20	0.20
Total	100.00	100.00	100.00	100.00	100.00	100.00	100.00	100.00

Source: Tabulated from NSS Unit record data (60th Round).

(3) Representativeness, as measured by the percent of originally selected households in the sample, was higher for all-India than for all-Kerala and higher for North Kerala than for the South (Table 4).

Table 4
Representativeness of the Sample

Survey	*Rural*				*Urban*			
Survey Code	*North Kerala*	*South Kerala*	*All-Kerala*	*All-India*	*North Kerala*	*South Kerala*	*All-Kerala*	*All-India*
Original	94.83	92.16	93.42	97.67	94.17	93.17	93.54	95.39
Substitute	5.17	7.84	6.58	2.33	5.83	6.83	6.46	4.61
Total	100.00	100.00	100.00	100.00	100.00	100.00	100.00	100.00

Source: Tabulated from NSS Unit record data (60 Round).

ECONOMIC DEVELOPMENT AND HEALTH CARE: A MACRO PROFILE

The state of Kerala has received attention across the world for effective public intervention for human welfare, which has finally led to both high levels of human development and economic growth. Though there were doubts regarding the sustainability of Kerala's development strategy, recent evidence on economic growth has set at rest all such doubts. Today the level of living of every decile group of all-Kerala population is higher than that of its counterpart at the all-India level (Table 5). This holds good even when the comparison is made between South Kerala and all-India (Table 5). Only the rural sector of North Kerala is better off than its counterpart at the all-India level; not so as to its urban sector. This is confirmed by estimates of incidence of poverty (headcount ratio) across regions and by sectors also.

Given the status of economic development, it would be worthwhile to examine the extent of facilities available and their utilization pattern. Some available details are as follows:

(1) About 90 per cent of the illness is treated in both rural and urban areas of Kerala as against 82 per cent in rural all-India and 89 per cent in urban all-India (Table 6).

(2) However, their relative dependence on public and private medical sources differs. While 37 per cent of the ailments are treated in the government medical facilities in rural Kerala, it is just 20 per cent in its urban sector. Compared with rural Kerala, a relatively smaller proportion of the all-India rural population is

Table 5
The Average Monthly per Capita Expenditure by Decile Group of Population by Sector: Kerala (North, South and whole) and All India (2004)

(at current prices)

	North Kerala		*South Kerala*		*All-Kerala*		*All-India*					
MPCE Decile Group	*Rural*	*Urban*	*Comb.*	*Rural*	*Urban*	*Comb.*	*Rural*	*Urban*	*Comb.*	*Rural*	*Urban*	*Comb.*
1	284.58	290.69	301.6	346.47	418.09	366.72	314.8	351.6	322.35	211.83	324.21	222.54
2	384.66	406.54	412.95	441.43	536.8	484.83	416.42	481.39	428.02	280.62	452.67	299.26
3	446.61	475.69	481.6	511.88	627.99	576.75	480.82	546.5	494.68	323.56	520.67	350.34
4	493.32	515.16	535.04	577.13	742.37	682.65	529.06	623.45	551.13	364.33	611.65	397.85
5	534.32	561.05	611.84	653.61	863.3	787.98	595.63	728.33	620.97	403.64	711.57	446.58
6	592.66	625.95	711.33	727.92	1012.05	982.25	670.28	852.46	704.38	444.47	815.75	503.61
7	665.26	715.93	855.34	806.06	1234.28	1446.33	746.7	1026.64	789.4	497.04	967.08	576.57
8	746.67	851.55	1245.93	950.12	1444.7	943.23	848.44	1280.03	938.86	562.93	1114.37	687.49
9	873.51	1103.23	503.93	1180.37	1778.79	911.06	1046.48	1599.48	1199.09	672.96	1422.35	885.37
10	1528.84	1734.14	1051.95	1945.75	2764.86	1889.03	1820.4	2493.72	2071.09	1072.27	2424.52	1616.02
Total	654.77	727.37	670.96	813.96	1141.72	906.85	746.75	998.06	811.87	483.36	936.27	598.52
Gini ratio (%)	26.25	28.50	26.95	28.33	31.68	30.73	28.20	32.80	30.50	25.70	32.50	32.40
Headcount ratio (%)	22.06	45.13	27.21	14.2	16.14	14.75	17.52	26.19	19.77	32.82	27.81	29.50

Notes:

(1) 'Comb.' means 'Rural and Urban combined'.

(2) Estimates of poverty are with reference to the poverty lines estimated by the Planning Commission for the agricultural year 2004-05; hence, they are approximate and could be overestimates to some extent. The poverty lines are as follows: Rs 430.12 (Rural Kerala), Rs 559.39 (Urban Kerala), Rs 356.30 (Rural Indian) and Rs 538.60 (Urban India) (GoI, 2007b).

Source: Tabulated from the NSS Unit record data (60 Round)

dependent on the public institutions (22 per cent); both rural and urban sectors rely more on the private medical institutions (about 80 per cent) (Table 6).

Table 6
Percentage of Spells of Ailments Treated (Non-institutional) during 15 Days and Percentage Distribution of Treated Spells of Ailments by Source of Treatment in Major States

	Rural			*Urban*		
	% Spells of ailments treated	*Source of treatment (%)*		*% Spells of ailments treated*	*Source of treatment (%)*	
Major State		*Govt.*	*Pvt.*		*Govt.*	*Pvt.*
Andhra Pradesh	77	21	79	88	20	80
Assam	79	27	73	94	24	76
Bihar	81	5	95	88	11	89
Chattisgarh	89	15	85	90	20	80
Delhi	@	@	@	95	23	77
Gujarat	84	21	79	93	18	82
Haryana	94	12	88	95	20	80
Himachal Pradesh	94	68	32	92	86	14
Jammu & Kashmir	82	52	48	94	51	49
Jharkhand	92	13	87	96	24	76
Karnataka	78	34	66	87	16	84
Kerala	87	37	63	90	22	78
Madhya Pradesh	87	23	77	95	23	77
Maharashtra	88	16	84	92	11	89
Orissa	76	51	49	86	54	46
Punjab	94	16	84	96	18	82
Rajasthan	90	44	56	90	53	47
Tamil Nadu	78	29	71	87	22	78
Uttaranchal	89	18	82	98	35	65
Uttar Pradesh	77	10	90	88	13	87
West Bengal	80	19	81	83	20	80
India	82	22	78	89	19	81

Source: GoI (2006; p. 22).

(3) Such estimates for the years 1986-87, 1995-96 and 2004 show marginal variations in the role of public institutions in providing non-hospitalised treatment of ailments for both rural and urban populations. However, the profile is different for Kerala: Reliance

of the urban population on public intuitions has decreased but that of the rural population, though fluctuating decreased between 1995-96 and 2004 (Table 7).

Table 7
Percentage of Treated Ailments Receiving Non-Hospitalised Treatment from Government Sources

	Rural			*Urban*		
Major States	*2004*	*1995-96*	*1986-87*	*2004*	*1995-96*	*1986-87*
Andhra Pradesh	21	22	12	20	19	16
Assam	27	29	40	24	22	26
Bihar	5	13	14	11	33	17
Chattisgarh	15	*	*	20	*	*
Delhi	@	*	*	23	*	*
Gujarat	21	25	28	18	22	18
Haryana	12	13	15	20	11	19
Himachal Pradesh	68	*	*	86	*	*
Jammu & Kashmir	52	*	*	51	*	*
Jharkhand	13	*	*	24	*	*
Karnataka	34	26	32	16	17	30
Kerala	37	28	32	22	28	33
Madhya Pradesh	23	23	24	23	19	28
Maharashtra	16	16	21	11	17	15
Orissa	51	38	37	54	34	43
Punjab	16	7	12	18	6	11
Rajasthan	44	36	46	53	41	52
Tamil Nadu	29	25	28	22	28	31
Uttaranchal	18	*	*	35	*	*
Uttar Pradesh	10	8	*	13	9	14
West Bengal	19	15	16	20	19	20
India	22	19	21	19	20	24

Source: GoI (2006; p. 23).

(4) As regards hospitalization, the rate is the highest for Kerala across all states. The proportion of persons hospitalized is 10.1 per cent for rural Kerala and 9 per cent for urban Kerala while corresponding estimates for all-India are 2.3 and 3.1 per cent respectively (Table 8).

Table 8
Proportion (Per 1000) of Persons Hospitalised in Rural and Urban Areas and Population Per Bed Across States

Major State	*No. per 1000 Hospitalised*		*Population per Hospital Bed*
	Rural	*Urban*	
AP	22	28	1057
Assam	11	16	1782
Bihar	10	10	3029
Chhattisgarh	12	27	–
Delhi	–	11	493
Gujarat	29	36	709
Haryana	32	31	3026
HP	32	31	
J & K	18	20	4790
Jharkhand	9	22	–
Karnataka	23	26	1319
Kerala	101	90	325
MP	18	29	5582
Maharashtra	30	36	920
Orissa	23	30	3064
Punjab	30	30	1623
Rajasthan	18	25	3175
Tamil Nadu	37	37	1135
Uttaranchal	17	19	–
UP	13	20	2647
West Bengal	23	35	1464
India	23	31	1503

Source: GoI (2006; p. 25).

(5) Kerala along with Jammu & Kashmir are the two states where the percentage of hospitalized cases treated in government hospitals exceeds the percentage of beds in government hospitals (Table 9). This feature reflects quite favorably on the quality of service provided in public hospital in these two states.

(6) High levels of morbidity and the relatively higher reliance on the private sector in urban Kerala would have its own implications for the poor in an era of privatization and drug deregulation. The average medical expenses for non-hospitalised treatment per ailing person during the period of 15 days is Rs. 182

in rural Kerala and Rs. 193 in urban Kerala. A further break-up by source (govt. vs. private) shows that virtually the entire amount (Rs. 179 in rural Kerala and Rs. 189 in urban Kerala) was on treatment from private institutions. As against this, the all India estimates of medical expenses for rural and urban sectors are Rs. 257 and Rs. 285 respectively. The public vs. private break-ups are (11+2416) for rural and (7+299) for urban all-India (Table 10).

Table 9
Percentage of Hospitalised Cases Treated in Public Hospital and Private Hospital

	Rural		*Urban*		
Major States	*Govt. Hosp.*	*Pvt. Hosp.*	*Govt. Hosp.*	*Pvt. Hosp.*	*% of Beds in Govt. Hospitals*
AP	27.23	72.77	35.80	64.20	40
Assam	74.20	25.80	55.40	44.60	84
Bihar	14.40	85.60	21.50	78.50	71
Chhattisgarh	53.50	46.50	49.30	50.70	–
Delhi	@	@	37.30	62.70	64
Gujarat	31.30	68.70	26.10	73.90	42
Haryana	20.60	79.40	29.00	71.00	75
HP	78.10	21.90	89.50	10.50	91
J & K	91.30	8.70	86.50	13.50	75
Jharkhand	46.60	53.40	31.20	68.80	–
Karnataka	40.00	60.00	28.90	71.10	74
Kerala	35.60	64.40	34.60	65.40	31
MP	58.50	41.50	48.50	51.50	–
Maharashtra	28.70	71.30	28.00	72.00	57
Orissa	79.10	20.90	73.10	26.90	98
Punjab	29.40	70.60	26.40	73.60	75
Rajasthan	52.10	47.90	63.70	36.30	–
TN	40.80	59.20	37.20	62.80	78
Uttaranchal	43.10	56.90	34.20	65.80	–
UP	26.93	73.07	31.40	68.60	72
WB	78.68	21.32	65.40	34.60	86
India	41.70	58.30	38.20	61.80	62

Source: Based on Statement 24.1 in GoI (2006; p. 28).

Table 10

Medical and Non-Medical Costs (Per treated Person) Associated with Non-Hospitalised Treatment: Kerala and All-India

(Rs. during 15 days)

Major State	*Medical Expenses by Source of Treatment*			*Other Expenses*	*Total Expenditure*	*Loss of Household Income Per treated Person*
	Govt.	*Pvt.*	*All*			
Rural Sector						
All-Kerala	3	179	182	16	198	72
All-India	11	246	257	27	285	135
Urban Sector						
All-Kerala	5	189	193	13	206	83
All-India	7	299	306	20	326	96

Source: GoI (2006; pp. 40-41).

Table 11

Average Medical and Total Expenditure Per Hospitalisation Case by Type of Hospital and Loss of Household Income due to Hospitalization: Kerala and All-India

(Reference period: 365 days)

Major State	*Medical Expenses by Source of Treatment*			*Other Expenses*	*Total Expenditure*	*Loss of Household Income Per treated Person*
	Govt.	*Pvt.*	*All*			
Rural Sector						
All-Kerala	2174	4565	3717	342	4059	431
All-India	3238	7408	5695	530	6225	636135
Urban Sector						
All-Kerala	2600	6179	4954	247	5201	578
All-India	3877	11553	8851	516	9367	745

Source: GoI (2006; pp. 42-43).

(7) In addition, illness involves an opportunity cost for the household in terms of loss of income. Estimated loss of income per treated person (non-hospitalised cases) during the reference period of 15 days is Rs. 72 in rural Kerala and Rs. 83 in urban Kerala; the corresponding estimates for all-India were Rs. 135 and Rs. 96 respectively (Table 10). In a similar way,

hospitalization for different types of ailments too has its own monetary and opportunity costs as listed in Table 11.

MORBIDITY AND HEALTH IN KERALA

Current Scenario

To facilitate a proper understanding of issues and appreciation of welfare imperatives, this section provides a profile of the incidence of morbidity that is, Proportion of Ailing Persons across gender and by sector sex for Kerala along with that for all-India for the same reference period (January-June 2004) (Table 12). In fact, several studies have emphasized the gender and economic dimensions of inequality in health status in India (Sen. *et al.*, 2002) and from a policy perspective, one may consider other dimensions like occupation too. Some salient features of the gender, occupational and economic dimensions are presented in the same sequence below:

Table 12
Incidence of Morbidity by Gender and Sector
Kerala and All-India (2004)

(Per cent)

	Northern Kerala			*Southern Kerala*			*All-Kerala*			*All-India*		
Gender	*Rural*	*Urban*	*Comb.*	*Rural*	*Urban*	*Comb.*	*Rural*	*Urban*	*Comb.*	*Rural*	*Urban*	*Comb.*
Male	18.34	15.81	17.77	28.48	27.72	28.26	24.28	23.56	24.09	8.36	9.11	8.56
Female	18.15	15.74	17.62	33.06	29.13	31.93	26.66	24.51	26.10	9.30	10.86	9.69
Total	18.24	15.77	17.69	30.86	28.46	30.18	25.53	24.06	25.15	8.82	9.95	9.11

Note: Comb. means 'Rural and Urban combined'.
Source: Tabulated from NSS Unit record data (60th Round).

(a) Incidence of morbidity is higher in Kerala than India as a whole. For the population as a whole it is 25.11 per cent for Kerala as against 9.11 per cent for All-India.

(b) For both men and women, it is higher, though marginally, in the rural sector than in the urban in Kerala and the reverse at the all-India level.

(c) It is uniformly and marginally higher for women than for men across sectors both in Kerala and in India as a whole. Within Kerala, it is higher for women only in the South; it is the same as/marginally less for women than for men in North Kerala.

(d) Within Kerala, the incidence is much higher (almost twice) in the South than that in the North, whatever it may imply about the health status. This pattern holds good across gender in both rural and urban sectors.

That the magnitude of morbidity is much higher in Kerala than in India as a whole has serious budgetary and policy implications with respect to provision of health care, its volume as well as type, in Kerala.

If so, a moot question would be how far these estimates are reliable? Do they represent actual state of affairs or are they resultant of higher levels of awareness thanks to high levels of literacy in Kerala? One approach to verify this issue could be to juxtapose estimates of morbidity with those for infant mortality across states. This is because infant mortality is widely considered as a reliable indicator of the health status of a population. Sample Registration Scheme estimates by the Registrar-General of India of infant mortality for the year 2002 exhibit broad negative covariance with morbidity across states in India (Table 13).

Table 13

Number (per 1000) of Persons Reporting Ailment (PAP) and Number Reporting Commencement of any Ailment (PPC) during last 15 days, along with Infant Mortality Rate (IMR) for Major States

	Rural			*Urban*		
Major States	*PAP*	*PPC*	*IMR*	*PAP*	*PPC*	*IMR*
Andhra Pradesh	90	36	71	114	47	35
Assam	82	58	73	83	48	38
Bihar	53	32	62	63	30	50
Chhattisgarh	69	38	–	72	31	–
Delhi	@	@	@	16	7	–
Gujarat	69	29	68	78	29	37
Haryana	95	48	65	87	43	51
Himachal Pradesh	87	26	–	59	19	–
Jammu & Kashmir	70	30	–	78	34	–

Contd...

	Rural			Urban		
Major States	*PAP*	*PPC*	*IMR*	*PAP*	*PPC*	*IMR*
Jharkhand	33	21	–	50	21	–
Karnataka	64	32	65	57	20	25
Kerala	255	103	11	240	100	8
Madhya Pradesh	61	32	90	65	36	56
Maharashtra	93	44	52	118	50	34
Orissa	77	49	91	54	30	56
Punjab	136	61	55	107	44	35
Rajasthan	57	23	81	72	27	55
Tamil Nadu	95	54	50	96	49	32
Uttaranchal	52	31	–	65	25	–
Uttar Pradesh	100	55	83	108	55	58
West Bengal	114	56	52	157	62	36
India	88	45	69*	99	44	40*

Notes: (1) The data on Infant Mortality Rate (IMR) are estimates for 2002 obtained by the Sample Registration Scheme of the Registrar-General of India.

(2) IMR values in brackets are averages of IMRs estimated for 1995 and 1996 by the Sample Registration Scheme of the Registrar-General of India.

Source: GoI (2006; p. 18).

Occupational Profile

From a policy perspective, it would be important to examine the levels morbidity by occupational groups of households since the nature and extent of access to health facilities as well as insurance available varies by these groups (Tables 14 & 15):

(1) As regards the rural sector, incidence was the highest among 'other labour' in Kerala and 'Others' for all-India. Within Kerala, the North and the South differ with respect to both magnitude and profile. Incidence was the highest for self employed in agriculture in Northern Kerala but Other labour in South Kerala It was the lowest among self-employed in anon-agriculture in North Kerala, 'Others' in South Kerala, but agriculture labour' for Kerala as a whole. For all-India, it was lowest among 'agriculture labour' (Table 14).

(2) As regards the urban sector, morbidity was the highest among casual labouers in northern Kerala, other labour in South Kerala and Kerala as a whole and also

for all-India. Urban morbidity was the lowest among regular wage/salary earners in North Kerala, self-employed in non-agriculture in South Kerala, Kerala as a whole and also all-India (Table 15).

Table 14
Incidence of Morbidity by Type of Rural Household: Kerala Vs. India (2004)

(Per cent)

Household Type	*Kerala*			*India*
	North	*South*	*All*	
Self Employed (Non Agriculture)	15.90	31.05	26.06	9.16
Agriculture Labour	17.41	28.63	22.94	7.67
Other Labour	17.66	33.91	27.49	10.64
Self Employed (Agriculture)	21.92	28.95	26.08	8.14
Others	18.69	28.23	23.23	12.33
All Rural	18.27	30.86	25.54	8.83

Note: All means 'North and South combined'.
Source: Tabulated from NSS Unit record data (60th Round).

Table 15
Incidence of Morbidity by Type of Urban Household: Kerala Vs. India (2004)

(Per cent)

Household Type	*Kerala*			*India*
	Northern	*Southern*	*All*	
Self Employed (Non Agriculture)	14.20	24.93	21.91	9.31
Regular Wage/Salary	12.56	30.50	25.95	9.89
Casual Labour	17.99	26.44	22.59	9.58
Others	17.59	45.39	30.58	15.60
All Urban	15.77	28.46	24.06	9.95

Note: All means 'North and South combined'.
Source: Tabulated from NSS Unit record data (60th Round).

Economic Class Profile

Given the general perception that level income and health status co-vary in the same direction, it would be interesting to examine the incidence of morbidity by population decile groups formed with reference to levels of consumer expenditure in Kerala as well as country as a whole. The extent of inequality in health status is generally measured in terms of different measures. For instance, Sen. *et al.* (2002) regress morbidity on fractile group and use estimated slope parameter as a measure of extent of inequality. However, one limitation of this study is that the fractile groups are of unequal size involving heteroscedasticity and giving scope for specification error and hence, inefficient regression slope estimates. Hence, we overcome this problem by estimating morbidity rates across equi-frequency decile groups and pseudo-Gini rations based on unit record data. The estimates bring out the following features (Table 16):

Table 16
Incidence of Morbidity by Sector: Kerala and All India (2004)

(Per cent)

	Northern Kerala			*Southern Kerala*			*Kerala*			*India*		
MPCE Decile Group	*Rural*	*Urban*	*Comb.*	*Rural*	*Urban*	*Comb.*	*Rural*	*Urban*	*Comb.*	*Rural*	*Urban*	*Comb.*
1	15.02	16.23	15.38	31.30	21.54	28.98	22.40	17.10	20.60	6.10	7.80	6.20
2	16.76	13.95	16.81	21.73	26.65	27.79	19.70	19.40	20.00	6.30	8.50	6.50
3	15.46	13.38	16.67	35.31	24.93	27.37	22.60	18.80	23.10	6.60	8.20	7.30
4	17.46	15.78	19.50	25.04	24.71	29.19	27.10	23.20	24.90	7.70	8.50	8.00
5	21.18	11.44	17.92	24.29	27.28	36.32	21.30	21.50	21.40	8.00	9.50	8.70
6	19.77	20.38	18.86	34.67	24.69	34.58	23.80	21.50	24.80	8.80	9.90	9.10
7	16.26	12.70	18.39	37.65	31.19	29.93	28.70	22.90	28.50	9.30	9.70	9.10
8	18.15	16.53	21.79	35.91	36.15	27.34	29.10	30.10	28.10	9.40	10.60	10.60
9	18.99	16.31	15.30	29.79	35.15	26.51	30.70	34.70	28.30	11.10	12.60	11.70
10	23.36	21.06	16.29	32.90	32.35	33.80	29.80	31.60	31.90	14.90	14.10	13.70
Total	18.24	15.77	17.69	30.86	28.46	30.18	25.50	24.10	25.10	8.80	9.90	9.10
Pseudo -Gini	6.10	5.71	5.60	4.45	9.39	4.97	7.20	12.20	7.90	15.10	10.30	13.70

Note: Comb. means 'Rural and Urban combined'.
Source: Tabulated from the NSS Unit record data (60th Round)

(1) Incidence of morbidity is higher in rural than in urban Kerala and vice versa for all-India. As regards inequality in morbidity, the extent in general is lower in Kerala than in India though levels of morbidity are higher in the former than in the latter. Within Kerala, contrary to the relative profile of morbidity levels, inequality was higher in urban than in rural sector in South Kerala and Kerala as a whole. Similarly, at the

all India level too, inequality in morbidity as against incidence was higher in the rural than in the urban sector.

(2) Within Kerala, relative levels of incidence of morbidity across sectors was the same as at the state level; and the incidence in general was less in the North than in the South.

(3) Estimates of relative inequality in morbidity distribution show explicit ordinal rankings of sectors; however, pseudo-Lorenz curves for sectors at different levels (state as well as all-India) intersect implying that relative levels of morbidity vary at different percentiles of expenditure (Figures 1-4).

(4) However, a binary classification into poor and non-poor categories tend to show that finding that the incidence of morbidity is uniformly higher among the poor than among the non-poor categories at all geographical levels (Table 17).

Table 17
Morbidity Incidence for Poor and Non-Poor by Sector: Kerala and All-India (2004)

(Per cent)

	Northern Kerala		*Southern Kerala*		*Kerala*		*India*	
Characteristic	*Rural*	*Urban*	*Rural*	*Urban*	*Rural*	*Urban*	*Rural*	*Urban*
Poor	15.51	14.47	29.31	23.18	21.97	17.98	6.47	8.17
Non-poor	19.01	16.84	31.11	29.48	26.28	26.22	9.97	10.61
Total	18.24	15.77	30.86	28.46	25.53	24.06	8.82	9.95

Source: Tabulated from NSS Unit record data (60th Round).

Given Panikar-Soman explanation for the Kerala's paradoxical experience, a moot question would be on type of diseases afflicting these two categories at different levels (Tables 18 & 19). This coupled with the information on their relative access to private and public medical institutions will facilitate a study of welfare costs and benefits (Tables 20 &21). These issues are discussed in the following sub-section.

Figure 1
Pseudo-Lorenz Curve for Morbidity: All-Kerala

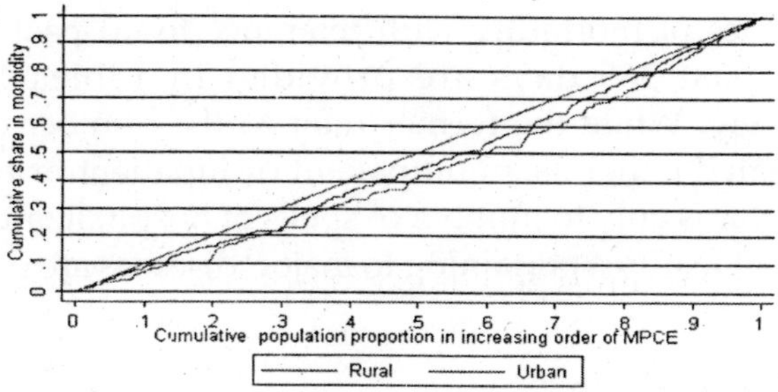

Figure 2
Pseudo-Lorenz Curve for Morbidity: North-Kerala

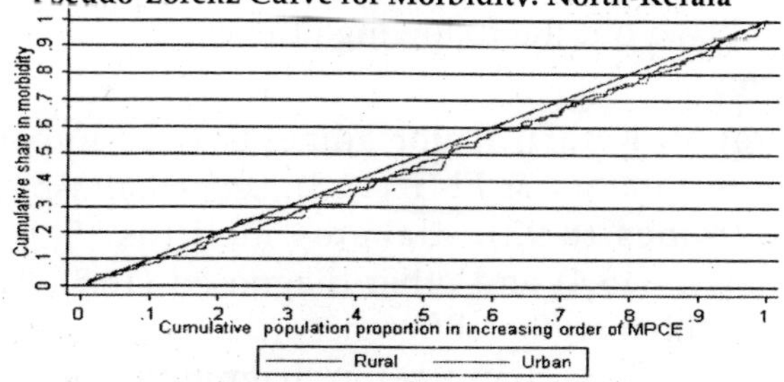

Figure 3
Pseudo-Lorenz Curve for Morbidity: South-Kerala

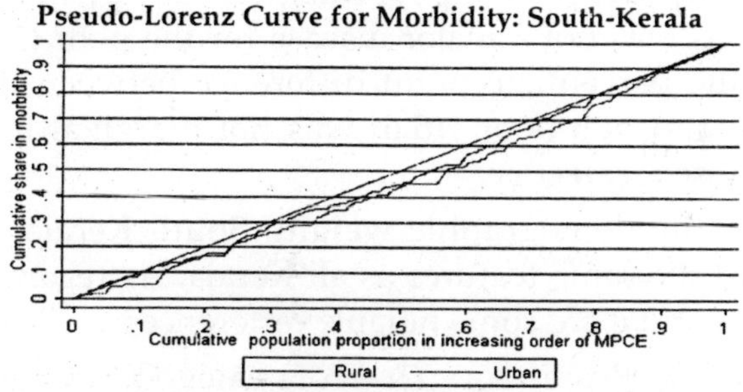

Figure 4
Pseudo-Lorenz Curve for Morbidity: All-India

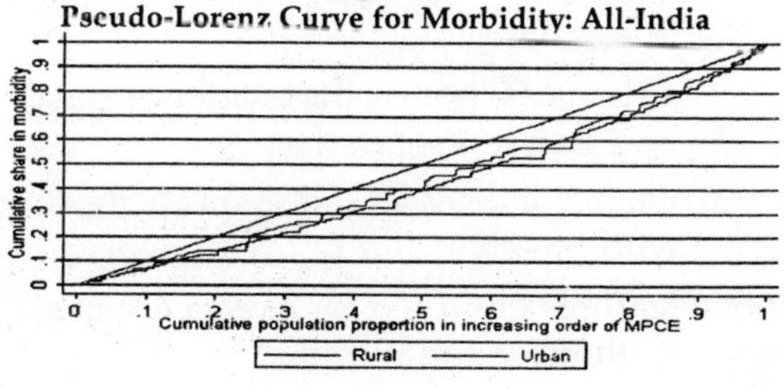

Morbidity: Profile and Treatment

The profiles of morbidity with reference to (a) past 15 days and (b) past 365 days are provided in Tables 18 & 19 respectively. While the former refer to the number of ailing cases treated either as an outpatient or inpatient or both, the latter pertains only to number of spells of hospitalization only. The salient features pertaining to major[3] diseases are presented below:

Short-run Scenario

The profile of self-reported morbidity with a reference period of 15 days bring out the following (Table 18):

Rural Sector

(1) In rural all-Kerala, major ailments were hypertension (7.61), respiratory & ENT (12.3), bronchial asthma (5.2), joints/bones (8.97), diabetes mellitus (5.92), fever (unknown) (15.4) and other diagnosed (16.5). The same profile, with marginal differences (that is, percentage point difference of less than five) in magnitude, held good for both the poor and non-poor categories except that diabetes mellitus was not a major disease for the poor (3.07) and that the percentage point difference between the poor (21.5) and non-poor (15.6) was not marginal for 'other diagnosed' category.

(2) Given the demographic weight, South Kerala exhibits almost the same features as all-Kerala. As regards North Kerala, there are some notable differences.

   (a) While Respiratory (& ENT) category accounted for only 5.11 per cent in North Kerala but 15.19 per cent in South Kerala.

   (b) As regards joints/bones, the incidence was 5.19 in the North and 10.5 in the South.

(1) In general, the major diseases in Kerala are those generally associated with life-style and not with deprivation.

(2) The above features observed for Kerala are in some sense in contrast with those for all-India:

(a) Diarrhoea/dysentery, gastric/peptic ulcer together account for about 10 per cent of the reported cases at the all-India level while the same for Keràla was about 3 per cent. Further malaria, which did not prevail in Kerala, afflicted the rest of India.

(b) Heart diseases and hypertension together accounted for about 11 per cent in Kerala but about 5 per cent at all-India rural sector.

(c) ENT related ailments afflicted one out of every eighth ailing case in Kerala but only one out of 14 at the all-India level.

Urban Sector

(1) Major ailments in urban all-Kerala were hypertension (9.84), respiratory & ENT (13.79), joints/bones (7.44), diabetes mellitus (8.52), fever (unknown) (17.47) and other diagnosed (13.36). All these diseases except 'other diagnosed' and 'fever (unknown)' categories, dominated for the non-poor than for the poor in the sense that the estimates for the former exceeded those for the latter by more than five percentage points.

(2) South Kerala exhibited nearly similar features as the state as a whole; however, the North differs by exhibiting near homogeneity of ailment profiles for the poor and non-poor.

(3) All-India features too were broadly similar to those for Kerala in some respects.

Long-run (Hospitalization Only) Scenario

Rural Sector

(1) For Kerala as a whole, major ailments for which hospitalization was undertaken were heart disease (5.62), respiratory (ENT) (5.36), fever (unknown) (18.52), fractures/poisoning (8.83) and 'other diagnosed' (18.29). As regards the poor, the profile differs in that other categories like diarrhoea/dysentery, gastric/peptic ulcer, joints/bones also dominate.

(2) A similar profile held for the North and the South but for the following: Ailments pertaining to 'joints/bones' were major in the South while diarrhoea was major in the North. Further, respiratory (ENT) was not major in the North.

Urban Sector

(1) Major ailments were heart disease (7.15), respiratory (ENT) (8.23), bronchial asthma (5.51), diabetes mellitus (5.34), fever of unknown origin (15.69), fractures/poisoning (10.03) and other diagnosed (12.29) (Table 19). The same holds good for both the poor and the non-poor with the following features:

    (a) The first three categories of ailments accounted for relatively larger percentage number of hospitalization among the non-poor than that among the poor; the estimates for the non-poor were heart disease (7.73), respiratory (ENT) (9.25), bronchial asthma (5.87).

    (b) The last four categories of ailments were relatively more dominant for the poor (diabetes mellitus (6.48), fever of unknown origin (19.07), fractures/poisoning (14.66) and other diagnosed (16.82).

(2) The urban profile was almost similar for the South. North Kerala had a similar profile but for the following features.

    (a) Hypertension (10.15) was another major ailment; respiratory (ENT) category (1.77) was a minor ailment.

    (b) The profiles of diseases between poor and non-poor were different: diarrhoea (6.13) was a major ailment that afflicted the poor while diabetes was major for the non-poor (8.43).

A summary profile of the preceding features is provided in Table 20. In general, the profile is the same between economic categories and across sectors. This is further corroborated by estimates of rank correlation coefficients between ailment profiles for both reference periods by sector and different regional levels (Tables 21 & 22).

Table 18
Distribution of Morbidity by Illness and Sector (2004)

	Northern Kerala						Southern Kerala						Kerala						India					
	Rural			Urban			Rural			Urban			Rural			Urban			Rural			Urban		
Population Sub-group	NP	Poor	All	NP	Poor	All	NP	Poor	All	NP	Poor	All	NP	Poor	All	NP	Poor	All	NP	Poor	All	NP	Poor	All
Diarrhoea/ dysentery	0.14	0.00	0.11	0.49	1.68	0.97	1.27	0.58	1.18	0.59	0.00	0.51	0.96	0.37	0.87	0.57	0.78	0.61	4.97	7.11	5.48	3.25	5.35	3.71
Gastric/ pepticulcer	2.50	4.35	2.85	0 00	3.64	1.47	2.45	3.36	2.57	2.05	1.14	1.93	2.46	3.72	2.65	1.72	2.30	1.83	4.17	3.64	4.04	2.60	3.03	2.70
Worm infestation	0.00	3.31	0.62				0.25	0.00	0.21	0.91	0.00	0.79	0.18	1.20	0.33	0.76	0.00	0.62	0.45	0.44	0.45	0.34	0.44	0.37
Amoebiosis	0.00	1.32	0.25				0.37	0.00	0.32	0.15	0.00	0.13	0.27	0.48	0.30				0.44	0.47	0.44	0.22	0.22	0.22
Hepatitis/ Jaundice																0.13	0.00	0.10	0.36	0.62	0.42	0.46	0.69	0.51
Heart disease	2.77	1.86	2.60	7.38	1.18	4.88	3.99	3.81	3.96	4.91	3.73	4.75	3.65	3.11	3.57	5.30	2.55	4.78	2.21	0.85	1.89	5.40	2.43	4.75
Hyper-tension	7.75	7.45	7.70	16.23	7.72	12.80	8.14	3.96	7.58	9.82	3.71	9.03	8.03	5.22	7.61	10.83	5.56	9.84	4.24	1.25	3.53	10.93	3.91	9.40
Respiratory (& ENT)	5.72	2.50	5.11	4.93	6.43	5.53	15.45	13.48	15.19	17.83	4.02	16.05	12.78	9.51	12.29	15.79	5.13	13.79	7.32	6.15	7.04	7.51	6.15	7.22
Tuberculosis	0.79	0.90	0.81	0.43	0.00	0.25	0.56	0.52	0.55	0.56	2.43	0.80	0.62	0.66	0.63	0.51	1.31	0.68	1.25	1.60	1.33	0.55	1.45	0.74
Bronchial asthma	5.45	5.63	5.48	2.56	3.81	3.06	4.99	5.66	5.08	2.97	5.74	3.33	5.12	5.65	5.20	2.91	4.84	3.27	4.08	2.95	3.81	3.14	3.19	3.15
Joints/ bones	5.01	5.93	5.19	6.68	3.90	5.56	10.69	9.32	10.50	8.50	4.27	7.95	9.13	8.09	8.97	8.21	4.10	7.44	7.00	4.71	6.46	7.32	5.01	6.81
Kidney/ urinary	0.97	0.00	0.79	1.16	1.12	1.15	0.57	1.51	0.69	1.09	2.82	1.31	0.68	0.96	0.72	1.10	2.03	1.27	1.01	0.65	0.92	1.24	0.69	1.12
Prostatic disorders							0.00	1.03	0.14				0.00	0.66	0.10				0.13	0.20	0.14	0.11	0.02	0.09

Contd...

	Northern Kerala						Southern Kerala						Kerala						India					
	Rural			Urban			Rural			Urban			Rural			Urban			Rural			Urban		
Population Sub-group	*NP*	*Poor*	*All*	*NP*	*Poor*	*All*	*NP*	*Poor*	*All*	*NP*	*Poor*	*All*	*NP*	*Poor*	*All*	*NP*	*Poor*	*All*	*NP*	*Poor*	*All*	*NP*	*Poor*	*All*
Gynaecological	0.91	0.00	0.74	2.25	1.59	1.99	0.76	0.51	0.72	1.14	0.29	1.03	0.80	0.33	0.73	1.31	0.89	1.23	1.28	1.36	1.30	0.97	0.90	0.95
Neurological disorders	3.14	2.30	2.98	3.39	2.12	2.88	2.45	2.30	2.43	3.44	1.20	3.15	2.64	2.30	2.59	3.44	1.63	3.10	2.04	1.50	1.91	2.41	2.01	2.32
Psychiatric disorders	2.56	1.58	2.37	1.02	0.00	0.61	1.14	1.90	1.24	0.32	3.88	0.78	1.53	1.79	1.57	0.43	2.09	0.74	0.66	0.81	0.70	0.60	0.74	0.63
Conjunctivitis	0.49	0.65	0.52				0.04	0.40	0.09	0.39	1.51	0.54	0.16	0.49	0.21	0.33	0.81	0.42	0.42	0.38	0.41	0.43	0.62	0.47
Glaucoma	0.42	0.00	0.34	0.95	0.00	0.56	0.15	0.00	0.13				0.22	0.00	0.19	0.15	0.00	0.12	0.21	0.33	0.24	0.32	0.34	0.32
Cataract	1.21	0.57	1.09	1.40	0.00	0.83	1.13	2.35	1.29	0.73	0.98	0.76	1.15	1.70	1.23	0.83	0.53	0.78	1.64	1.64	1.64	1.17	2.17	1.39
Diseases of skin	1.90	2.61	2.04	0.14	0.00	0.08	2.03	1.80	2.00	1.28	0.98	1.24	2.00	2.09	2.01	1.10	0.52	0.99	2.28	2.97	2.44	1.49	2.69	1.75
Goitre	0.00	0.29	0.05	2.12	0.00	1.26	0.37	0.00	0.32	0.08	0.00	0.07	0.27	0.10	0.24	0.40	0.00	0.32	0.13	0.07	0.11	0.13	0.10	0.13
Diabetes mellitus	9.04	3.09	7.91	10.16	7.39	9.04	5.43	3.06	5.11	8.92	4.62	8.37	6.42	3.07	5.92	9.12	5.90	8.52	2.71	0.81	2.26	7.95	2.75	6.82
Under-nutrition							0.05	0.00	0.04				0.03	0.00	0.03				0.11	0.10	0.11	0.26	0.11	0.22
Anaemia	0.77	0.89	0.79	0.00	2.28	0.92	0.06	0.00	0.05	0.00	0.52	0.07	0.25	0.32	0.26	0.00	1.33	0.25	0.40	0.67	0.47	0.37	0.95	0.50
STDs																			0.08	0.11	0.09	0.01	0.00	0.00
Malaria																			1.95	2.39	2.06	0.91	1.12	0.96
Eruptive	0.10	0.00	0.08				0.70	0.00	0.61				0.53	0.00	0.45				0.53	0.73	0.58	0.19	0.24	0.21
Mumps							0.11	0.00	0.10				0.08	0.00	0.07				0.25	0.41	0.29	0.16	0.45	0.22
Diphtheria										0.00	1.76	0.23				0.00	0.95	0.18	0.09	0.28	0.14	0.19	0.38	0.23

Contd...

	Northern Kerala						*Southern Kerala*						*Kerala*						*India*					
	Rural			*Urban*			*Rural*			*Urban*			*Rural*			*Urban*			*Rural*			*Urban*		
Population Sub-group	*NP*	*Poor*	*All*	*NP*	*Poor*	*All*	*NP*	*Poor*	*All*	*NP*	*Poor*	*All*	*NP*	*Poor*	*All*	*NP*	*Poor*	*All*	*NP*	*Poor*	*All*	*NP*	*Poor*	*All*
Whooping cough	0.52	1.00	0.61	0.41	0.00	0.25	1.23	1.06	1.21	1.53	0.00	1.33	1.04	1.04	1.04	1.35	0.00	1.10	2.53	2.76	2.59	2.19	2.46	2.25
Fever (Unknown)	15.23	16.47	15.46	16.86	16.78	16.83	15.00	17.74	15.37	16.51	25.34	17.65	15.06	17.28	15.40	16.57	21.38	17.47	19.34	24.42	20.55	13.65	19.82	15.00
Tetanus							0.09	0.00	0.08				0.07	0.00	0.06				0.05	0.01	0.04	0.02	0.00	0.02
Filariasis/ Elephantiasis				0.00	0.40	0.16				0.00	2.81	0.36				0.00	1.70	0.32	0.11	0.13	0.12	0.10	0.26	0.13
Locomotor	3.17	2.18	2.98	1.88	5.51	3.35	0.91	0.46	0.85	0.73	1.48	0.83	1.53	1.09	1.46	0.91	3.34	1.37	1.88	2.35	1.99	1.48	2.00	1.60
Visual/ blindness (no cataract)	0.71	0.29	0.63				0.99	0.00	0.85	0.19	0.51	0.24	0.91	0.10	0.79	0.15	0.28	0.19	1.12	1.59	1.23	0.64	1.15	0.75
Speech	0.36	0.00	0.29				0.23	0.51	0.27	0.00	2.58	0.33	0.27	0.33	0.28	0.00	1.38	0.26	0.18	0.39	0.23	0.41	0.22	0.37
Hearing	0.19	0.52	0.26	0.74	0.00	0.44	0.63	1.02	0.68	1.45	0.51	1.33	0.51	0.84	0.56	1.34	0.28	1.14	0.95	1.05	0.97	0.98	0.78	0.94
Mouth/ Teeth/Gum	0.32	1.59	0.56	0.22	0.00	0.13	0.84	0.00	0.72	0.29	0.00	0.25	0.69	0.58	0.68	0.28	0.00	0.23	1.12	0.51	0.97	1.14	0.94	1.10
Fractures/ Poisoning	1.68	5.25	2.35	2.49	3.30	2.81	2.06	1.18	1.94	1.49	6.99	2.20	1.95	2.65	2.06	1.65	5.28	2.33	2.69	2.84	2.73	2.36	3.48	2.60
Cancer/ tumours	0.49	0.26	0.45	1.89	0.73	1.42	0.41	0.53	0.43	0.09	0.23	0.11	0.43	0.43	0.43	0.37	0.46	0.39	0.53	0.41	0.50	0.62	0.47	0.58
Other diagnosed	23.44	25.47	23.82	13.67	29.40	20.02	12.59	19.27	13.48	11.46	12.04	11.53	15.57	21.51	16.46	11.31	20.07	13.36	14.41	15.22	14.61	13.89	17.50	14.68
Other un-diagnosed	2.25	1.75	2.16	0.56	1.03	0.75	1.90	2.67	2.00	0.59	3.92	1.02	1.99	2.34	2.04	0.58	2.58	0.96	2.70	3.11	2.80	1.89	2.76	2.08
Total	100	100	100	100	100	100	100	100	100	100	100	100	100	100	100	100	100	100	100	100	100	100	100	100

Table 19

Hospitalization (during the past 365 days) by Type of Disease: An Economic Profile (2004)

(per cent)

	Northern Kerala						Southern Kerala						Kerala						India					
	Rural			Urban			Rural			Urban			Rural			Urban			Rural			Urban		
Population Sub-group	*NP*	*Poor*	*All*	*NP*	*Poor*	*All*	*NP*	*Poor*	*All*	*NP*	*Poor*	*All*	*NP*	*Poor*	*All*	*NP*	*Poor*	*All*	*NP*	*Poor*	*All*	*NP*	*Poor*	*All*
Diarrhoea/ dysentery	6.16	1.85	5.33	3.45	6.13	4.52	3.40	7.99	4.10	4.12	0.91	3.53	4.23	5.74	4.48	3.99	3.14	3.78	7.09	11.19	7.93	5.66	9.55	6.47
Gastric/ pepticulcer	3.46	4.48	3.66	1.69	0.66	1.28	2.84	7.59	3.56	2.07	3.17	2.28	3.02	6.45	3.59	2.00	2.10	2.02	4.89	5.14	4.94	3.92	4.76	4.10
Worm infestation	0.47	0.00	0.38				0.29	0.00	0.25	1.02	0.00	0.83	0.35	0.00	0.29	0.81	0.00	0.61	0.39	0.46	0.40	0.44	0.55	0.46
Amoebiosis				0.00	0.66	0.26	0.72	0.85	0.74	0.12	1.56	0.39	0.50	0.54	0.51	0.10	1.18	0.35	0.31	0.33	0.32	0.36	0.47	0.38
Hepatitis/ Jaundice	0.62	0.00	0.50				0.31	0.81	0.39	0.83	7.04	1.98	0.40	0.51	0.42	0.66	4.03	1.47	1.58	1.18	1.50	2.03	2.66	2.16
Heart disease	5.90	6.77	6.06	6.46	4.01	5.48	5.57	4.51	5.41	8.06	6.27	7.73	5.67	5.34	5.62	7.73	5.30	7.15	4.26	2.97	3.99	8.02	4.51	7.29
Hyper- tension	3.03	4.79	3.37	13.69	4.80	10.15	3.05	2.75	3.00	3.24	0.00	2.64	3.04	3.50	3.12	5.37	2.05	4.58	2.07	1.17	1.89	3.36	2.80	3.25
Respiratory (& ENT)	1.64	7.85	2.84	0.00	4.45	1.77	6.58	6.13	6.51	11.62	5.42	10.48	5.08	6.76	5.36	9.25	5.01	8.23	3.54	2.43	3.31	3.30	2.26	3.08
Tuberculosis	0.88	0.74	0.85	0.00	0.66	0.26	1.35	0.61	1.24	0.34	1.51	0.56	1.21	0.66	1.12	0.27	1.15	0.48	2.46	3.76	2.73	1.49	2.67	1.74
Bronchial asthma	3.17	4.19	3.37	5.35	5.63	5.46	4.25	5.33	4.42	6.00	3.44	5.53	3.92	4.91	4.09	5.87	4.38	5.51	3.29	2.77	3.18	2.98	3.35	3.05
Joints/ bones	0.91	2.44	1.20	3.14	1.07	2.32	6.20	7.06	6.33	4.99	1.26	4.30	4.59	5.37	4.72	4.61	1.18	3.79	2.72	1.89	2.56	2.80	2.33	2.70
Kidney/ urinary	2.33	2.75	2.41	4.40	1.04	3.06	2.49	2.10	2.43	5.39	0.89	4.56	2.44	2.34	2.42	5.19	0.95	4.17	3.79	3.43	3.72	5.50	2.79	4.94
Prostatic disorders				0.00	0.66	0.26				0.21	0.00	0.17				0.16	0.28	0.19	0.38	0.39	0.38	0.46	0.10	0.38

Contd...

Population Sub-group	Northern Kerala						Southern Kerala						Kerala						India					
	Rural			Urban			Rural			Urban			Rural			Urban			Rural			Urban		
	NP	Poor	All	NP	Poor	All	NP	Poor	All	NP	Poor	All	NP	Poor	All	NP	Poor	All	NP	Poor	All	NP	Poor	All
Gynaeco-logical	3.67	1.88	3.33	3.03	7.61	4.86	2.64	3.02	2.70	5.40	1.46	4.67	2.95	2.60	2.89	4.92	4.09	4.72	5.60	4.72	5.42	5.33	4.98	5.25
Neurolo-gicaldisorders	3.13	2.69	3.05	2.33	1.58	2.03	2.13	5.64	2.66	1.18	0.41	1.04	2.43	4.56	2.78	1.42	0.91	1.30	3.32	2.59	3.17	3.08	2.82	3.02
Psychiatric disorders	1.99	1.02	1.80				1.58	0.00	1.34	0.13	0.53	0.21	1.70	0.37	1.48	0.11	0.30	0.15	1.09	0.90	1.05	0.65	0.36	0.59
Conjunctivitis																			0.21	0.16	0.20	0.15	0.44	0.21
Glaucoma	0.05	0.00	0.04				0.14	0.00	0.12				0.11	0.00	0.09				0.53	0.26	0.48	0.87	0.34	0.76
Cataract	0.85	2.21	1.11	1.09	1.28	1.17	1.44	0.00	1.22	0.52	0.00	0.43	1.26	0.81	1.18	0.64	0.55	0.62	2.90	3.35	2.99	2.52	2.47	2.51
Diseases of skin	0.96	0.32	0.84				0.20	1.31	0.37	2.07	1.94	2.05	0.43	0.95	0.52	1.65	1.11	1.52	0.62	0.61	0.62	0.66	0.51	0.63
Goitre	0.18	0.00	0.15							0.85	0.00	0.69	0.05	0.00	0.05	0.67	0.00	0.51	0.06	0.13	0.08	0.17	0.09	0.15
Diabetes mellitus	4.62	0.00	3.73	8.53	2.99	6.32	4.08	0.00	3.46	4.06	9.10	4.99	4.24	0.00	3.54	4.97	6.48	5.34	2.11	0.26	1.73	2.48	1.75	2.33
Under-nutrition							0.17	0.00	0.14				0.12	0.00	0.10				0.08	0.07	0.08	0.09	0.03	0.08
Anaemia	0.00	1.18	0.23							0.94	0.00	0.77	0.00	0.43	0.07	0.75	0.00	0.57	0.92	0.82	0.90	1.16	0.95	1.12
STDs																			0.17	0.09	0.15	0.07	0.03	0.06
Malaria							0.00	1.01	0.15				0.00	0.64	0.11				2.52	5.99	3.22	3.82	3.71	3.80
Eruptive	0.20	0.00	0.16				0.27	0.80	0.35				0.25	0.51	0.29				0.09	1.00	0.28	0.09	0.12	0.10
Mumps																			0.09	0.08	0.09	0.02	0.05	0.02
Diphtheria																			0.10	0.32	0.15	0.54	0.06	0.44
Whooping cough	0.65	0.00	0.52				0.94	0.72	0.90	0.17	0.00	0.14	0.85	0.46	0.78	0.14	0.00	0.10	0.70	0.59	0.68	0.66	0.39	0.61
Fever (Unknown)	19.02	18.49	18.91	18.28	16.48	17.56	17.59	22.56	18.34	13.69	21.02	15.04	18.02	21.06	18.52	14.63	19.07	15.69	8.35	7.28	8.13	6.51	8.73	6.97

Contd...

	Northern Kerala						Southern Kerala						Kerala						India					
	Rural			Urban			Rural			Urban			Rural			Urban			Rural			Urban		
Population Sub-group	*NP*	*Poor*	*All*	*NP*	*Poor*	*All*	*NP*	*Poor*	*All*	*NP*	*Poor*	*All*	*NP*	*Poor*	*All*	*NP*	*Poor*	*All*	*NP*	*Poor*	*All*	*NP*	*Poor*	*All*
Tetanus							0.37	0.00	0.31	0.12	2.68	0.59	0.26	0.00	0.22	0.10	1.53	0.44	0.21	0.64	0.30	0.19	0.26	0.21
Filariasis/ Elephantiasis				0.00	0.82	0.33	0.12	0.00	0.10				0.08	0.00	0.07	0.00	0.35	0.08	0.14	0.11	0.14	0.11	0.20	0.13
Locomotor	1.10	0.25	0.93	0.00	1.85	0.74	0.21	0.00	0.18	0.09	0.00	0.07	0.48	0.09	0.42	0.07	0.79	0.24	1.47	1.05	1.38	0.86	1.05	0.90
Visual/ blindness (no cataract)							0.24	0.00	0.21	0.90	0.00	0.74	0.17	0.00	0.14	0.72	0.00	0.55	0.32	0.90	0.43	0.35	0.17	0.31
Speech																			0.08	0.06	0.07	0.03	0.00	0.03
Hearing	0.16	0.00	0.13	0.00	1.71	0.68	0.23	0.00	0.20	0.15	0.00	0.12	0.21	0.00	0.18	0.12	0.73	0.27	0.16	0.25	0.18	0.04	0.22	0.08
Mouth/ Teeth/Gum	0.00	0.75	0.15				0.21	0.00	0.17				0.14	0.28	0.16				0.25	0.28	0.26	0.20	0.11	0.18
Fractures/ Poisoning	10.11	8.73	9.85	6.18	11.09	8.13	9.09	4.32	8.36	9.17	17.34	10.69	9.40	5.94	8.83	8.56	14.66	10.03	10.28	9.45	10.11	8.61	10.59	9.02
Cancer/ tumours	2.89	6.41	3.57	5.83	1.49	4.10	2.83	2.12	2.72	1.22	0.00	1.00	2.85	3.69	2.99	2.17	0.64	1.80	2.64	1.89	2.49	3.00	1.43	2.67
Other diagnosed	21.40	20.20	21.17	14.89	23.32	18.25	17.97	11.48	16.98	9.83	11.95	10.22	19.01	14.67	18.29	10.86	16.82	12.29	16.83	16.31	16.72	16.51	17.20	16.66
Other undiagnosed	0.46	0.00	0.37	1.65	0.00	0.99	0.53	1.30	0.65	1.47	2.11	1.59	0.51	0.82	0.56	1.51	1.21	1.44	1.40	2.71	1.66	0.90	2.14	1.16
Total	100	100	100	100	100	100	100	100	100	100	100	100	100	100	100	100	100	100	100	100	100	100	100	100

Table 20

Morbidity and Treatment: A Summary Profile

Spells of ailment	*Past 15 days*		*Hospitalization during past 365 days*					
Sector	*Rural*	*Urban*	*Rural*	*Urban*				
Economic category	*Non-poor*	*Poor*	*Non-poor*	*Poor*	*Non-poor*	*Poor*	*Non-poor*	*Poor*
North-Kerala	HT, ENT, asthma, Bones,	HT, asthma, bones, fever, frac:ures,	HD, HT, bones, diabetes, fever, OD	HT, ENT, diabetes, fever, locomotor, OD	Dirrahoea, HD, fever, fractures, OD	HD, ENT, fever, fractures,	HD, HT, asthma, diabetes,fever, fever, fever, cancer, OD	diabetes, asthma, gynecological, fractures, OD
South-Kerala	HT, ENT, asthma, bones, diabetes, fever, OD	ENT, asthma, bones, fever, OD	HD, HT, ENT, bones, diabetes, fever, OD	Asthma, fever, fracture, OD	HD, ENT, bones, fever, fractures, OD	Diarrhoea, gastric, ENT, asthma, bones, neuro, fever,	HD, ENT, athma, bones, kidney,genaci, fever, fractures, OD	Jaundice, HD, ENT, diabetes, fever, OD fractures, OD
All-Kerala	HT, ENT, asthma, bones, diabetes, fever, OD	HT. ENT. Asthma, bones, fever, OD	HD, HT, ENT, bones, diabetes, fever, OD	HT, ENT, asthma, diabetes, fever, fractures, OD	HD, ENT, fever, fractures, OD	Diarrhoea, gastric, HD, ENT, asthma, bones, fever, fractures, OD	HD, HT, ENT, asthma, kidney, gynaeco, diabetes, fever, fractures, OD	HD, ENT, diabetes, fever, fractures, OD
All-India	Diarrhoea, ENT, bones, fever, OD	Diarrhoea, ENT, fever, OD	HD, HT, ENT, asthma, diabetes, fever, OD	Diarrhoea, ENT, bones, fever, OD	Diarrhoea, gastric,gynaeco, fever, fractures, OD	Diarrhoea, gastric malaria, fever, fractures, OD	Diarrhoea, HD, kidney, gynaeco, fever, fractures, OD	Diarrhoea, gynaco, fever, fractures, OD

Notes:
- HD: heart disease
- HT: hypertension
- ENT: Respiratory & ENT
- Fever: Fever of unknown origin
- OD: Other diagnosed

Table 21
Association between Morbidity Profiles for different Economic Categories by & Across Sectors: 2004
(Outpatient scenario; reference period of 15 days)

Rank Correlation for Incidence of Hospitalization across Diseases between	*Kerala*			*All-India*
	North	*South*	*All*	
Poor and non-poor: Rural Sector	0.7095*	0.8396*	0.8644*	0.9361*
Poor and non-poor: Urban Sector	0.6426*	0.5141*	0.6373*	0.9421*
Poor: Rural and Urban	0.6550*	0.7687*	0.7679*	0.9275*
Non-poor: Rural and Urban	0.6430*	0.8527*	0.8480*	0.9548*

Note: *indicates p-value = 0.01.

Table 22
Association between Morbidity Profiles for different Economic Categories by & Across Sectors: 2004
(Hospitalization scenario; reference period of 365 days)

Rank Correlation for Incidence of Hospitalization across Diseases between	*Kerala*			*All-India*
	North	*South*	*All*	
Poor and non-poor: Rural Sector	0.7169*	0.7431*	0.8035*	0.9038*
Poor and non-poor: Urban Sector	0.6429*	0.5834*	0.6928*	0.9349*
Poor: Rural and Urban	0.4836	0.4888*	0.6546*	0.9090*
Non-poor: Rural and Urban	0.7581*	0.7890*	0.7840*	0.9611*

Note: *indicates p-value = 0.01

Finally, a factor that has some relevance from a policy perspective is the finding that in general the poor rely relatively more on the public sector than on the private for treatment of illness as well as for hospitalization. If so, the pursuit of privatization and public sector reform has to be carried out with due regard to the welfare costs associated with them.

SUMMING UP

India has much to realize with reference the goals for the sectors on education and health, particularly the latter. Of course, the country has initiated reform measures like revisions in the scope for public health centers, cost recovery and privatization. Such measures will bear upon the welfare pursuits of the poor

Table 23
Share of Public Sector in Treatment of Ailmenst during the Past 15 Days: North Vs. South Kerala (2004)

MPCE Decile Group	Northern Kerala						Southern Kerala					
	Rural		Urban		Total		Rural		Urban		Total	
	Govt	Others	Govt	Others	Govt	Others	Govt	Others	Govt	Others	Govt	Others
1	53.17	46.83	24.03	75.97	47.07	52.93	64.15	35.85	52.14	47.86	60.62	39.38
2	43.58	56.42	22.37	77.63	36.88	63.12	58.95	41.05	25.84	74.16	52.88	47.12
3	16.55	83.45	39.52	60.48	28.86	71.14	50.49	49.51	30.40	69.60	53.21	46.79
4	37.44	62.56	51.67	48.33	19.98	80.02	54.70	45.30	15.74	84.26	41.57	58.43
5	18.70	81.30	8.79	91.21	18.26	81.74	38.41	61.59	35.22	64.78	45.04	54.96
6	18.65	81.35	41.36	58.64	23.24	76.76	48.12	51.88	35.05	64.95	41.37	58.63
7	21.78	78.22	11.41	88.59	15.77	84.23	40.89	59.11	10.99	89.01	22.75	77.25
8	20.96	79.04	23.73	76.27	17.19	82.81	44.09	55.91	9.38	90.62	25.93	74.07
9	16.04	83.96	33.91	66.09	32.65	67.35	23.36	76.64	19.72	80.28	27.87	72.13
10	15.88	84.12	1.58	98.42	19.63	80.37	20.23	79.77	17.15	82.85	14.34	85.66
Total	25.12	74.88	25.32	74.68	25.16	74.84	43.53	56.47	23.58	76.42	38.13	61.87

Table 24
Share of Public Sector in Treatment of Ailmenst during the Past 15 Days: All Kerala vs. All India (2004)

	All Kerala						*India*					
	Rural		*Urban*		*Total*		*Rural*		*Urban*		*Total*	
MPCE Decile Group	*Govt*	*Others*	*Govt*	*Others*	*Govt*	*Others*	*Govt*	*Others*	*Govt*	*Others*	*Govt*	*Others*
1	61.57	38.43	40.01	59.99	56.37	43.63	33.03	66.97	25.57	74.43	30.78	69.22
2	44.82	55.18	33.99	66.01	44.80	55.20	28.74	71.26	29.83	70.17	29.32	70.68
3	43.96	56.04	32.42	67.58	45.14	54.86	29.96	70.04	24.02	75.98	24.79	75.21
4	48.65	51.35	27.73	72.27	36.31	63.69	22.49	77.51	27.80	72.20	25.38	74.62
5	28.75	71.25	14.21	85.79	33.32	66.68	24.55	75.45	18.18	81.82	25.44	74.56
6	35.65	64.35	34.47	65.53	34.69	65.31	24.36	75.64	22.38	77.62	22.93	77.07
7	43.18	56.82	34.57	65.43	35.61	64.39	22.59	77.41	21.94	78.06	24.56	75.44
8	37.25	62.75	13.72	86.28	37.20	62.80	24.13	75.87	15.10	84.90	21.62	78.38
9	30.25	69.75	9.15	90.85	21.02	78.98	22.56	77.44	17.17	82.83	22.13	77.87
10	16.61	83.39	18.87	81.13	16.00	84.00	21.27	78.73	12.56	87.44	16.37	83.63
Total	38.03	61.97	23.98	76.02	34.48	65.52	24.35	75.65	20.26	79.74	23.09	76.91

Table 25
Share of Public Sector in Hospitalised Treatment across Decile Groups by Sectors: North Vs. South Kerala (2004)

(per cent)

MPCE Decile Groups	Northern Kerala						Southern Kerala					
	Rural		Urban		Total		Rural		Urban		Total	
	Private	Public	Private	Public	Private	Public	Private	Public	Private	Public	Private	Public
1	47.19	52.81	28.40	71.60	50.37	49.64	53.65	46.35	44.41	55.59	58.38	41.62
2	50.13	49.88	44.01	55.99	54.48	45.52	60.09	39.91	52.01	47.99	51.52	48.49
3	74.88	25.12	42.52	57.48	75.08	24.92	55.65	44.34	34.00	66.00	69.84	30.16
4	70.92	29.08	67.59	32.41	69.77	30.22	69.34	30.56	58.21	41.79	58.27	41.73
5	68.35	31.65	61.47	38.53	61.19	38.81	65.78	34.21	74.39	25.61	65.58	34.42
6	58.20	41.80	53.73	46.27	60.38	39.62	61.28	38.72	61.63	38.36	52.77	47.23
7	65.08	34.92	79.96	20.04	64.01	35.99	62.07	37.93	89.37	10.63	77.47	22.53
8	57.63	42.37	40.49	59.51	78.95	21.05	55.53	44.47	92.05	7.95	60.07	39.93
9	68.75	31.25	55.97	44.03	49.85	50.15	63.20	36.80	89.38	10.62	69.14	30.87
10	87.69	12.31	100.00	0.00	66.81	33.19	90.44	9.56	97.24	2.76	92.33	7.67
Total	64.98	35.02	56.21	43.78	63.25	36.75	64.30	35.69	68.51	31.49	65.33	34.67

Source: Tabulated from NSS Unit record data (60th Round).

Table 26
Share of Public Sector in Hospitalised Treatment across Decile Groups by Sectors: Kerala and India (2004)

(per cent)

	Kerala						*India*					
	Rural		*Urban*		*Total*		*Rural*		*Urban*		*Total*	
MPCE Decile Group	*Private*	*Public*	*Private*	*Public*	*Private*	*Public*	*Private*	*Public*	*Private*	*Public*	*Private*	*Public*
1	54.30	45.70	39.44	60.56	52.16	47.84	39.11	60.88	42.55	57.45	40.00	60.00
2	57.82	42.18	42.86	57.14	56.04	43.97	47.14	52.86	47.82	52.18	49.15	50.85
3	59.47	40.54	66.01	34.00	54.84	45.16	50.70	49.30	47.24	52.76	49.34	50.66
4	65.90	34.10	38.55	61.45	71.45	28.55	51.67	48.32	59.60	40.40	49.24	50.77
5	66.88	33.12	67.99	32.01	50.56	49.44	48.96	51.05	57.34	42.65	54.41	45.59
6	61.96	38.04	61.86	38.14	65.84	34.16	56.24	43.77	60.83	39.17	55.20	44.79
7	60.33	39.68	61.11	38.89	61.53	38.47	56.33	43.67	62.58	37.42	59.32	40.68
8	57.17	42.83	93.48	6.52	61.29	38.71	60.10	39.90	69.51	30.49	63.86	36.14
9	67.14	32.86	89.33	10.67	74.33	25.67	66.48	33.52	73.59	26.41	65.15	34.85
10	85.73	14.27	98.28	1.72	91.50	8.50	72.49	27.51	84.00	16.00	76.97	23.03
Total	64.51	35.49	65.34	34.67	64.70	35.30	58.69	41.31	62.45	37.54	59.87	40.13

Source: Tabulated from NSS Unit record data (60th Round)

Notes:

i. 'Public' refers to public hospital (including PHC/Sub centre/CHC), public dispensary (incl. CGHS/ESI); and

ii. 'Private' refers to private hospital.

and hence would call for appropriate cost-effective strategies for improving health in India.

It is this reason, which has motivated this study on Kerala, which is unique for several reasons like the following: (i) Levels of morbidity in Kerala are quite high despite remarkable achievements in human development (including life expectancy); (ii) Hypothesis that high levels of morbidity along with low rates of mortality could be due to a poor health status associated with low levels of income and hence, inadequate nutrition; and (iii) need for verification of such hypotheses given the evidence that Kerala has caught up and has even done better than most of states in terms of growth and levels of living during the post-1973 scenario.

This study has taken up issues pertaining to the health sector in Kerala in a comparative perspective in the Indian context. Its focus is on the incidence of morbidity across socio-economic dimensions and their implications for economic policy. Its major findings are as follows:

- The level of living of every decile group in Kerala is higher than that of the corresponding group at the all-India level. The same result holds good for South Kerala versus all-India. However, only the rural population of North Kerala is better off than its counterpart at the all-India level.
- Extent of inequality in consumption distribution is higher in rural Kerala (North, South and combined) than in rural all-India and higher in urban Kerala (combined only) than in urban all-India.
- Within Kerala, the southern region is better off in terms of levels of living in both rural and urban sectors. The extent of inequality is also higher in South Kerala than in the North; still incidence of absolute poverty is higher in the North than in the South, reflecting the relatively lower level of standard of living in the former.
- As regards institutional facilities for health care, proportion of illness treated is higher in Kerala than in India as a whole.

- Extent of dependence on the public sector for health care is higher in Kerala than in all-India.
- Opportunity costs of illness is lower in Kerala than in India as a whole.
- Incidence of morbidity is higher in Kerala than in all-India. Within Kerala as a whole, it is (i) higher among women than men; (ii) higher in the rural than in the urban sector; and (iii) higher in the in the South than in the North.
- Incidence of morbidity is higher in rural than in urban Kerala and vice versa for all-India. As regards inequality in morbidity, the extent in general is lower in Kerala than in India though levels of morbidity are higher in the former than in the latter. Within Kerala, contrary to the relative profile of morbidity levels, inequality was higher in urban than in rural sector in South Kerala and Kerala as a whole. Similarly, at the all India level too, inequality in morbidity as against incidence was higher in the rural than in the urban sector.
- Incidence of morbidity is uniformly higher among the poor than among the non-poor categories in South as well as North Kerala.
- The short-run and long run profiles of morbidity are as follows:
- As regards the short-run estimates based on self-reported morbidity for the reference period of 15 days, the major diseases in Kerala are those generally associated with life-style and not with deprivation.
- For rural Kerala as a whole, major ailments for which hospitalization was undertaken were heart disease, respiratory (ENT), fever (unknown), fractures/ poisoning and 'other diagnosed'. As regards the poor, the profile differs in that other categories like diarrhoea/dysentery, gastric/peptic ulcer, joints/ bones also dominate.

- For urban Kerala, major ailments were heart disease, respiratory (ENT), bronchial asthma, diabetes mellitus, fever of unknown origin, fractures/poisoning and other diagnosed.
- In general, the poor rely relatively more on the public sector than on the private for treatment of illness as well as for hospitalization. Hence, the pursuit of privatization and public sector reform has to be carried out with due regard to the welfare costs associated with them.

NOTES

1. For a critical perspective, see Subramanian (2006).
2. Morbidity has increased at the all-India level too from 5.5 to 8.8 per cent and 8.4 to 9.9 per cent between the same two periods (GoI, 2000 and 2006).
3. Identification of ailments as major/minor is carried out with reference to their percentage share criterion: ailments, which accounted for more than or about 5 per cent of the total number of ailing cases or spells of hospitalization are called major.

REFERENCES

Ahluwalia, M. S. (2000), "Economic Performance of States in Post-Reforms Period", *Economic and Political Weekly*, Vol. No., pp. 1637-1648.

Centre for Development Studies (2006), *Human Development Report 2005: Kerala*, State Planning Board, Thiruvananthapuram.

Chen, Lincoln C. and Claire van Schaik (1986), 'Book Review: *Health Status of Kerala: Paradox of Economic Backwardness and Health Development* by P. G. K. Panikar; C. R. Soman', in *Population and Development Review*, Vol. 12, No. 4., pp. 805-810.

Government of India (1983), "Survey Results: Per capita Per Diem Intake of Nutrients, NSS 27th Round: October 1972-September 1973", *Sarvekshana: Journal of National Sample Survey Organisation*, Vol. VI, Nos. 3-4, Issue No. 18, pp. S1-S88.

Government of India (1986): "Results on the Third Quinquennial Survey on Consumer Expenditure: NSS 38th Round", Sarvekshana: *Journal of National Sample Survey Organisation*, Vol. IX, No. 4, pp. S1–S102.

Government of India (1989), 'Results on Per Capita Consumption of Cereals for Various Sections of Population: NSS 38th round (1983)', *Sarvekshana: Journal of National Sample Survey Organisation*, Vol. XIII, No. 2, pp. S-1-S-176.

Government of India (1996), *Level and Pattern of Consumer Expenditure, 5th Quinquennial Survey 1993-94*, Report No. 402, National Sample Survey Organisation, Department of Statistics, Government of India, New Delhi.

Government of India (1997), "Survey Results on Nutritional Intake in India-NSS 50th Round (July 1993-June 1994)", *Sarvekshana: Journal of National Sample Survey Organisation*, Vol. XXI, No. 2, pp. S-1-S-214.

Government of India (2000), "A Note on Morbidity and Treatment of Ailments, NSS 52nd Round (July 1995–June 1996), *Sarvekshana: Journal of the National Sample Survey Organisation*, Vol. XXIII, No. 3, Issue, No. 82, pp. 43-78.

Government of India (2006), *Morbidity, Health Care and The Condition of the Aged, NSS 60th Round (January–June 2004)*, NSS Report No 507, National Sample Survey Organisation, New Delhi.

Government of India (2007a), *Nutritional Intake in India 2004-2005:* NSS 61st Round (July 2004–June 2005), NSS Report No 513, National Sample Survey Organisation, New Delhi.

Government of India (2007b), *Poverty Estimates for 2004-05*, Press Information Bureau, New Delhi.

International Institute for Population Sciences and ORC Macro (2000), *National Family Health Survey (NFHS-2) 1998-99 India*, IIPS, Mumbai.

Kabir, M. and T. N. Krishnan (1992), *Social Intermediation and Health Transition: Lessons from Kerala*, Working Paper No 251, Centre for Development Studies, Thiruvananthapuram.

Kannan, K. P. (2005), "Kerala's Turnaround in Growth: Role of Social Development, Remittances and Reform", *Economic and Political Weekly*, Vol. XL, No. 6, pp. 548-554.

Kannan K. P., K. R. Thankappan, Raman Kutty V. Aravindan K. P. (1991), *Health and Development in Rural Kerala: A Study of the Linkages Between Socio-Economic Status and Health Status*, Kerala Shasthra Sahitya Parishad, Thiruvananthapuram.

Kunhikannan, T.P. and K. P. Aravindan (200), *Changes in the Health Status of Kerala: 1987-1997*, Discussion Paper No. 20, Kerala

Research Programme on Local Development, Centre for Development Studies, Thiruvananthapuram.

Krishnaswami, P. (2004), *Morbidity Study–Incidence, Prevalence, Consequences and Associates,* Discussion Paper No. 63, Kerala Research Programme on Local Development, Centre for Development Studies, Thiruvananthapuram.

Panikar, P. G. K. (1999), *Health Transition in Kerala,* Discussion Paper No. 10, Kerala Research Programme on Local Development, Centre for Development Studies, Thiruvananthapuram.

Panikar, P. G. K. and C. R. Soman (1984), *Health Status of Kerala: The Paradox of Economic Backwardness and Human Development,* Centre for Development Studies, Trivandrum.

Purohit, B. J. and T. A. Siddiqui (1995), "Cost Recovery in Diagnostic Facilities", *Economic and Political Weekly,* XXX , No. 27, pp. 1700-1705.

Sen, Gita, Aditi Iyer and Asha George (2002), "Structural Reforms and Health Equity: A Comparison of NSS Surveys, 1986-87 and 1995-96", *Economic and Political Weekly,* Vol. XXXVII, No. 14, pp. 1342-1352.

Subramanian, K. K. (2006), Economic Growth in the Regime of Reforms", *Economic and Political Weekly,* Vol. XLI, No. 10, pp. 885-890.

Suryanarayana, M. H. (2003), "Policies for Nutrition: How Imperative are They?" in Dev, S. Mahendra, K.P. Kannan and Nira Ramachandran (Eds): *Towards A Food Secure India: Issues & Policies,* Institute for Human Development, New Delhi, pp. 406-432.

The World Bank (1993), *World Development Report 1993: Investing in Health,* Oxford University Press, New York, NY 10016.

CHAPTER-5

CONSOLIDATION OF PRIVATE HOSPITALS IN KERALA: POLICY IMPLICATIONS

T. R. Dilip

INTRODUCTION

India is one of the countries with the highest private sector participation in delivery of health care services. Kerala is no exception, where about 87 per cent of total health expenditure being incurred by the private sector (MOHFW 2006). The development of health care facilities in Kerala between 1980's and mid 1990's is well documented (Kutty 2000). According to the author, rising disposable incomes and lack of barriers in opening up a private hospital has led to an unexpected growth of private health care sector. The private hospitals are better equipped in terms of technical resources and were reported to be encashing on the long term illnesses in the state. Despite this overwhelming presence of private sector, Kerala is always proved to be having one of the most equitable health systems in India (Krishnan 2000; Peters et al 2001; Mahal et al 2002). Perhaps equity has more do with higher purchasing power of the state's population than on the health system composition and characteristics.

As in the case of India, it is the private sector that dominated the provisioning of health care services. The only divergence in Kerala is that the private sector participation in provision of inpatient care is above the national average, but the same is below the all India average in the case outpatient care services (NSSO 2006). The presence of voluntary/ charitable sector is limited as only about 1.2 per cent users reported to have sought inpatient treatment from this sector (Narayana and Dilip, 2007). Here they figure out that the majority of the not for profit hospitals in charitable sector in Kerala seems to have gone the private by charging for services at rates generally charged by the private sector. Hence a user identify them as private hospital and not as a hospital in not for profit sector managed by charitable organisations.

All the existing national level surveys report that majority of inpatient and outpatient treatment in India and in Kerala are provided by the private health care sector (NSSO, 1992; NCAER, 1992; Sundar 1995; NSSO 1998; NSSO 2006). In fact all these survey reports documents the class differentials in utilisation health care services from public/private sector. Further these studies point out that the average out of pocket expenditure is higher in private sector than in public sector and the rich poor divide in utilisation of health care services is often attributed to this. As noted in the national level surveys, these state specific health survey also brings out the rich poor divide in access to private health care facilities and attribute the same to the pricing services in private sector (Kannan *et al* 1991; Aravindan and Kunhikannan 2000 and KSSP 2006). Levesque *et al* (2007) while acknowledging the vital role played by private sector in delivery of health care services, caution about it's capacity in serving the poorer sections and under developed regions in Kerala. Here the issue is that private health care sector has grown on its own and is already the major provider of health care and it is time for policy planners to take a serious note of private health system's capacity in provisioning of health care services to all sections of the society.

Here one should also take a note of existing evidence on preference for private hospitals in the state According to Raman Kutty (1989) the utilisation of private medical care in Kerala state is primarily determined by 'money prices' as 'travel time' and 'waiting time' are relatively lower in private sector. The recent KSSP (2006) study finds that better facilities is the reason reported for preference of private sector, while economic reasons is cited as major reason for seeking care from a government hospital. The NFHS-3 shows that lack of facility in nearby locality (48 per cent) as a major reason for not seeking care from a government hospital (IIPS and Macro International, 2007). Poor quality of care were also treated as reason for avoiding government facilities by a substantial number of persons. In this background the paper attempts to document the trends in distribution of private hospitals in Kerala and its capacity in reaching all sections of the society.

DATA

Present analysis is based on data from two sources (1) Directorate of Economics and Statistics (DES), Government of Kerala and (2) National Sample Survey Organisation (NSSO), Government of India. The DES, has undertaken censuses of private medical institutions in the state during the years 1986, 1996 and 2004. Report based on each of this census gives information on size, location, ownership, facilities, in the private medical institutions in Kerala. Data on utilisation of private hospitals and its implications is indirectly captured from the NSSO household surveys on morbidity and utilisation of health care services carried out during 1986-87 (42nd round), 1995-96 (52nd round) and 2004 (60 round). NSSO Kerala sample was 2471, 4928 and 2829 households for this topic of enquiry during 1986-87, 1995-96 and 2004 respectively. Even though the private hospitals are providing inpatient and outpatient treatment, the recent data (NSSO 2006) does not give information on proportion seeking outpatient care from private hospitals, separately. Due to this data constrain, the present analysis is restricted to provisioning of inpatient treatment in private hospitals. These NSSO data sets provides information on instances of hospitalisation and treatment details for household member, who was hospitalised during last 365 days prior to the survey date.

CHANGES IN SIZE OF PRIVATE HOSPITALS

The trends in availability of private hospitals and public hospitals during the study period is presented in Table 1. The study period witnessed an actual decline in number of number of private institutions having inpatient facilities in the state. The number of institutions in the private sector having inpatient treatment facility increased from 2042 in the year 1986 to 2274 by the year 1995 and then declined to 1942 in 2004. The same is true for hospitals under the allopathic system of medicine.

Trends were almost similar in the case of bed availability under private sector. There was a rapid increase in number of beds in private sector between 1986 and 1995. A slight decline in total number of beds from 112,088 in 1995 to 108,684 in 2004 is also noticed. For comparison purposes the bed availability in public hospitals is also presented. In fact there is an absolute increase in number of beds available in public sector, with population served per bed keeping pace with population growth. About 59 per cent of total hospital beds are in private sector.

The regional variation in availability of private hospitals are sizeable. The presence of private sector is limited in northern districts of Palakkad, Kozhikode, Malappuram and Kasargod. Private sector participation is relatively higher in other districts of state ie Idukki, Pathanamthitta, Ernakulam and Kottayam. Presence of private hospitals is relatively lesser in Trivandrum district which has a huge concentration of public hospitals. Ernakulam, Thrissur, Pathanamthitta, Kottayam, Malappuram and Kozhikode are districts where there has been an un-accounted for increase in access to private hospitals beds between 1986 and 1996 and where there has been a decline in bed population ratio between 1996 & 2004. Incidentally these are the districts, which have benefited considerably from remittances through international migration, which may be reason for sudden fluctuations in population served per bed in the profit driven private sector.

Average number of beds per private hospital is presented to get approximate idea of size of private hospitals in the state.

Table 1

Number of Hospital Beds in Public and Private Sector, Kerala 1986-87, 1995-96, 2004

	1986/1986-87			*1995 / 1995-96*			*2004/ 2004-05*		
	Public	*Private*	*Total*	*Public*	*Private*	*Total*	*Public*	*Private*	*Total*
Thiruvananthapuram	6682	4198	10880	7050	5225	12275	8245	6811	15056
Kollam	2018	4787	6805	2345	7519	9864	2129	4886	7015
Pathanamthitta	3573	3745	7318	4105	4496	8601	681	4323	5004
Alapuzha	1132	3203	4335	1196	3847	5043	3827	2922	6749
Kottayam	3155	6382	9537	3583	7888	11471	3075	5285	8360
Idukki	619	3535	4154	1003	4004	5007	1238	5149	6387
Ernakulam	3558	8796	12354	4083	11602	15685	4144	9850	13994
Thrissur	4096	5259	9355	4341	8893	13234	4795	7272	12067
Palakkad	1768	1099	2867	2214	2231	4445	2486	2653	5139
Malappuram	1556	2150	3706	2355	3948	6303	2870	4108	6978
Kozhikode	4339	2497	6836	4553	4053	8606	5432	3081	8513
Wayanad	625	1594	2219	933	1806	2739	1108	1521	2629
Kannur	2439	2570	5009	2571	4099	6670	3133	5081	8214
Kasaragode	698	951	1649	832	1313	2145	1030	1549	2579
Kerala	36258	50766	87024	41164	70924	112088	44193	64491	108684

Source: (1) Private Beds from Survey of Private Medical Institutions in Kerala, Department of Economics and Statistics and (2) Public Beds from Economic Review, State Planning Board (respective years)Note: Data for number of hospital beds in government hospitals from Economic Review, published by the State Planning Board (respective years) Figure varies from the number given in Economic Review because institutions receiving government grant are excluded.

Increase in this ratio indicates that the large hospitals with more number of beds are increasing, while the smaller hospitals and nursing homes are either closed down or getting transformed into larger hospitals. We have already seen that there is a decline in number of allopathic hospitals in private sector. However an increase in average number hospital beds per hospital from 26 in 1986 to 41 in 2004 indicates a consolidation of larger hospitals in the state. One reason for this type of consolidation is public policy on privatisation of medical education that facilitated opening up number of private medical colleges. For example, until the year 1994 there were only 5 medical colleges in the state under the allopathic system of medicine, all owned by the government. Since then 13 more new self financing medical colleges were started in the state, in the private sector. In addition 5 Ayurvedic medical collages, 13 Dental collages and 2 Homeopathic collages were started in the self financing sector during this period.

The change in size of private hospitals over the three time periods is presented in the Table 2. Ernakulam and Thrissur were the two districts that have a concentration of large private hospitals in the state. The chart indicates that Alapuzha, Kollam, Malappuram and Palakkad have small or medium sized hospitals. Consolidation of large private hospitals or the phenomenon of expansion of large hospitals and marginalisation of smaller hospitals and nursing homes was largely in Trivandrum, Kannur, Pathanamthitta, Idukki and Kasaragod districts. Data limitation is one reason for the under estimation in the level of consolidation districts with better private health facilities like Ernakulam, Thrissur and Kottayam.

DEMAND FOR INPATIENT CARE SERVICES

Below we examine the nature of increase in demand for inpatient care services over time. When factors like population ageing and shifting disease pattern from communicable to chronic degenerative diseases could pave the way for an increase in the demand for inpatient care services, there is yet another factor associated with improvements in medical

Table 2

Number of Institutions, Total Number of Beds and Average Beds Per Institution under Allopathic System of Medicine Kerala, 1986, 1995, 2004

	1986		*1995*		*2004*		*Beds per institution*		
	Institutions	*Beds*	*Institutions*	*Beds*	*Institutions*	*Beds*	*1986*	*1995*	*2004*
Thiruvananthapuram	246	3744	236	4807	157	5728	15	20	36
Kollam	218	4504	240	7194	158	4236	21	30	27
Pathanamthitta	137	3720	122	4391	64	3801	27	36	59
Alapuzha	154	3157	151	3633	92	2342	21	24	25
Kottayam	182	6189	191	7642	126	4873	34	40	39
Idukki	152	3521	130	3944	109	4973	23	30	46
Ernakulam	186	8646	189	11418	145	8770	46	60	60
Thrissur	124	5101	120	8345	99	6612	41	70	67
Palakkad	63	1013	81	2105	78	2192	16	26	28
Malappuram	101	1931	125	3313	110	3000	19	27	27
Kozhikode	108	2411	127	3714	86	2908	22	29	34
Wayanad	54	1594	62	1769	44	1429	30	29	32
Kanmur	96	2550	127	3952	95	4766	27	31	50
Kasaragode	43	949	57	1290	42	1441	22	23	34
Total	1864	49030	1958	67517	1405	57071	26	34	41

Source: (1) Private Beds from Survey of Private Medical Institutions in Kerala, Bureau of Economics and Statistics (respective years).

technology that neutralise such demand. With improvements in medical technology, diseases which required hospitalisation in earlier years can now be cured through procedures which do not require the same. Annual hospitalisation is the ratio of total estimated number of hospitalisations in a year to the corresponding mid year population.

Table 3
Trends in Annual Hospitalization Rates by MPCE Quintile, Kerala 1986-87, 1995-96 & 2004

MPCE Quintile	*Number Hospitalized per 1000 Persons*		
	1986-87	*1995-96*	*2004*
0-20	76	69	112
20-40	71	65	136
40-60	71	84	126
60-80	55	84	118
80-100	70	115	141
Total	69	81	126

Source: Estimated using NSSO Unit level data for respective years* Hopitalisations relating to pregnancy and child birth are excluded.

Table 3: above shows that there has been a consistent increase in annual hospitalization rates from 69 per 1000 population 1986-87 to 81 per thousand population in 1995-96 to 126 per thousand population by the year 2004. Differentials by MPCE quintile were only marginal in 2004, while same was highest during 1995-96. Perhaps the poorer sections have avoided hospitalisations during this period to avoid catastrophic payments. Risk of hospitalisation is highest among richest quintile and lowest among the poorest quintile. However no such differentials were noted in the year 1986-87.

LEVEL OF UTILIZATION OF INPATIENT CARE FROM PRIVATE HOSPITALS

The national sample survey data provides information on source of treatment for persons who had undergone hospitalisation during last one year prior to the survey period. Based on source of treatment the inpatients were classified into (1) those who had undergone treatment in a public/government hospital and (2) those who has undergone treatment in private institutions. Inequalities in the proportion of the illness episodes involving hospitalisation, where treatment was sought from private hospital is presented in Table 4.

Table 4
Percentage of Inpatient Episodes Treated in Private Hospitals by MPCE Quintiles, Kerala 1986-87, 1995-96 & 2004

MPCE Quintile	*1986-87*	*1995-96*	*2004*
0-20	53.5	45.5	54.8
20-40	50.3	57.7	60.7
40-60	53.3	63.6	63.7
60-80	58.5	63.5	66.6
80-100	68.9	72.2	82.5
Total	55.4	60.3	64.6

Source: NSSO Unit level data for respective years.

Majority of inpatient treatments (65 per cent) are in private hospitals. There has been a periodic increase in proportion seeking care from private hospitals between 1986-87 and 2004. The well known rich poor divide in access to private hospitals, was utmost during 1995-96 and lowest during 1986-87.

CORRELATES OF UTILIZATION OF INPATIENT CARE SERVICES FROM PRIVATE HOSPITALS

We have already noted that there is an increase in proportion of persons seeking inpatient care from private hospitals. This is an attempt to understand the trends in nature of gender, rural-urban, caste and class wise differentials in access to private hospitals. The of bi-variate tables for variables used in logistic regression are presented in appendix Table 1.

Since all the variables identified are categorical in nature, logistic regression analysis has been performed to study the trends and determinants of utilisation of inpatient care services in the private sector. Here the dependent variable "type of hospital", coded as 1, if it is private hospital and 0, if in private hospital. The same set of independent variables have been used for the period 1986-87, 1995-96 and 2004 and the relative importance of each variable is understood from the changes in odds ratio [exp (b)] itself. Since variations in household size and duration of stay at the hospital could be confounders, these variables-household size and duration of stay (as proxy for seriousness of ailment) have been used as covariates in the model.

Table 5
Odds Ratio from Logistics Regression Analysis for Use of Inpatient Care from Private Hospitals, Kerala 1986-87, 1995-96 & 2004

	1986-87		*1995-96*		*2004*	
	S.E. (B)	*Odds Ratio Exp (B)*	*S.E. (B)*	*Odds Ratio Exp (B)*	*S.E. (B)*	*Odds Ratio Exp (B)*
Age (Reference = 60+)						
0-14	0.183	0.762	0.166	1.680**	0.153	1.079
15-59	0.147	0.928	0.124	1.03	0.123	0.987
Sex (Ref =Male)						
Female	0.114	1.260*	0.102	0.862	0.103	0.869
Residence (Ref = Rural)						
Urban	0.189	0.566**	0.232	0.798	0.122	1.084
Caste (Ref = SC/ST)						
Non-SC/ST	0.185	1.752**	0.162	2.294**	0.165	2.635**
MPCE (Ref =0-20 quintile)						
20-40	0.161	0.853	0.159	1.962**	0.146	1.185
40-60	0.168	0.947	0.157	2.542**	0.156	1.408*
60-80	0.192	1.177	0.165	2.495**	0.168	1.550**
80-100	0.217	2.005**	0.176	4.268**	0.196	3.828**
Region (Ref = North Kerala)						
South Kerala	0.13	1.467**	0.255	1.518	0.115	1.031
Household size@	0.021	1.018	0.027	1.117**	0.024	1.084**
Duration of stay@	0.005	0.974**	0.003	0.992**	0.007	0.959**
Constant	0.314	0.693	0.271	0.202	0.273	0.508
N	1336	1755	1860			

* $p < 0.05$, ** $p < 0.01$
@ used as covariates in the model

Here the odds ratio presented in the Table 5 indicate the variation in likelihood of seeking inpatient care from a private hospital, when the effect of all other independent variables in the model are kept constant. For the period 1986-87, the variables sex, residence, caste and MPCE category were significant. During this period, it can be seen that odds of using inpatient care from a private hospital was significantly higher for females than males. Results indicate odds of seeking care from private hospital is significantly higher in rural areas than in urban areas, where majority of the specialised hospitals in public sector are located. When compared to a person from SC/ST household, the odds of seeking treatment from private hospital was 1.8 times higher for a person from non-SC/ST household. It is to be noted that household income/MPCE wise variation in access to private hospitals was significant only in the case of richest quintile.

Analysis for the period 1995-96 showed that the variables sex, caste and MPCE background of hospitalised person are having significant impact in selection of private hospital for inpatient treatment. There is a preference for private hospitals in case of treatment of children than those in other age groups. Odds of seeking inpatient care from a private hospital are 2.3 times higher for a person from 'non SC/ST" category from a person from SC/ST subgroup. The positive relationship between economic background and use of inpatient care from a private hospital is highly significant. As compared to a person in poorest quintile, persons in 80-100, 60-80, 40-60 and 20-40 are 4.3 times, 2.5 times and 2.5 times and 2 times likely to seek care from private hospital, respectively

By the year 2004, only variables - caste and economic background of the ailing person are having a significant impact on selection of source for treatment involving hospitalisation. It appears that the poor social groups are increasingly getting alienated from the private hospitals. When compared to a patient of the SC/ST denomination, a patient from a 'non SC/ST' category is 2.6 times more likely to seek inpatient care from a private hospital. The relationship between MPCE and selection of source of treatment remained the same as in 1995-96, but there is a marginal decline in this inequality in access to private hospital between these two time periods.

DISCUSSION

There has been considerable changes in availability of hospital facilities in Kerala. While expansion of public bed facilities is

Appendix I

Source for Inpatient Treatment, Kerala 1986-87, 1995-96 & 2004

	1986-87			*1995-96*			*2004*		
	Public	*private*	*Total*	*public*	*private*	*Total*	*public*	*private*	*Total*
Age group									
0-14	46.9	53.1	100	30.9	69.1	100	31.1	68.9	100
15-59	43.8	56.2	100	41.4	58.6	100	37.3	62.7	100
60+	44.7	55.3	100	42.0	58.0	100	35.6	64.4	100
Sex									
Male	47.4	52.6	100	38.1	61.9	100	34.0	66.0	100
Female	41.8	58.2	100	41.3	58.7	100	36.8	63.2	100
Place of residence									
Rural	43.3	56.7	100	40.1	59.9	100	35.6	64.4	100
Urban	55.7	44.3	100	38.4	61.6	100	34.6	65.4	100
Social Group									
SC/ST	57.6	42.4	100	60.3	39.7	100	62.8	37.2	100
Non-SC/ST	43.0	57.0	100	37.2	62.8	100	32.2	67.8	100
MPCE Quintile									
0-20	46.5	53.5	100	54.5	45.5	100	45.2	54.8	100
20-40	49.7	50.3	100	42.3	57.7	100	39.3	60.7	100
40-60	46.7	53.3	100	36.4	63.6	100	36.3	63.7	100
60-80	41.5	58.5	100	36.5	63.5	100	33.4	66.6	100
80-100	31.1	68.9	100	27.8	72.2	100	17.5	82.5	100
Region									
Northern Kerala	48.9	51.1	100	40.4	59.6	100	37.0	63.0	100
Southern Kerala	42.8	57.2	100	36.4	63.6	100	34.7	65.3	100
Total	44.6	55.4	100	39.7	60.3	100	35.4	64.6	100
N	629	712	1341	640	1119	1806#	651	1218	1869

\# Information on source not available in 47 cases

Source: NSSO Unit level data respective years

in tune with the population growth, the private sector witnessed a consolidation of larger units meant for delivery of inpatient care. The fact that the private health care sector is the major provider and their increasing presence in provisioning of health care services needs to be acknowledged. However the capacity of market driven unregulated private hospitals in meeting health care needs of poor and vulnerable is doubtful. This is a typical case which demonstrates the unpredictability in private sector participation in delivery of health care services. Closure of smaller hospitals and nursing homes night have affected the population who were depending on them, However improvements in transport and communication over time might have enabled them to over come this hurdle, by seeking care from other nearest inpatient care units. This gets substantiated due to the fact that despite the urban bias and north-south divide in existence of health care facilities, it doesn't get reflected in utilisation pattern.

Trends indicate that the economic background of the patient is gradually becoming the single most important predictor of use of inpatient care services from private hospitals. The effect of physical access related variables (regional or rural/urban) are negligible. This could be due to the widening geographical spread of private hospitals and improvements in road and transport facilities. The reason for the increasing isolation of the SC/ST from private hospitals even after controlling for their economic background is still unexplained. Perhaps this could be due to their relative backwardness in attaining better standards of living over time. Hence one has to cautious while acknowledging while accounting their contribution in Kerala's health system performance, from an equity perspective.

To conclude, the public policy favouring increased private sector participation in medical education coupled with opening of super speciality hospitals has lead to a situation where small hospitals or nursing homes loosing their significance and a large number them have been phased out. Considering the age structural transition induced epidemiological profile of Kerala, the demand for long term nursing care as well as rehabilitative care for chronic illness is likely to come up in future. Adding to this is ageing of population, out migration of working population, and shift from nuclear to joint family system. The large private medical collages and super speciality hospitals will not be able to met these type demand for long terms nursing and rehabilitative care services in a cost effective manner. Therefore the so called "consolidation" of large private hospitals is expected to be a temporary phenomenon and demand for small hospitals and nursing homes are likely to remerge in near future.

REFERENCES

Department of Economics and Statistics 'Report on Private Medical Institutions in Kerala,' Trivandrum: Department of Economics and Statistics, Government of Kerala. (for the years 1986, 1995 & 2004).

International Institute for Population Sciences and Macro International 'National Family Health Survey (NFHS-3)', 2005-06, Mumbai: IIPS; 2007.

Kannan K. P. *et al.* (1991), Health and Development in Rural Kerala: A Study of Linkages between Socio-Economic Status and Health Status, Trivandrum: Kerala Shastra Sahithya Parishad.

Kerala Shasthra Sahithya Parishad (2006), *Kerala Padanam.* Kozhiode: Kerala Shasthra Sahithya Parishad.

Krishnan, T. N. (2000), Access to Health Care and Burden of Treatment in India: An Interstate Comparison, In Rao (eds.) *Investing in Health*: New Delhi, Sage Publications: 212-230.

Kunhikannan T. P. and K. P. Aravindan (2000), Changes in Health Status of Kerala 1986-1997. *KRPLLD Discussion Paper No 20,* Thrivananthapuram: Centre For Development Studies.

Kutty V. R. (1989), Rationing of Medical Care in Kerala-Price and Non Price Mechanisms, *Economic and Political Weekly,* 9:1922-1933.

Kutty V. R. (2000), Historical Analysis of Development of Health Care Services in Kerala. *Health Policy and Planning,* 15(1):103-109.

Ministry of Health and Family Welfare (2006), *National Health Accounts India–2001-02,* New Delhi: Ministry of Health and Family Welfare, Government of India.

Levesque J. F., Haddad S. Narayana, D and Fournier, P. (2007), "Insular Pathways to Health Care in the City: A Multilevel Analysis of Access to Hospital Care in Urban Kerala, India", *Tropical Medicine & International Health*, 12 (7), 802–814.

Mahal, A. *et al.* (2000), Who Benefits from Public Health Spending in India, New Delhi National Council for Applied Economic Research.

Narayana, D and Dilip T. R. (2007), Not for Profit Sector in Health Care: What is Good for Tamil Nadu is not Good for Kerala?, Paper Presented at the National Seminar on "Expanding Freedom: Towards Social and Economic Transformation in a Globalising World" Institute of Economic Growth, Delhi, April, 11-13.

National Council for Applied Economic Research (NCAER) (1992) Household Survey on Medical Care, NCAER: NewDelhi.

National Sample Survey Organisation (1992), Morbidity and Utilisation of Medical Services, NSS 42nd Round July 1986-June 1987, *Sarvekhshana*, April 1992, pp. 55-75, pp. S134-S.

National Sample Survey Organisation (1998), *Morbidity and Treatment of Ailments*. Report No. 441, New Delhi: Ministry of Statistics and Programme Implementation.

National Sample Survey Organisation (2006), *Morbidity Health Care and The Condition of Aged*. Report No. 507, New Delhi: Ministry of Statistics and Programme Implementation.

Peters, D., A. Yazbeck, *et al.* (2001), Better Health Systems for India's Poor. Findings, Analysis and Options. Washington DC, World Bank.

State Planning Board. '*Economic Review*,' Trivandrum: State Planning Board, Government of Kerala. (for the years 1986, 1995 & 2005).

Sundar, Ramamani (1992), Household Survey of Medical Care', *Margin* 24(2): 169-175.

CHAPTER-6

POLICY REFORMS AND HEALTH SECTOR IN INDIA

V. Anbumani & M. Saravanakumar

INTRODUCTION

Health sector reforms are a part of economic reforms. Health sector reforms have been implemented in an effort to improve health services management and supervision. These reforms are intended to decentralize health systems, reduce bureaucracy, and increase cost-effectiveness and efficiency by reorganizing services, streamlining management, and allocating resources to better meet local needs. However, due care will have to be taken to ensure that the poorer segments of the population are able to access services they need.

INDIA'S HEALTH CARE SYSTEM

- *Medicine Systems:* Allopathy, Ayurvedic, Unani, Siddha and Homeopathy.
- *Major Groups:* Public, Private and Households.
    - *Public:* Union Government, State Government, Local Government and ESIs.
    - *Private:* Not for Profit Organizations.
        - For Profit Organizations.
        - NGOs, Trusts, Charities, Missions, etc.

Players

- *Formal:* Licensed General Practitioners (GPs).
  - Super Specialists.
  - Consultants.
  - Paramedics.
  - RMPs.
- *Informal:* Faith healers, Indigenous medical men, quacks.

HEALTH POLICIES AND HEALTH SECTOR REFORMS

A health policy is defined as a program of action whose aim is to improve health conditions of the people. Health sector reforms are part of the overall economic, social and political reforms that began two decades ago.

Health sector reforms in developing countries have largely focused on health financing, user fees, health insurance, changes in health system organization, delivery and management of health systems, regulation of public–private partnerships and contracting out services. They have been implemented to improve efficiency and cost effectiveness in public health services (Jeppsson *et. al.* 2004).

Major health reforms that have been instituted include: Decentralization of governance to districts; health sub district approaches; civil service reforms; user fees; Sector-Wide Approaches (SWAPs); Unification of health and family planning services, and health care financing (Stella Neema).

COMPOSITION OF THE HEALTH SYSTEM

As far as the composition of the health system in the country is concerned, we know that the health system is highly heterogeneous and complex with multiple actors, the large number of treatment providers belonging to different apathies and in different settings. We have a wide range of providers: formal and non formal, qualified and less than qualified, registered medical practitioners etc. They are working in the outreach, home settings, stand alone dispensaries, nursing homes and corporate sector world-class hospitals. We have preventive and promotive care services in terms of immunizations, family planning, maternal health services, vertical disease control programme to name the few. We have a range of financing mechanisms to support health care. The Government spending on health is an attempt to subsidize health care.

USER CHARGES IN THE PUBLIC HEALTH SECTOR IN INDIA

(1) Reforms in health sector in India, initiated in early 1990s, included levying of user charges for services in public health facilities as one of the initiatives. User charges came to be levied from patients belonging to families above poverty line for diagnostic and curative services, while free or highly subsidized services continued to be provided to the poor and needy patients.

(2) States where user fees are being levied include Assam, Gujarat, Haryana, Himachal Pradesh, Karnataka, Kerala, Madhya Pradesh, Maharashtra, Orissa, Punjab, Rajasthan, Tripura, Uttar Pradesh Uttaranchal and West Bengal. There are inter-State differences in the levy, collection and utilization of such charges.

(3) Some States like Haryana levy rates for various services in all public health institutions from Primary Health Centre upwards. In West Bengal, user charges apply only in secondary and tertiary level health facilities. In case of Madhya Pradesh and Kerala, the charges for various services are approved by Rogi Kalyan Samitis (RKS)/Hospital Development Committees at the facility level, and hence vary across institutions. In Orissa, lower rates are levied in less developed and tribal districts. Cost recovery ratio varies across States, but seldom exceeds a quarter.

(4) There is also variation in the nature of services for which user charges are levied. For example, in Orissa user charges is limited to accommodation, transportation and laboratory/diagnostic services, while in West Bengal, user charges are collected for diagnostic, curative services in

both outpatient and inpatient departments, as well as ancillary services like diet. In most States, services for which user fees are charged include registration, diagnostic tests (pathological and radiological), bed charges, operation theatre charges amongst others. All States implementing user charges, exempt the poor, treatment under National Health Programmes and emergency cases.

(5) The funds collected by way of user charges are meant to be utilized for improving the quality of services in health facilities, such as maintenance of hospital buildings, improving the cleanliness and hygiene, minor repairs and construction work, maintenance and repair of equipment, purchase of medicines and consumables, and improving facilities for patients and attendants. Available literature on experiences of user charges in states indicate that user charges is definitely a means to raise resources to support the health care delivery system as well as improve the quality of health services and financial sustainability in health care system.

WORLD CLASS IN HEALTH

What do we mean by 'world class in health,' health services should achieve international standards in terms of state of-the-art medical technology, specialists, and corporate hospitals with five-star comfort? Or appropriate, trustworthy health care through user-friendly primary level health services accessible to all, with equally trustworthy secondary and tertiary level public hospitals? Or that the Indian people attain the highest international indices for health status, e. g., life expectancy reaches the 80 years of Japan, infant mortality and maternal mortality decrease to the 3 per 1,000 and 5 per 1,00,000 live births respectively of Sweden [UNDP 2002].

The first goal will provide world class medical care for those who can afford it (or who get it as employees in the organised sector institutions). It will also set 'high' standards for all health services and bring the country financial resources and foreign currency through medical tourism. The second goal will provide the common people with affordable, comprehensive, preventive and curative health services. The third is, of course, the final outcome of all developmental activities. The National Health Policy-2002 [GoI 2002] speaks of all three, but has been criticised for favouring the first and distorting the second.

COMMON MINIMUM PROGRAMME

It is within this scenario that the thrust of health service development has to be decided. The Common Minimum Programme (CMP) of the new government contains four measures for the health sector:

(1) Increasing allocation to 2-3 per cent of GDP;

(2) major expenditure on primary health care and communicable diseases with political backing for AIDS control;

(3) health insurance for the poor; and

(4) regulation of drug prices for 'lifesaving' drugs and revival of public sector production units. These are all significant commitments. Now their details need to be worked out.

Some tough moves towards 'an Indian model of reforms' in the health services are necessary if the dream to become 'world class' is to be achieved. Merely increasing funding for the current programmes will do little to improve health if the structure, content and functioning of the public services are not revamped. While restructuring the health services, lessons learnt from the 'reforms' of the 1990s should be heeded. We need to set priorities and the most cost-effective ways to address them, ensuring that issues of quality are not undermined in the name of cost cutting and feasibility. Optimal criteria for quality will have to be set for our context.

DEMOGRAPHY AND HEALTH

Table 1 presents the Technical Group on Population Projections constituted by the National Commission on Population, May

2006. Annual population growth is expected to be gradually decelerate from 1.6 per cent in the five years ending in 2006 to 0.9 per cent in the five years ending in 2026. India's population, which is estimated to have gone up from the Census 2001 figure of 1029 million to 1112 million in 2006, is projected to increase to 1400 million by 2026.

Table 1
India: Population Projections (in millions)

Year	*2001*	*2006*	*2011*	*2016*	*2021*	*2026*
Total	1.029	1,112	1,193	1,269	1,340	1,400
Below 15 years	365*(364)	357	347	340	337	327
15-64 Years	619*(613)	699	780	851	908	957
Above 65 Years	45*(49)	56	66	78	95	116

Notes: *Figures are as per smoothing of age-groups for working out population projections.

Source: Population projections for India and States 2001-2026-Census of India 2001: Report of the Technical Group on Population projections constituted by the National Commission on Population, May 2006.

The well-known 'demographic dividend' will manifest in the proportion of population in the working age group of 15-64 years increasing steadily from 62.9 per cent in 2006 to 68.4 per cent in 2026. The actual tapping of this demographic dividend will, however, depend a lot on ensuring proper healthcare and other human resource development such as education.

Table 2 explains that healthcare is important not only for reaping the demographic dividend, having a healthy productive workforce and general welfare, but also for attaining the goal of population stabilization that is proposed to be achieved by addressing issues like child survival, safe motherhood and contraception. There has been some improvement in the quality of health care over the years, but wide inter-State, male-female and rural-urban disparities in outcomes and impacts continue to persist. While population stabilization is in the Concurrent List, health is a State subject.

Table 2
India-Selected Health Indicators

Parameter	*1951*	*1981*	*1991*	*Current level*
Crude birth rate (CBR) (Per 1000 population)	40.8	33.9	29.5	23.8 (2005)
Crude death rate (CDR) (Per 1000 population)	25.1	12.5	9.8	7.6 (2005)
Total fertility rate (TFR) (per woman)	6.0	4.5	3.6	2.9 (2005)
Maternal mortality ratio (MMR) (per 100,000 live births)	NA	NA	437 (1992-93) NFHS	301 (2001-03
Infant mortality rate (IMR) (per 1000 live births)	146 (1951-61)	110	80	58 (2005)
Child (0-4) mortality rate (per 1000 children)	57.3 (1972)	41.2	26.5	17.0 (2004)
Couple protection rate (per cent)	10.4 (1971)	22.8	44.1	48.2 (1998-99) NHFS
Life expectancy at birth				
8.1 Male	37.2	54.1	59.7 (1991-95)	63.87 (2001-06)
8.2 Female	36.2	54.7	60.9 (1991-95)	6691 (2001-06)

Source: Office of Registrar General India; NFHS: National Family Health Survey; NA: Not Available.

The reproductive and child health services reach community and household levels through the primary health care infrastructure. Inadequacies in the existing health infrastructure have led to gaps in coverage and outreach services in rural areas. Empirical studies suggest that education, income and the overall quality of the State administration are often more important than specific public health interventions in explaining the differences in demographic and health indicators.

India's position on health parameters compared even to some of its neighbours continues to be unsatisfactory. India compares poorly not only with China and Sri Lanka, but also Bangladesh and Nepal with respect to some indicators (Table 3).

Table 3
Some Health Parameters: India and its Neighbours

Country	*Life Expectancy at birth (Years)*	*Under-five mortality rate (per 1,000 live births)*		*Infant mortality rate (per 1, 000 live births)*		*Maternal mortality ratio (per 100,000 live births)*
	2000-05	*1990*	*2004*	*1990*	*2004*	*2004*
China	71	49	31	38	26	51
India	63	123	85	80	62*	540*
Nepal	61	145	76	100	59	740
Pakistan	63	128	101	96	80	530
Sri Lanka	74	23	14	19	12	92
Bangladesh	63	144	77	96	56	380
South Asia	63	126	84	84	62	NA

NA: Not available

* Figures shown for India are at variance with the official figures of the office of Registrar General of India.

Source: UNDP, Human Development Report 2006.

NATIONAL RURAL HEALTH MISSION (NRHM)

NRHM is the main vehicle for giving effect to the mandate of the NCMP. Operationalized throughout the country, its special focus is on 18 states with weaker health infrastructure and health status indicators. Provision of accessible, affordable, accountable, effective and reliable primary health care facilities especially to the poor and vulnerable sections of the population, bridging the gap in rural health care services through creation of a cadre of Accredited Social Health Activists (ASHA), improved hospital care, decentralized planning, ensuring population stabilization, intersectoral convergence and maintaining gender balance constitute the basic features of the NRHM.

The mission envisaged selection of a trained female community health worker called ASHA in each village in the ratio of one per 1000 population in all 18 high-focus States and in tribal and under-served areas of other States. ASHA would reinforce community action for universal immunization, safe delivery, newborn care, prevention of waterborne and other communicable diseases, nutrition and sanitation. ASHAs would work in close coordination with the Anganwadi Workers (AWW). ASHAs would also provide immediate and easy access for the rural population to essential health supplies like Oral Rehydration Solution (ORS), contraceptives, a set of ten basic drugs, and a health communication kit developed villages.

STRENGTHENING OF PRIMARY HEALTH INFRASTRUCTURE AND IMPROVING SERVICE DELIVERY

Table 4 shows that there has been a steady increase in health care infrastructure available over the plan period as per the Rural Health Infrastructure Bulletin 2006, there is a shortage of 19,269 Sub-centres (SCs), 4,337 Primary Health Centres (PHCs) and 3,206 Community Health Centres (CHCs) as per 2001 population norm. Further, almost 50 per cent of the existing health infrastructure is in rented buildings. Last but not the least poor upkeep and maintenance, and high absenteeism of manpower in rural areas, have eroded the credibility of the health delivery system in the public sector. NRHM seeks to strengthen the public health delivery system at all levels. All the facilities are also being provided untied funds to enable the local management committee to carry out locally relevant initiatives for better service delivery. Flexible, decentralized planning is the pivot on which the entire concept of the Mission revolves.

The NRHM seeks to strengthen service delivery by ensuring community ownership of the health facilities. The success of decentralized planning process under NRHM hinges on the capacity of the districts and the states. The management capacity at the states, districts and blocks is being strengthened with the constitution of the Programme Management units (PMUs) with professionals including MBAs, chartered Accountants, and computer experts etc. these professionals have been assigned specific roles and a training component has been built in to make management effective.

The UNICEF evaluation conducted over 2006 has indicated that the coverage of immunization has improved from 52.8 per cent for full immunization in 2000-01 to 54.5 per cent during 2004-05. Janani Suraksha Yojana (JSY) has been launched all over all over country to promote safe delivery, and incentives are being provided to BPL families for institutional delivery. During 2005-06, over 6 lakh beneficiaries of JSY were reported by the States and during 2006-07, 12 lakh beneficiaries have been reported under JSY by the States. Outlay on NRHM has gone up by 23 per cent from Rs. 6,731 crore in 2005-06 (RC) to Rs. 11,505 crore in 2006-07 (BE).

Table 4
Trends in Health Care Infrastructure

	1951	*1991*	*2005 (period/Source)*
SC/PHC/CHC	725	57353	171608*
Dispensaries and Hospitals (all)	9209	23555	27770**
Beds (Private and Public)	117198	569495	914543 (all types)**
Nursing Personnel	18054	143887	865135@
Doctors (Modern System)	61800	268700	656111 @

* RHS: Rural Health Statistics, 2006
** Health information of India, 2004.
@ National Health Profile, 2005.

REPRODUCTIVE AND CHILD HEALTH (RCH-II) PROGRAM

The second phase of Reproductive and Child Health Program, launched on April 2005 for a period of 5 years, intends to improve the performance of family welfare in reducing maternal and infant morbidity and mortality, and unwanted pregnancies, and thus lead to population stabilization. Reoriented and revitalized to give a pro-poor focus, the programme is envisaged as an umbrella programme by integrating all the related and inter-linked stand alone schemes into a single composite programme. With a sector-wide approach to family welfare, it adopts a decentralized process by inviting each State/UT to prepare its own implementation plan on the basis of a situational analysis of ground realities and requirements. Funds approved for RCH-II went up from Rs. 1, 523.75 crore to Rs. 1,871.67 crore between 2005-06 (RE) and 2006-07 (BE).

Table 5
Expectation of Life at Birth

Year	*Male*	*Female*
1980	54.10	54.70
1990	58.60	58.70
1991	58.10	58.60
1992	58.60	59.00
1993	59.00	59.70
1994	59.40	60.40
1995	59.70	60.90
1996-2001 (p)	62.30	65.27
2001-2006 (P)	63.87	66.91
2006-2011 (P)	65.65	67.67
2011-2016 (P)	67.04	69.18

Source: Office of Registrar General India and Statistical Abstract India 1997, CSO, New Delhi.
P–Projected levels of the expectation of life at Birth as per report of the Technical Group on Population, RG, India.

Table 6
Total Fertility Rate for 16 Major States of India

States	*1981 (Census)*	*1991 (Census)*	*1999 (SRS)*	*2000 (SRS)*
Andhra Pradesh	4.0	3.0	2.4	2.3
Assam	4.1	3.5	3.2	3.1
Bihar	5.7	4.4	4.5	4.5
Gujarat	4.3	3.1	3.0	2.9
Haryana	5.0	4.0	3.2	3.2
Karnataka	3.6	3.1	2.5	2.4
Kerala	2.8	1.8	1.8	1.9
Madhya Pradesh	5.2	4.6	3.9	4.0
Maharashtra	3.6	3.0	2.5	2.5
Orissa	4.3	3.3	2.7	2.8
Punjab	4.0	3.1	2.5	2.4
Rajasthan	5.2	4.6	4.2	4.1
Tamil Nadu	3.4	2.2	2.0	2.1
Uttar Pradesh	5.8	5.1	4.7	4.7
West Bangal	4.2	3.2	2.4	2.4
Himachal Pradesh	3.8	3.1	2.4	2.3
India	4.5	3.6	3.2	3.2

Source: Registrar General, India.
SSR–Sample Registration System.

PLAN OUTLAY

Plan outlay of the Department of Health was increased from Rs. 5118 crore during IX Plan toRs.9253 crore during X Plan. However with the transfer of Rs.999 crore from Department of Family Welfare the X Plan Outlay Department of Health has been increased to Rs. 10252 crore. Plan outlay of the Department of Health for 2006-07 has been enhanced to Rs. 3328 crore as against Rs. 2908 crore for the year 2005-06.

Table 7
Trends in Plan Outlay and Expenditure from 2000-01 to 2006-07

	Approved Outlay	*Expenditure*
20001-01	1300	1120.3
2001-02	1450	1307.94
2002-03	1550	1359.83
2003-04	1550	1325.81
2004-05	2208#	1772.36
2005-06	2908	2239.52*
2006-07	3328	694.86**

* Provisional ** Provisional upto 30.9.2006
# Additionality of Rs. 408 crore has crore has been provided by

Source: Annual Report 2006-07.

PUBLIC PLUS PRIVATE EXPENDITURE

The public plus private out-of-pocket expenditure on health in India is 5.1 per cent of GDP, higher than most 'developing' countries including China and several Latin American countries which spend 3.5-4.5 per cent and close to Japan and the west European countries that spend 5.5-8 per cent [UNDP 2002]. However, the public share of expenditure on health in the country is only 17.5 per cent, among the lowest in the world (0.9 per cent of GDP).

Countries with much lower per cent of GDP spent on health but a greater share of it through the public sector have achieved much better health indices, such as Sri Lanka and China. However, the much lower levels of poverty in Sri Lanka and China, i e, 6.6 per cent and 18.8 per cent of population living below $1per day compared to India's 44.2 per cent, could be responsible for their better health indices.

The relative importance of levels of poverty and public expenditure as determinants of health status is debated, but that both need urgent attention for improving health status is well accepted.

An equally serious consideration is the nature of expenditure of public funds for health. For instance, the US has the highest GDP, spends the maximum on health through both public and private sectors, has the most hi-tech medical care and generates the maximum state-of-the-art medical technology. Paradoxically, it has lower health indices than Japan and Sweden. It also has extremely high levels of iatrogenic ill health, i e, disease and death due to medical treatment [Steel *et al* 1981; Brennan *et. al.* 1991].

IMPROVEMENT IN THE QUALITY OF HEALTH CARE

(1) The improvement in the quality of health care over the years is reflected in respect of some basic demographic indicators. The Crude Birth Rate (CBR) declined from 40.8 births per thousand population in 1951 to 29.5 in 1991 and further to 23.8 in 2005. Similarly there was a sharp decline in Crude Death Rate (CDR) which decreased from 25.0 deaths per thousand population in 1951 to 9.8 in 1991 and further to 7.6 in 2005. Also, the Total Fertility Rate (average number of children likely to be born to a woman between 15-40 years of age) has decreased from 6.0 in 1981 to 2.9 in 2004 as per the estimate from the Sample Registration System (SRS) of Registrar General India, Ministry of Home Affairs.

(2) The Maternal Mortality Rate has also declined from 437 per one lakh live births in 1992 – 93 to 301 in 2001-03.

(3) Infant Mortality Rate, which was 110 in 1981, has declined to 58 per 1000 live births in 2004. Child Mortality Rate has also decreased from 57.3 in 1972 to 17.0 in 2004.

(4) In so far as family planning is concerned, the District Level Household Survey DLHS) conducted in 2002-04, has revealed that 45.7% eligible couples are currently using any one of the family planning methods as against 22.8% in 1981.

(5) The total number of acceptors of different Family Planning methods enrolled in the country during the year 2006-07 as per provisional performance figures available so far was 29.44 million. The table (Table 2) below summarizes the position in regard to family planning achievements during 2005-06 and 2006-07 (up to September 2006) at all India level.

HOUSEHOLD EXPENDITURE ON HEALTH

The various studies conducted have revealed that households spend a substantial amount on health care and the poorer class spends more on health care in terms of their proportion to consumption expenditure and income. Household health expenditure works out to 8.4%. The upper class spends only 4% of their consumption expenditure, while the lowest and lower middle classes spend as much as 8% and 10% respectively on health care. A study in rural Kerala in 1987 found that the per capita cost per year incurred by the household on health was $ 5. The percentage of the reported income spent on health was found to be around 7%. Comparing it across class it found that the lowest class spends as high as 14% of their income on health as compared to the highest class which spent only 4.4% s. (Kannan, Thankappan, Raman Kutty, and Aravindan, 1991).

PRIVATE HOUSEHOLD EXPENDITURE

Findings from various studies make it evident that a substantial financial burden of the household is borne for meeting health care needs. Compared to government expenditure on health the private household expenditure is nearly 4 to 5 times more. A substantial portion of their income and consumption expenditure is spent on health. This certainly is not a happy state of affairs, since such expenditure on health care would mean cutting down on the household food consumption.

This gains significance when we realize that nearly half of the country's population does not have enough resources to meet their food requirements, and worse still the capacity to earn if the patient happens to be the sole earning member.

Given this socio economic situation in the country the purchasing power becomes a crucial factor. As we have seen above the accessibility of the public health service is poor especially in rural areas of the country. The private health sector becomes unaffordable for the vast majority of the poor. There is impoverishment of the lower class or middle class due to illness which could be of a chronic nature or that involving hospitalization or surgery. The high cost of health care makes the poor more marginalised. There is a need to question the dominant role of the private health sector and the consequently high health care expenditure.

The issues raised above need to be addressed by the planners, policy makers, funders, NGO's, researchers among others. In the new lexicography of Indian economics privatisation and liberalization are the new panacea for ills in the economy. Privatisation and liberalization being undertaken in the country has to be viewed in the broad context of majority of the Indian people living under extreme poverty conditions, non-availability of basic amenities for the majority of the people, poor nutritional status, impoverishment due to health, poor availability of public services, presence of a dominant and unregulated, unaccountable private health sector along with strengthening of market forces and helplessness of the consumer against various odds. In India no single system can work. The health sector reforms that are undertaken in India are diametrically opposite to the people's needs. What we need is a combination of social insurance, employment related insurance for the organised sector employees, voluntary insurance for other categories who can afford to pay and finally, taw and related revenues.

Issues that need to be questioned in India's health policy

- Priorities within the health sector need to be changed.
- More funds need to be made available for the rural areas especially with regard to curative services.
- Additional resources, especially for non-salary expenditures.
- Greater decentralisation on a priority basis.

- Questioning of increasing support for population control.
- Wastage reduction and improving efficiency by better management practices.
- Establishment of proper referral systems.
- Regulatory intervention and monitoring of the government in the private sector and market.
- Geographical distribution of physicians through licensing and other means.
- Legislation should be enacted where there is no legislation.
- Standardisation of fees charged by the practitioners and fixation of reasonable charges.
- Trend favouring user charges should be countered.
- Additional revenues earmarked for the health sector could be generated through taxing health-degrading products.
- Those with a capacity to pay should be mandated to contribute to health care through insurance and other pre-payment programs.

The Share of the Poor in Health Care

- In recent times there has been stagnation in the number of rural public health institutions and beds in public hospitals, with a decrease relative to population.
- Simultaneously, there has been an increase in beds in private hospitals.
- The National Sample Survey data shows that respondent perceptions of not accessing care due to financial constraints increased from 10 per cent to 20 per cent in rural areas and 15 per cent to 25 per cent in urban areas.
- The rate of untreated ailments increased by 40 per cent for the poorest expenditure decile.
- The Government has over the years committed not more than 3.5 per cent of its resources to the health sector.

- The expenditure on health as a percentage to GDP is around 0.9 per cent woefully short of the WHO's recommendation of 5 per cent.
- The grants from Government to the State Governments declined drastically from 19.9 per cent in 1974-84 to 3.3 per cent in 2003-05.
- The population control program stands as the highest priority activity.
- Family Planning expenditures are spent mostly in rural areas.
- 43 per cent of the total expenditure on public health was spent on salaries.
- Government takes care of preventive and promotive health services and left the curative care to private health sector.
- 70-80 per cent of the investment and expenditure reaches 30 per cent of the population in urban areas.
- Of all hospitals and beds in the country, only 32 per cent and 20 percent respectively were in the rural areas i.e., 20 beds per 1,00,000 population in rural areas as compared to 238 beds per 1, 00, 000 population in urban areas.
- Also, the poor still resort to the public services for more of their secondary and tertiary level care than do the better off (Iyer and Sen 2000).
- Even 2-3 per cent of India's GDP is not enough for the public sector to provide comprehensive health services to all its citizens. Therefore the imperative for private services will remain.
- Ths issues is what kind of private services should the government promote–the 'informal' providers that the poor access most easily, formally trained generalist private practitioners who are a varied group and cater to different classes, or the corporate sector that does no cater to the poor even when it avails of government subsidies.
- The Share of central grants for public health declined from 28 percent 17 per cent during reform periods.

- Three fourth of those qualifying from public funded medical colleges practice in the private sector. 40 per cent of the doctors migrate out of the country.
- The poor in the villages were given inferior health services in the name of Primary Health Care, National Programs. For the rural population there is very little provision of state funded curative care though these services are most demanded.
- The percentage of the reported income spent on health was found to be around 7 per cent. Comparing it across class it found that the lowest class spends as high as 14 per cent of their income on health as compared to the highest class which spent 4 per cents.
- The share of private health sector at today's price works out 15714 millions per year.

Abuses in Private Practice

- Surgeries are more profitable.
- 30 per cent of the deliveries were by cesarean section.
- Unnecessary investigations, tests, consultations, etc.
- The profit ratio is 40 percent in Bombay and 30 per cent other areas.
- Doctor Associations have standardized the profit ratios to be given to referring doctors.
- Pressure on the doctors to ensure that the beds are occupied and hospital equipment fully utilized.
- Collection of compulsory deposit before hand.

CONCLUSION

Thus the focus of reforms and health sector in India, decentralization is going to be the key element of the reform process. One size doesn't fit all is clearly the mantra. Alternate ways of financing health care should receive policy attention in a major way. Clearly there is scope of formulating demand side financing mechanisms so as to provide access to poor.

Private sector should be seen as a national asset and alternate service delivery systems e.g. social franchising should be considered. It is also critical to work with private sector in terms of certification and accreditation systems.

Thus, within available resources we can move towards achieving the optimum in health services for all Indians, given the resolve to rethink prevailing paradigms and take some hard steps.

REFERENCES

Agarwal D. (2006), "Health Sector Reforms: Relevance in India," *Indian Journal of Community Medicinc*, Vol. 31, No. 4, Oct.-Dec. pp. 202-222.

Jesani A., Ananthraman S. (1993), "Private Sector and Privatization in the Health Care Services", FRCH, Bombay.

Kannan, K. P. *et al*, (1991), "Health and Development in Rural Kerala", K. S. S. P., Thiruvananthapuram.

Kannamma Raman (2006), "A Critique of Healthcare Policy in India," *Economic and Political Weekly*, Vol. 41, No. 43 and 44, Nov. 4. pp. 4579-4583.

Ritu Priya *et al*, (2004), "CMP on Health: Making India World Class," *Economic and Political Weekly*, Vol. 39, No. 27, July 3. pp. 2971-2974.

CHAPTER-7

MALNOURISHED INDIAN CHILDREN: THE POST REFORM SCENARIO

K. P. Vipin Chandran

INTRODUCTION

One of the major issues of discussion relating to the economic reforms launched in the country in 1991 has been their impact on the lives of ordinary people, particularly those belonging to the weaker sections. Much of the discussion on the effects of economic reforms in India has centered on the temporal movement in the poverty and inequality magnitudes. The economic reforms initiated in 1991 did not directly call for any change in the commitment of the nation to the weaker sections or to the government's role in translating it into concrete action. In fact the reforms, belatedly at least, emphasized the continuing role that the state should play in eradicating poverty and conceded the fact that the state has to play a positive role in the social sector generally, including social security, education and public health. Nutritional deficiencies and poor health of children are major public health concerns in developing countries, where they represent both a cause and a manifestation of poverty ((UN 2000; World Bank 1998; NSSO 61st Round 2004-05).

Increasing health is seen as a dimension of poverty in its own right and child health is known to have important long-term effects on productivity during adulthood. As children are the future of every country, their situation is always of concern to policy makers, their parents and the general public. Ensuring children's health is a universally supported goal of development. After India become independent in 1947, several steps were taken for the improvement of the health situation and well-being of the children. But still malnutrition is a major problem in India, according to NFHS-3 (2005-06), 46 per cent of India's children under the age of three are underweight. Better nutritional status among children is the nucleus for child survival and optimal cognitive development of the current as well as succeeding generations. It is estimated that nearly 54% of children deaths are associated with malnutrition (WHO 2004). The corresponding levels of child malnutrition are much lower in most other countries-28 per cent in Sub-Saharan Africa and 8 per cent in china (UNICEF 2007). Malnutrition rates from primarily inadequate food intake, illness and harmful child care practices such as delayed supplementary feeding. The main responsible factors underlying these are household food insecurity, inadequate preventive and curative health care services, and poor perception of health care (World Bank 1998).

Preventing undernutrition has emerged as one of the most critical challenges to India's development planners in recent times. General undernutrition, characterized by under-weight among children is more prevalent amongst rural children, scheduled castes and tribes, and amongst children with illiterate mothers. The threat of communicable diseases, as well as prenatal morbidity and mortality, looms larger because of the poor nutritional status of a substantial part of the population (Michale Gragnolati *et. al* 2005). The present challenges of communicable diseases and maternal and child survival reveals the weaknesses of the health system. Amartya Sen points out that "while the case for economic reforms may take good note of the diagnosis that India has too much government interference in some fields, it ignores the fact that India also has insufficient and ineffective government activity in many others fields, including basic education, health care, social security, land reform, and the promotion of social change"(Economic Survey 1999-2000).

Over the last decade, countries across the world have been changing their existing economic models in favour of one driven by the free market, incorporating processes of liberalization, privatization and globalization. The direct impact of free trade on children may not leap to the eye, but we do know that globalised India is witnessing worsening levels of basic health, nutrition and shelter. Over the periods, India has invested sizable funds in health and nutritional across the country to improve health and nutritional care delivery services to children, both in terms of quantity and quality. Generally, it is expected that harmonizing returns would be visible in overall health and nutritional status of the children in the country. However, reality speaks something different. Complete elimination of malnutrition and curable yet, dreadful communicable diseases are still an "unfinished agenda. Significantly, inequalities in undernutrition increased during the 1990s, between demographic segments, and socio-economic groups. The consequences of malnutrition are multi-dimensional having impinged on survival, development, health, productivity and economic growth. The various direct and indirect nutritional interventions make the state of affairs even worse situation in India especially public distribution system and ICDS.

CONCEPTUAL FRAMEWORK OF THE CAUSES OF UNDERNUTRITION

Child undernutrition is a consequence of the complex interactions of multiple determinants. It traces the causal pathways of undernutrition through different levels – the most immediate, the underlying, and the basic causes. The first level is composed of the most immediate causes of malnutrition and highlights the importance of both food intake and the absence of infection for improving child nutritional status. Inadequate dietary intake and infections create a vicious cycle that is responsible for much of the high morbidity and mortality among children in developing countries. On the one hand, when children do not consume enough, immune response is lowered, rendering them more susceptible to infectious diseases. On the other hand, ill children deplete their nutritional stores and are in poor health because of reduced intake, poor absorption of nutrients and the increased demands of combating disease (UNICEF 1990, Jonsson 1993, smith and Haddad 2000).

MEASUREMENT OF CHILD MALNUTRITION

Malnutrition is measured in terms of input and output indicators. Food energy intake is the input indicator, which measures the magnitude of malnutrition by comparing the food energy intake of the person with proposed norms. Output indicators are closely related to health and functional capability (Mortell and Ho 1984). The nutritional outcome measures are anthropometric measures, bio-chemical and clinical indicators.

Three commonly used anthropometric measures: height-for-age, weight-for-height and weight-for-age. Each index provides different information about a child's nutritional status. Height-for-age measures linear growth retardation, primarily reflecting chronic (long-term) malnutrition. Weight-for height measures body mass in relation to height, primarily reflecting acute (short-term) malnutrition. Weight-for-age reflects both chronic and acute malnutrition. These three indices are expressed in terms of standard deviations from the median for an international reference population specified by WHO. (Peter Svedberg 1987, Seckler 1982, Ratzan *et. al* 2000). Children whose height-for-age falls more than two standard deviations below the reference median are defined as 'stunted'. Those whose weight-for-height falls more than two standard deviations below the reference median defined as 'wasted', and those whose weight-for-age falls more than two standard deviations below the reference median are defined as 'underweight'. Children who fall more than three standard deviations below the reference median on any of these indices are defined as severely stunted, wasted or underweight.

HOW SERIOUS IS MALNUTRITION?: A GLOBAL PERSPECTIVE

Nearly three-quarters of the world's underweight children live in just ten countries, and over half in just three South Asian countries–Bangladesh, India and Pakistan. Together, Bangladesh, India and Pakistan account for half of all the world's underweight children. In fact, India has more undernourished children that Africa, at 51 million, compared to the continent's 47 million. South Asia is the only region which shows a gender bias with regard to child nourishment, with girls more likely to be underweight than boys (UNICEF 2007a, 2008b). Globally, the proportion of children under age five who are underweight has fallen only slightly since 1990– proof that the world is failing to address children's issues. The 'first Millennium Development Goal' (MDG) to achieving this goal means halving the proportion of children who are underweight for their age, the most visible sign of undernutrition. But current trends show the world is still far off track. Undernutrition is the result of insufficient food intake, repeated infectious diseases and lack of care. It stunts children's growth and development and, in girls, their later ability to bear healthy children. Hunger and undernutrition lead and contribute to some of the world's most intractable problems. It contributes significantly to a cycle of poverty. It hurts children in their ability to learn. It hurts children in their ability to develop and it hurts children in their ability to resist serious diseases (Veneman 2006).

Whether undernutrition is measured as the prevalence of underweight, stunting or wasting, it is clear that the nutritional situation in India is amongst the worst in the world. India's prevalence of underweight (47%) compares to Bangladesh (48%) and Nepal (48%), but is much higher than all other countries within south Asia and far higher than the averages for other regions of the world. (See Table 1).

THE SOUTH ASIAN ENIGMA

South Asia has the doubtful difference of having the highest prevalence of malnutrition in children–higher than even Sub-Saharan Africa which in many ways is lesser developed

Table 1
Child Deprivation in India and South Asia (2004)

Country	*Bangladesh*	*Bhutan*	*India*	*Nepal*	*Pakistan*	*Sri Lanka*
Immunization (% of children under 3 years who have not received the stated vaccine)						
BCG	5	8	27	15	20	1
DTP3	15	11	36	20	35	3
MCV	23	13	44	27	33	4
Polio	15	10	30	20	35	3
Child undernutrition (% of children with the stated condition)						
Underweight	48	19	47	48	38	29
Stunting	43	40	46	51	37	14
Wasting	13	3	16	10	13	14
Infant and child mortality (per 1,000 live births)						
Infant mortality rate	56	67	62	59	80	12
Under-5 mortality Rate	77	80	85	76	101	14

Source: UNICEF (2006), 'State of the World's Children'. In each row, the 'worst' figure is highlighted.

than south Asia. Ramalinaswami.et.al refers to this as the 'South Asian Enigma'. 'The South Asian Enigma' can be explained by three key differences between South Asia and Sub-Saharan Africa. Firstly, low birth weight is the single largest predictor of under nutrition; and over 30% Indian babies are born with low birth weights, compared to approximately 16% in Sub-Saharan Africa. Secondly, women in South Asia tend to have lower status and less decision-making power than women in Sub-Saharan Africa. This limits women's ability to access the resources needed for their children's health and nutrition, and has been shown to be strongly associated with low birth weight, as well as poor child feeding behaviours in the first twelve months of life. Thirdly, hygiene and sanitation standards in South Asia are well below those in Africa, and have a major role to play in causing the infections that lead to undernutrition in the first two years of life.

TRENDS OF CHILD MALNUTRITION: RECENT EVIDENCES FROM INDIA

Over the periods, India has invested sizable funds in health and nutritional across the country to improve health and nutritional care delivery services to people, both in terms of quantity and quality. Over the last decade, countries across the world have been changing their existing economic models in favour of one driven by the free market, incorporating processes of liberalization, privatization and globalization. The direct impact of free trade on children may not leap to the eye, but we do know that globalised India is witnessing worsening levels of basic health, nutrition and shelter.

The very survival of the Indian child is a matter of concern. Around 2.5 million children die in India every year, accounting for one in five deaths in the world, with girls being 50% more likely to die. 87 children of every 1,000 born still have the probability of dying between birth and 5 years of age. According to a UNICEF report on the state of India's newborns, the health challenges faced by a newborn child in India are bigger than those experienced by any other country. Malnutrition and starvation one in every three malnourished children in the world lives in India. The major cause is lack of public health services in remote and interior regions of the country, poor access to subsidized healthcare facilities, declining State expenditure on public health, and lack of awareness about preventive child healthcare (Census of India, 2001).

Table 2
State of Children in India

State of children in India	*NFHS-2 (1998-99)*	*NFHS-3 (2005-06)*
Proportion (%) of young children with the following characteristics:		
Low birth weight (about 30) not breastfed within an hour after birth	84	*
Undernourished	47	46
Stunted	46	38
Wasted	16	19
Not fully vaccinated+	58	56
Not vaccinated at all+	14	NA
Birth was not preceded by any antenatal checkup	34	*
Suffer from anaemia	74	79
Proportion (%) of young children who suffered from the following, during the last two weeks		
Fever	30	NA
Diarrhea	19	NA
Acute respiratory infection	19	NA

Source: NFHS-2, NFHS-3 and Human Development Report 2006
+ Age: 12-23 months

Generally, it is expected that harmonizing returns would be visible in overall health and nutritional status of the children in the country. However, reality speaks something different. Complete elimination of malnutrition and curable yet, dreadful communicable diseases are still an "unfinished agenda". This is a serious problem through-out the country but with large disparities between states and groups. Bihar, Madhya Pradesh, Uttar Pradesh, and Rajasthan account for more than 43 per cent of all underweight children. Furthermore, inequalities in nutritional status worsened in the 1990s, between income groups, urban and rural dwellers, castes and genders. Undernutrition is concentrated in a relatively small number of districts and 10 per cent of villages and districts account for almost 30 per cent of all underweight children; a quarter of districts and villages account for more than half of all underweight children (FOCUS Report 2006).

Table 3
Child Indicators from NFHS

Indicators	*NFHS-1*	*NFHS-2*	*NFHS-3*
IMR (per '000 births)	77.3	67.3	55.5
% of children under-weight (age<3 years)	51.1	46.7	43.3
Children fully immunized (%)	38.3	44.2	46.0
ABC Index	36.6	43.3	49.0

Source: Calculated as weighted average of 22 states for which data is available.

Consider the well being of children under six. Since they constitute the most marginalized group, an improvement in well-being of children can be taken as improvement in well-being of the average population. On the basis of the three important indicators of IMR, the percentage of children who are underweight and have been immunized, then FOCUS report (2006) created an "Achievement of Babies and Children (ABC) index".

While the ABC index increased by 6.7 points (18.4%) between NFHS-1 and NFHS-2, the increase in the later period was only 5.7 points (13.1%). Further, some other indicators point towards deterioration in conditions of children between NFHS-2 and NFHS-3. The percentage of children under age 3 who are categorized as wasted, increased in 18 of the 22 states for which data is available,(the only states reporting a reduction in wasting were Assam, Chhattisgarh, Himachal Pradesh, Karnataka, Maharashtra and Orissa.) with the all India incidence rising from 14% to 17%. Children suffering from anemia increased from 74% to 79% (the states where the percentage increased are Andhra Pradesh, Assam, Gujarat, Karnataka, Kerala, Madhya Pradesh, Orissa, Tamilnadu and Uttar Pradesh).

Levels of undernourishment vary widely across Indian States. Punjab, Kerala, Jammu and Kashmir, and Tamilnadu report the lowest proportions of underweight children (27% to 33%); whereas Chhattisgarh, Bihar, Jharkhand, and Madhya Pradesh report the highest levels of underweight children (52% to 60%). The first set of four States with the lowest proportion of underweight children, provisioning of health services, care of children especially of newborns, and the nutritional status of women are better than in the second set of four high malnutrition States. For instance, 60% to 81% of children aged six to 35 months were fully immunized in the low malnutrition States, whereas the proportion is much lower - 33% to 49% - in the high malnutrition States. Reach of maternal care services is also poorer in the high malnutrition States. In the low malnutrition States, 63% to 97% of mothers receive at least three antenatal care visits; this proportion varies between 17% and 55 % in the high malnutrition States. Again, 53% to 100% of births were assisted by a trained birth attendant in the low malnutrition States whereas in the high malnutrition States the proportion varied between 17% and 55% and, the nutritional status of women is better in States where children had lower levels of malnutrition. For instance, whereas 14% to 24% of women in the low malnutrition States have a BMI below normal, the proportion varies from 40% to 43% in the high malnutrition States.

The important policies associated with globalization affected the health sector; it reduced overall government

Table 4
Indicators of Children's Nutritional Status: State-wise Trends

	Percentage of children							
	Stunting		*Wasting*		*Underweight*		*Children age 6-35 months who are Anaemic*	
States	*NFHS-2 1998-99*	*NFHS-3 2005-06*	*NFHS-2 1998-99*	*NFHS-3 2005-06*	*NFHS-2 1998-99*	*NFHS-3 2005-06*	*NFHS-2 1998-99*	*NFHS-3 2005-06*
Andhra Pradesh	39	34	9	13	38	37	72.3	79
Assam	50	35	13	13	36	40	63.2	76.7
Bihar	55	42	20	28	54	58	81.1	87.6
Chhattisgarh	58	45	19	18	61	52	87.7	81
Delhi	37	35	13	16	35	33	69	63.2
Goa	18	21	13	12	29	29	53.4	49.3
Gujarat	44	42	16	17	45	47	74.5	80.1
Haryana	50	36	5	17	35	42	83.9	82.5
Himachal Pradesh	41	27	17	19	44	36	69.9	58.8
Jharkhand	49	41	25	31	54	59	82.4	77.7
Jammu & Kashmir	39	28	12	15	35	29	71.1	68.1
Karnataka	37	38	20	18	44	41	70.6	82.7
Kerala	22	21	11	16	27	29	43.9	55.7
Madhya Pradesh	49	40	20	33	54	60	71.3	82.6
Manipur	31	25	8	8	28	24	45.2	52.8

Contd...

	Percentage of children							
	Stunting		*Wasting*		*Underweight*		*Children age 6-35 months who are Anaemic*	
States	*NFHS-2 1998-99*	*NFHS-3 2005-06*	*NFHS-2 1998-99*	*NFHS-3 2005-06*	*NFHS-2 1998-99*	*NFHS-3 2005-06*	*NFHS-2 1998-99*	*NFHS-3 2005-06*
Meghalava	45	42	13	28	38	46	67.6	68.7
Mizoram	35	30	10	9	28	22	57.2	51.7
Maharashtra	40	38	21	15	50	40	76	71.9
Nagaland	33	30	10	15	24	30	43.7	na
Orissa	44	38	24	19	54	44	72.3	74.2
Punjab	39	28	7	9	29	27	80	80.2
Rajasthan	52	34	12	20	51	44	82.3	79.6
Sikkim	32	29	5	13	21	23	76.5	56.9
Tamilnadu	29	25	20	22	37	33	69	72.5
Tripura	40	30	13	20	43	39	61.8	67.9
Uttaranchal	47	32	8	16	42	38	77.4	61.5
West Bengal	42	33	14	19	49	44	78.3	69.4
INDIA	46	38	16	19	47	46	74.2	79.2

Source: NFHS-2 and NFHS-3

spending means government spending on health falls. Since governments are the main providers of mother and child health services, AIDS prevention work, leprosy control programmes and anti-smoking campaigns, these and other primary health care initiatives are particularly badly affected. In government services which remain after the cuts, user charges are often introduced. This method of introducing the market mechanism into the provision of health care obviously makes services less available to the poor. The privatization of health and hospital services also makes the poor suffer as services become more oriented towards those who can pay. In addition, essential drug policies, which aim to make necessary pharmaceuticals available to all at an affordable price, are threatened by increasingly liberal policies towards pharmaceutical companies. Finally, increasing unemployment and poverty add to the nation's health problems by creating extra demands on reduced government services.

EFFECTIVENESS OF FOOD INTERVENTION PROGRAMMES TO ADDRESS CHILD MALNUTRITION

The Government of India has been implementing a wide range of nutrition intervention programmes for achieving food and nutritional security at the household and individual levels. The important food-based interventions include Public distribution system (PDS), Integrated child development services (ICDS) and mid-day meal programmes (MDM).

(1) *Public Distribution System (PDS)*: The public distribution system (PDS) supplies food items, such as, food grains and sugar at administered prices through fair price shops. In the wake of economic reforms, the PDS is perceived to be the main safety net to protect the poor from the potential short-run price-induced adverse effects. The recently abnormally large increases in procurement prices and the consequent upward revisions in the central issue prices have had an adverse impact on the efficacy of the PDS. One of the consequences of the change in the policy of the central government, arising out of the

economic reform, has been on the PDS. The decision to limit the PDS subsidy to those 'below the poverty line' from 1997 has meant a decline in the availability of food grains at subsidized price to the status for their public distribution systems.

(2) *Integrated child development services (ICDS)*: The ICDS launched in 1975, is centrally sponsored, state-administered, nation-wide direct nutrition intervention programme, which integrates supplementary nutrition with primary health care and informal education. It provides various services to children under six years old, and their mothers. These include: (a) supplementary feeding, (b) immunization, (c) health check-ups, (d) referral services, (e) health and nutrition education to adult women, and (f) non-formal pre-school education to 3-6 year old. The overall impact of ICDS on malnutrition is very limited, which could be due to a meager allocation of budgetary resources and faulty project design. The programmes are regressively distributed between the states. The states with a high incidence of malnutrition like Bihar, Madhya Pradesh and Uttar Pradesh have a relatively low coverage.

(3) *Mid-day meal programme (MDM):* The national programme of nutritional support to primary education, commonly known as the mid-day meal programme, it is a nation-wide central scheme intended to improve the enrollment and regular attendance and reduce dropout in schools. It also intended to improve the nutritional status of primary school children. There are shortcomings in the implementation of the programme. The central allocations of food grains have fallen short of the entitlement. Moreover, many state governments do not even spend the norm of Rs. one per child per day fixed by the central government for states.

The performance of food-based interventions needs to be improved by making them more demand driven. Merely scaling up the coverage of the programmes without improving their quality may not be the best way to reduce malnutrition. It is essential to reform the PDS and simultaneously release some resources needed by the ICDS and MDM. In essence, all the current food-based interventions play a complementary role in justifying malnutrition over the life cycle of an individual.

GOVERNMENT INITIATIVES ON CHILD HEALTH AND NUTRITION

On November 20, 1989, the UN General Assembly adopted the Convention on the Rights of the Child (CRC). On January 26, 1990, the opening day of the session, 61 countries signed it. The CRC covers all children under the age of 18 years, regardless of sex, colour, language, religion or race. India ratified the CRC in 1992. Prior to the Fifth Five-Year Plan, the government's focus was on child welfare through the promotion of basic minimum services for children. This culminated in the adoption of the National Policy for Children, in 1974.

The Fifth Five-Year Plan (1974-79) saw a shift of focus from welfare to development and the integration and co-ordination of services after the Integrated Child Development Services (ICDS) 1975.The Sixth Five-Year Plan strengthened child welfare and development. It led to the spatial expansion and enrichment of child development services through a variety of programmes. The focus of the Eighth Five-Year Plan (1992-97) shifted to human development through advocacy, mobilization and community empowerment. The Government of India declared its commitment to every child in the Ninth Five-Year Plan (1997-2002). The Tenth Five-Year Plan advocated a convergent/ integrated rights-based approach to ensure the survival, development, protection and participation of children. The Eleventh Five-Year Plan (2007-2012) prepared by the Planning Commission emphatically stated that 'Development of the child is at the centre of the Eleventh Plan'. While continuing with the rights-based approach to child development, the plan recognizes the importance of a holistic approach, focusing both on outcomes and indicators for child development as well as macro-perspective trends and governance issues.

The very survival of the Indian child is a matter of concern. Around 2.5 million children die in India every year, accounting for one in five deaths in the world, with girls being 50% more likely to die Eighty-seven children of every 1,000 born still have the probability of dying between birth and 5 years of age. According to a report on the state of India's newborns, the health challenges faced by a newborn child in India are bigger than those experienced by any other country.

THREATS AND REASONS FOR HIGH MALNUTRITION IN INDIA

Several misconceptions cloud public opinion. Many people believe that India's low per capita income is the major underlying cause. This is entirely true. A majority of the countries in Sub-Saharan Africa report lower levels of per capita income than India-and most of them report lower rates of child malnutrition as well. Other argument that income poverty is a major underlying cause of child malnutrition. Here too, it finds no obvious linkage between levels of child malnutrition and income poverty. 26% of India's population lives below the poverty line and yet 46% of children under the age three are malnourished.

The important reasons for high levels of malnutrition in India; first hint is found in the proportion of low birth weight babies. Estimates for India reveals that 20 to 30 per cent of babies weight less than 2,500 grams at birth. Adversely affecting the birth of well- nourished babies is also the poor health and nutritional status of women. According to NFHS-3, close to one-third of Indian women suffer from chronic energy deficiency and have a body mass index (BMI) of less than 18.5kg/m2. The second factor has to do with the limited reach of public health services. In 2005-06, for instance, only 44% of children aged 12 to 23 months were fully immunized. NFHS-3 reveals some glaring shortfalls. In 2005-06, 515 of mothers across the country received at least three antenatal care visits during pregnancy; and less than half (48%) of births are attended to by a trained birth attendant , which includes a doctor, nurse, women health worker, and other health professional.

The third reason is related to care of the child. Breast milk provides vital nutrients throughout the first year of life; but it alone is not sufficient. Despite the importance of breastfeeding and appropriate feeding for preventing malnutrition, only 23 per cent of children under the age of three were breastfed within one hour of birth and less than half the babies (46 per cent) up to five months old were exclusively breastfed and only 56 per cent of children aged six to nine months received solid or semi-solid food and breastfed. The fourth dilemma related to the limited opportunities available to women. According to NFHS-3, malnutrition among Indian children below the age of three born to illiterate mothers (55 per cent) is more than twice the levels (26 per cent) reported among mothers who have completed more than 10 years of schooling.

CONCLUSION

India's high levels of child malnutrition reflect the continuing neglect of health, the inadequate reach and efficacy of health and child care services, and the failure of strategies to reach newborn children and those under the age of three. These deficiencies need to be addressed right away. The most serious obstacles to improving child nutrition do not relate directly to food availability, even at the household level. Distribution of food within the household, child-rearing practices, the nutritional quality of the food, clean water and reducing infections all require a much more comprehensive and integrated approach and implement all 'nutrition safety net schemes' in an integrated manner on a life-cycle basis.

The nutrition aspects of "food and nutrition security" need more specific attention. This applies to both reducing the number of malnourished and to accelerating the rate of decline. Economic growth and continuation of existing programmes will not be sufficient to overcome the problem of child malnutrition in particular. It also will require more state, district and even village-level differentiation and emphasis. The risk of growing inequality between groups, districts, regions, etc. is increasing as economic growth accelerates. This requires specific attention in districts where poverty is concentrated and greater attention on "forward looking" vulnerability reduction and risk management by households that target specific livelihood profiles. Improving programme implementation that targets BPL families is important but so is recognition of the much larger number of households that move above or below the poverty in any given year. Avoiding the fall and accelerating the rise out of poverty call for different strategies. Another suggestion is continue, strengthen and spread the on-going 'self-help revolution' (SHGs) by ensuring backward linkages with technology and credit and forward linkages with markets and also ensure access to clean drinking water, environmental hygiene, primary health care and elementary education.

REFERENCES

Economic Survey 1999-2000, GOI Based on NSSO 1999-2000.

Michale Gragnolati *et. al.* (2005), *"India's Undernourished Children-A Call for an Action"*, Health, Nutrition and Population (HNP) Discussion Paper, World Bank.

Monica Das Gupta et. al. (1996), *'Health, Poverty and Development in India'*, Oxford University Press, Delhi.

Mortell. R and T. J. Ho (1984), *"Malnutrition, Morbidity and Mortality"*, Population Development Report, 10: 49-68.

National Family Health Survey, India: Various issues *http://www.nfhsindia.org/:* International Institute for Population Sciences and ORC Macro, India, Mumbai.

Nirmala Lakshman (2007), *Where are the Children? The Hindu*, National Daily, August 15.

NSSO (National Sample Survey Organization) (2006), NSS 61st Round 2004-05, NewDelhi, NSSO

Peter Svedberg (1987), *"Undernutrition in Sub-Saharan Africa: A Critical Assessment of the Evidence"* WIDER Working Paper No. 15, June.

Radhakrishana R., K. Hanumantha Rao *et. al.* (2004), *'Chronic Poverty and Malnutrition in 1990's- Economic and Political Weekly*, July 10, pp. 3121-3130.

Radhakrishana R. and Ravi (2004), *'Malnutrition in India–Trends and Determinants', Economic and Political Weekly*, pp. 671-675, February 14.

Ramalingaswamy *et. al* (1996), *'The Asian Enigma, The Progress of Nations'*, UNICEF, pp. 11-17.

Seckeler D. (1982), *"Small but Healthy: A Basic Hypothesis in the Theory, Measurement and Policy of Malnutrition"*, in P.V. Sukhatme, Ed. (1982), Newer Concepts in Nutrition and their Implications for Policy.

UN (2000), United Nations Administrative Committee on Coordination/Standing Committee on Nutrition, Fourth Report on the World Nutrition Situation: Nutrition Throughout the Lifecycle. Geneva: ACC/SCN.

UNICEF (2007), *"The State of World Children 2007"*, South Asia Edition.

World Bank (1998), *"India: Wasting Away"*, Washington D.C.

Section–II

EDUCATION

CHAPTER-8

UNIVERSAL EDUCATION FOR THE VULNERABLE AND MARGINALIZED CHILDREN: BRIDGING THE POLICY INTENTIONS WITH MEANINGFUL OPERATIONAL STRATEGIES

M. D. Usha Devi

Many students especially those who are poor intuitively know what the schools do for them. They school them to confuse process and substance. Once these become blurred a new logic is assumed; the more treatment there is, the better are the results or escalation leads to success. The pupil is thereby 'schooled' to confuse teaching with learning, grade achievement with education, a diploma with competence and fluency with the ability to say something new (Illich, Ivan, 1973).

A look at the education system across the globe suggests that 21st Century is characterized by constant waves of reforms in school education. The backdrop for this reform activism was a broad social agreement to bring all children & young people into the education system and make their stay in the education system longer & more significant.

We notice that this wave of reform is not only confined to education system in the developing countries but also in advanced countries as well. Besides, the intensity and consistency of this reform is found to vary from country to country. The US current reform policy of 'No Child Left Behind' after its 'Nation at Risk' focuses on addressing educational needs of multicultural & racial ethnic minorities in American schools and also making school system fight violence, drug abuse, teenage pregnancy and HIV AIDS among young adolescents. Countries such as Australia, New Zealand and other European countries have also launched reforms such as school based management, self managed schools in order to make schools more autonomous and relevant to the community in which they function. In all these countries the central focus is to move towards excellence in educational standards & achieving greater equity.

In Latin & South American countries, the reform approach has been towards decentralized governance for expanding provision of educational services and impressive innovations such as educational vouchers, public and private partnerships, teacher evaluation, curriculum reform etc. Both 'equity' and 'quality' dimensions have been critical concerns in these countries.

Thus there is so much of richness & dimensions to these reforms in countries across the world that it becomes rather difficult to make any significant attempt to synthesize as there is diverse educational conditions & different developmental context in terms of social & economic conditions. However it is noticed that three important aspects the State reforms have transformed the education system (Navarro, 2007). They are:

(1) the level of government responsibility for providing & regulating education has been diversified (decentralization reforms)

(2) public capacities have been built as a result of the strengthening of central/state government institutions in critical areas (such as assessment)

(3) the role of the State as a direct provider of education has changed in some cases, for the most part, within the boundaries of programs that do not directly challenge the mainstream public education.

In the Indian context, it is noticed that the post economic reform period is considered as the most active period of educational development since the basic education received tremendous impetus during this time. India's 42nd amendment to the constitution effected in 1976 made education a concurrent responsibility, investing parliament with the authority to legislate on education and thus to facilitate the evolution of national policies for education. Subsequently, based on a dialogue and consensus process to promote education development, the National Policy of Education (NPE) was evolved for the first time in India in 1986. The policy, with a major emphasis on quality improvement within the framework of universalisation of elementary education strongly articulated the need for decentralized approach to school education and recommended for both academic and administrative decentralization. Subsequently, the Programme of Action (POA, 1987) for the NPE (1986) came out with strategies of action for setting up sub-state level academic support structures such as the District Institute of Education and Training (DIET), Block Resource Centre (BRC), Cluster Resource Centre (CRC) and the Village Education Committees (VEC) as a part of governance reform initiatives.

The 73rd and 74th amendments to the Indian Constitution in 1992 have provided further impetus to decentralization governance reforms in school education through creation of academic support institutions and grassroots participatory structures. These were intended for not only enhancing accountability of school system but also enabling the community to own up school systems so that no child in the community is deprived of elementary education. Clearly, in the post NPE period, there are deliberate attempts to bring systemic reforms in the school education through empowerment and enhanced participation of the community for realization of goals of universalisation of elementary education.

In fact it is the National Policy on Education, 1986, having recognized the critical importance of education in accelerating national progress recommended for a wide range of policy interventions, which set in motion clear-cut nation-wide efforts to hasten the goal of universalisation of elementary education. Within this framework, although the major focus was on ensuring elementary education to every child in the age group 6-14 years there was an added emphasis on making elementary education easily accessible for the most vulnerable children such as girls, deprived children from poorest of the poor households, socially and economically disadvantaged, scheduled castes, scheduled tribes, minorities, backward communities, migrant families and physically and mentally challenged children. Such a national effort was further catalyzed by the global declaration on basic education adopted in Jomtein in 1990 and in Dakar and also the Millennium Development Goal Declaration in 2000.

We notice that during the decade the country registered significant gains in literacy as well as substantial expansion in the elementary education sector. The overall literacy rate improved by a substantial 13.1 per cent, (from 52.2% in 1991 to 65.4% in 2001). For the first time during the 50 years since independence the absolute number of illiterates also came down by 32 million. Not only this, for the first time during the 50 years since independence more than half of female population in the country were declared literates. There was also reduction in the male-female literacy gap between 1991 and 2001 (25.0 % to 21.0%). All these achievements could be traced to the national and state efforts to expand access to elementary education.

The increase in number of lower primary and upper primary schools registered a gain of 14.0 per cent and 36.0 per cent respectively clearly suggesting enhanced access to institutional facilities. Altogether 24.3 million more children entered with opening of 130,000 new schools and appointment of 530,000 additional teachers during this period. The proportion of girls in the total enrolment went up from 41.0 per cent to 44.0 per cent in primary and from 38.0 per cent to 40.0 per cent in upper primary schools. The expenditure on education in the government sector went up from 3.84 to 4.11 per cent of GDP during the 1990s (GoI, 2006). An added dimension to the national effort to universalize elementary education also comes from the historic declaration of elementary education as a fundamental right through 86th amendment in the Indian constitution in 2002.

The new millennium has witnessed an emergence of new perspective at the national and international levels so far as fulfilling the goal of Education For All (EFA). The framework of action for EFA adopted by the global conference of 2000 in Dakar presents a renewed focus for action to provide education for all. In pursuance to this, major initiatives for strengthening policies and programmes related to EFA have been on the anvil in the country. While the SSA, a national flagship programme promises to achieve the goal of EFA by 2010 (5 years ahead of the international commitment made at Dakar), the revised framework of the NLM promises to reach a literacy rate of 75 per cent by the year 2007. The task of planning to achieve these goals became more concrete with the formulation of Tenth Five Year Plan beginning in 2002. Even the approach paper to eleventh five year plan (2007-2012) while focusing on faster and more inclusive growth emphasizes the need to enhance quality in schools for arresting dropout phenomenon in schools. Currently there is a National Plan of Action which creates a convergent perspectives on the EFA goals set out by the Dakar framework of action and the ongoing policies and programmes of India to reach the goals of universal elementary education, eradication of illiteracy and other related aspects (GOI, 2006).

Recognizing the importance of elementary education, the Government of India has been working with state government for achieving the goals of Universalization of Elementary Education. In this context, the major initiative has been the launch of Sarva Shiksha Abhiyan, a national flagship programme to implement the fundamental right to free and compulsory education. Under the national flagship programme of Sarva Shiksha Abhiyan Mission, the education of the marginalized groups has received further impetus. The Goals of SSA are:

(i) All children of 6-14 age in school/EGS (Education Guarantee Scheme) center/bridge course by 2005;

(ii) Bridge all gender and social category gaps at primary stage by 2007 and at elementary education level by 2010;

(iii) Universal retention by 2010;

(iv) Focus on elementary education of satisfactory quality with emphasis on education for life.

Implemented in partnership with the States, SSA addresses the needs of 194 million children in the age group of 6-14 years. There has been a significant reduction in the number of out of school children on account of SSA interventions. State/UTs have reported that as on March 31, 2006, there were 70.5 lakh children in the 6-14 age group who were not enrolled in a school. Allocation for SSA was increased by 41.0 per cent from Rs. 7,800 crore in 2005-06 (RE) to Rs. 11,000 crore in 2006-07 (BE).

Notwithstanding the above positive developments, there are certain disturbing trends in the participation of children in elementary education programme across different age groups, sex, region and social categories. Despite expanding access to formal schooling facilities, still a small chunk of population stay away from schooling in almost all the states across the country. Persistence of out of school children phenomenon in the country is a sad reflection on the policy efforts to universalize elementary education.

In certain areas which are most backward, this chunk of population may be substantially big. The following table reveals the magnitude of out of school children state-wise in India.

From the above table, it is clearly seen that the phenomenon of out of school children is prevalent in all the states in India. However the magnitude of this phenomenon varies from state to state. States such as Uttar Pradesh (15.7 million), Bihar (8.2 million), Andhra Pradesh (2.9 million), Madhya Pradesh (2.4 million) and West Bengal (2.8 million) reveal high incidence of the phenomenon. Where as states from the North East regions, Kerala, Himachal Pradesh, Goa and other Union territories reveal this incidence to a small extent. In the country as a whole more than 30 million children (as on 30th September 2000) in the school age continue to remain outside the elementary education system.

Further on, it is also noticed that this phenomenon is more prevalent at higher primary stage rather than at lower primary

Table 1
Proportion of out of School Children across States in India

(In Millions)

	Primary		*Upper Primary*	
States	*Projected child population (6-11) as on March 2000*	*Out-of-School children (6-11)*	*Projected child population (11-14) as on March 2000 population (11-14)*	*Out-of-school children School (11-14)*
Andhra Pradesh	8,558	0	5.768	2.945
Arunachal Pradesh	0.139	0	0.076	0.023
Assam	3.481	0	2.091	0.586
Bihar	13.238	2.665	8.154	5.603
Goa	0.187	0.063	0.101	0.029
Gujarat	5.367	0	3.344	1.12
Haryana	2.558	0.54	1.48	0.545
Himachal Pradesh	0.784	0.089	0.428	0.015
Jammu & Kashmir	1.158	0.095	0.634	0.209
Karnataka	5.862	0	3.705	0.949
Kerala	2.977	0.383	1.838	0.049
Madhya Pradesh	9.974	0	5.925	2.442
Maharashtra	10.616	0	6.265	0.927
Manipur	0.294	0.008	0.16	0.039
Meghalaya	0.284	0	0.155	0.061
Mizoram	0.11	0	0.061	0.016
Nagaland	0.196	0	0.107	0.039
Orissa	4.183	0	2.637	1.172
Punjab	2.672	0.56	1.535	0.544
Rajasthan	7.074	0	4.233	0.955
Sikkim	0.066	0	0.037	0.01
Tamil Nadu	5.92	0.211	3.827	0.276
Tripura	0.441	0	0.241	0.086
Uttar Pradesh	21.557	7.397	13.284	8.314
West Bengal	9.348	0	5.849	2.796
Andaman & Nicobar	0.045	0.005	0.025	0.003
Chandigarh	0.102	0.035	0.057	0.017
Dadar & Nagar Haveli	0.023	0	0.012	0.003
Daman & Diu	0.016	0	0.009	0.002
Delhi	1.625	0.629	0.893	0.418
Lakshadweep	0.008	0	0.004	0
Pondicherry	0.128	0.025	0.071	0.007
Total	118.991	5.164	73.006	30.196

Source: Selected Educational Statistics 2000-01, GoI, 2001].

stage in almost all the states as revealed by high proportions of children in 11-14 years age group. In fact the states which reveal this phenomenon to a higher extent also reveal highest proportion of children among this age group. Thus the likelihood of children falling into the trap of out of school phenomenon increases at the higher primary stage rather than at the lower primary stage.

THE VULNERABLE AND THE MARGINALIZED CHILDREN-TYPOLOGY

Considering the typology of vulnerable children, it is noticed that vulnerability manifests itself in several forms and in different degrees. It is also noticed that vulnerability is not confined to certain deprived sections of population such as S.C, S.T. Backward tribe, Minorities, girls etc,. although the prevalence of this problem may be more among these category of children. Despite primary education being free and compulsory and the provision of wide range of incentives such as noon meal, free uniforms, fee waive, scholarships, free supply of textbooks, stationery and other accessories and aids for children studying in government schools, yet poor families who do not have any sustainable livelihood are compelled to withdraw their children prematurely from schools, because of the opportunity cost involved. Landless households and families having uncultivable land and solely dependent upon rain fed agriculture often get into poverty trap. In such households, children are forced to leave school and engage in paid labour work for family subsistence. Sometimes, ill health, accidental handicaps and deaths of parents can also force withdrawal of children from schools prematurely, if there is no other source of earning member in the family. Sibling care, caretaking of cattle and household when both parents are forced to go out for work quite often force the elder children to leave school. For these families, services of children inside households are immensely important and sparing them continuously for 6-7 hours a day in school indeed is unaffordable.

The typology of marginalized children does not indicate any homogeneity. Rather they fall into an assorted group revealing different characteristic features under different circumstances and in different context and geographic locations. Large majority of them are dropouts from formal schools, although some of them may attend formal schools often irregularly depending on the circumstance in which they are situated. Eventually due to learning gap, there is likelihood that these children may also end up as dropouts. The typology and distinctive characteristic features of some major categories of marginalized children are discussed hereunder.

DROP OUTS

Children enrolled in formal schools who prematurely leave school without completing the first cycle of primary education are termed dropouts. It is seen that the overall drop out rate at elementary stage in India has declined from 78.3 per cent in 1960-61 to 50.8 per cent in 2004-05. However, this rate is unacceptably high. Although, in the earlier times, the dropout among girls was much higher as compared to boys, in recent times, interestingly enough, lesser proportion of girls (25.4%) is found to dropout at primary stage as compared to boys (31.8%). At the elementary stage, over the years not only the girls' dropout rate has come down, but also their dropout rate, which was always higher than that of boys until 2001-02 reveals a reverse trend from 2002-03 onwards. However, at the higher primary and secondary stage, the dropout rate among both boys and girls is found to be more than 50.0 per cent and 60.0 per cent respectively in 2004-05. Besides, the dropout among girls is found to be more than that of boys at these stages.

Considering the dropout phenomenon among SC and ST boys and girls, it is noticed that there is reduction among these groups over the years. However, the overall dropout rate is much higher as compared to general population at primary, higher primary and secondary stages (42.3 %, 65.9% and 79.0% respectively). Above all, the drop out among girls in these two groups is found to be higher. This is a cause of concern as caste dimension compounds the problem for girls particularly in rural areas.

Evidence suggests that both supply side and demand side factors are responsible for this persisting problem. It is noticed that lack of interest in studies, the private cost of education, and the compulsions of work and poverty, poor teaching standards account for almost 75 percent of the dropout cases (PROBE, 1998; NFHS-II, 1999). Over the years, the supply side dimensions of education covering physical, material and human resource facilities in schools have seen considerable augmentation and also wide range of educational incentives are provided to every child from this category for encouraging their participation in education. However the other supply side dimensions like the organizational structures, curriculum, school management, pedagogical practices at the school stage have not undergone any substantial reform with the result children from these categories do not seem to be attracted to stay in school to even complete full cycle of primary education. Recent survey findings of poor learning attainments among children studying in government schools reconfirm the same.

WORKING CHILDREN

India has the largest number of the working children in the world. Estimates of working children in the country vary quite widely. According to 1991 census, about 11.28 million child workers were found to be present in India. Of these children, 91.0 per cent were found to be living in rural areas. Further, out of the total 11.28 million children, 9.08 million children were classified as main workers and 2.2 million as marginal workers. Besides, 7 million are involved in household work, 88.0 per cent of whom are girls. Thus, if a comprehensive definition of work is taken, then the total incidence of child workers is quite substantial and merit serious attention (GoI, 2006).

There is a clear link between child labour and school dropout. Children by the time they attain the age of 9 or 10 years they become serviceable to the families in many ways. This is also the time when children enrolled in schools are pulled out from the schools either to supplement the family income or to assist in household chores and other activities of the family. Once children drop out of schools, they may be either serviceable to families in many ways in unpaid work or useful in supplementing the family income through participation in child labour in factories, automobile workshops, construction sites, brick kilns, shops and small offices, hotels, farm fields, domestic service, unorganized production and service sectors such as fishing, textiles, packaging, silk production, transport, fireworks etc,. While existence of regulatory framework prohibits employing children in organized labour, it continues to surface in quite a number of worksites such as the domestic, hotel, farm and other non farm labour intensive sectors, albeit in clandestine form.

MINORITY CHILDREN

Another vulnerable group, which reveals inadequate participation in schools is the children from minority groups. Most minority schools are in bad state of affairs and the curriculum and other programmes of Madrassas and Maktabs (religious schools) and similar institutions catering to these groups are found to be dated. There are exclusive schools run by the state for the minority children. However, these schools fare very badly as compared to mainstream schools in terms of facilities, human resource inputs and students' participation. Particularly girls' participation continues to pose bigger challenge as the religious and social dimensions compound the gender problem.

CHILDREN WITH SPECIAL NEEDS

Children with special needs are also vulnerable to risks of non participation in education. It is estimated that out of the total 200 million child population in the age group 6 to 14 in 2001, there are about 6 to 10 million children with special needs in India. Out of these many children, only about 1 million with disabilities are found to be attending schools. Children in the school age with orthopedic problems are supplied with aids and appliances free of cost under the SSA programme. Similarly, special interventions are launched to address educational needs of even mentally disabled children in the school going age. Exclusive home based education programmes are introduced under SSA for the children with severe neurological disabilities. Even resource centres are at the sub-district level for training children with psychomotor disabilities, visual, hearing and speech defects.

GIRLS FROM MOST DISADVANTAGED SECTIONS

Girls in general are more prone to vulnerability than boys particularly if they belong to most disadvantaged communities. Regional, economic and other socio cultural dimensions further compound the gender problem. Their services inside home and other household chores impose restrictions on them to participate in school education regularly. For such girls school education is a luxury. When choices have to be made to withdrawing a boy or girl from these families, it is always the girl who becomes the victim.

CHILDREN HARD TO REACH

Apart from the above categories, thee is also yet another group of children who are hard to reach, who despite all interventions may still be left out of elementary education. Children of sex workers, HIV/AIDS, children in juvenile homes, children living in coastal areas belonging to fishing communities, children living in hills and deep forest areas etc,.

CHILDREN OF MIGRANT FAMILIES

An other marginalized group is the children belonging to migrant families. These children after enrolling in formal schools are forced to be absent temporarily for some period due to their parents moving out in search of labour. These children obviously accompany them and when they return back to the village they are unwilling to attend the school. Besides, continuous long absence from school creates learning gaps ultimately leading to dropout.

THE POLICY INTENTIONS AND STRATEGIES UNDER SSA

In order to address the educational needs of the different groups of vulnerable children from the marginalized population segments the states have launched a number of strategies under the SSA programme. These strategies assume different names in different states such as Education Guarantee Scheme (EGS), non formal education (NFE) or alternative innovative education programmes (AIE). Further each one of this may again have different nomenclature depending on the target groups it serves such as the girls, S.C, S.T, backward tribes, minority, migrants, children hard to reach, child labourers, physically and mentally challenged etc,. Under the Sarva Shiksha Abhiyan, the current strategies for provision of elementary education for the poor and the marginalized largely include out of school strategies. In fact it is noticed that the allocations towards this is found to range around 10.0 per cent of the total SSA allocations across states in the country. Primarily, the strategies consist of the following types:

Education Guarantee Scheme (EGS);

Back to school campaign for girls, child labourers etc,.;

Residential bridge course of varying duration (4/6/10/12 months) depending upon the nature of clientele;

Non-Residential bridge course;

Feeder Schools;

Mobile schools;

Tent School;

Home based education support for the severely disabled;

Kasturba Gandhi Balika Vidyalaya;

National Programme for Education of Girls in Elementary Level

These strategies by and large are implemented with the support of either the local grassroot institutions such as the School Development & Monitoring Committees, Village Education Committees, Grama Panchayat or Self Help Groups etc,. The implementation process for these strategies consists of the following stages of action:

(1) Identification of children/target clientele

(2) Starting/locating a centre

(3) Provision of infrastructure facilities (building, teacher, equipment, Teaching Learning Materials, training of instructor/volunteers etc.)

(4) Admission of children

(5) Operationalising the centre on a regular basis.

Essentially the strategies for out of school children reveal two types of programmes, residential and non-residential.

RESIDENTIAL PROGRAMMES

Under this programme, effort is noticed to cover children with different vulnerability types. There are exclusive programmes which target the older age girl dropouts. One such programme is the Kasturba Gandhi Balika Vidyalaya (KGBV). KGBV is a residential type of school at upper primary level for dropout girls belonging predominantly to the SC, ST, OBC and minority communities. It is being implemented in educationally backward blocks of the districts where female rural literacy is below the national average and gender gap in literacy is above the national average. These schools are found to be receiving good response because of the better infrastructure facilities as well as better standards of residential facilities. In addition, the curriculum also makes provision for some vocational training. These are run with the support of the local NGO or any other grass roots organizations such as the Village Education Committees (VEC) or School Development and Monitoring Committees (SDMC).

The other type of residential programmes target dropout boys and girls in primary stage. They are operational either for full academic year or seasonally for specified period depending on the needs of children who are already studying in regular schools. While the former targets poor children belonging to different communities, who suffer from extreme form of deprivation at home, the latter targets specifically children of migrant families who move out in search of seasonal labour for specified period. Even these programmes are run with the help of the local NGO or VEC/SDMC.

NON-RESIDENTIAL PROGRAMMES

Some noteworthy strategies under this category include mobile schools, feeder schools, tent schools etc,. These institutions work during scheduled hours either as full time schools or as part-time schools. These centres will also have some basic and academic facilities. Children in these centres receive educational incentives including mid day meals. Many a times, even smaller children who accompany their elder siblings also receive mid day meals.

In addition, the National Programme for Education of Girls at Elementary Education (NPEGEL) launched under the SSA aims at enhancing girls' education through development of a "model school" in every cluster with more intense community mobilization and supervision of girls' enrolment in schools. The NPEGEL also supports an innovative Early Child Care Education (ECCE) for providing support to younger siblings of girls and also in outreach programmes for community mobilization.

GROUND REALITIES

The mission mode approach to elementary education under the SSA indeed has been able to raise educational awareness in communities and mobilize enrolment of children in schools, even from the marginalized sections. Besides, huge financial resources are offered to individual states by the Indian government to address educational needs of the marginalized children. Hence each district plans a variety of strategies depending upon the needs of the communities concerned. However, the field reality as observed during the monitoring of SSA work by the author indicates that these centres with the exception of KGBV suffer from complex problems. Huge shortfall in enrollment, poor attendance/low retention and most importantly poor quality of education appear to be the norm in most cases. In the first place, there appears to be some unrealistic estimations and expectations made with respect to the strategies and the target clientele. In spite of heterogeneity of their vulnerability, there is a tendency to treat the marginalized group children also on par with children in regular schools.

A look at the variety of strategies launched for out of school children reveal certain stereotypes in terms of organizational structures. Commonly all of these strategies are institutionalised with rigid time and space conditionality. Most importantly, they expect regular attendance of children during scheduled hours. Owing to these rigid conditions, it is noticed that even in these centres, there is often huge shortfall in enrolment and retention, clearly indicating lack of adequate planning and conceptualization of these programmes. In addition, the phenomenon of absenteeism also prevails in these centres. It is obvious that these strategies are meant for children who remained out of school due to various compulsions, which put severe constraints on them to be able to be present on a regular basis in certain locations during certain time and hours.

While residential institutions seem to be of considerable help for poor children in reducing their hunger, it also needs to be noted that not all parents are able to spare them on a continuous basis. Hence they expect the services of their children either at home or in other family activities during certain hours of the day or during certain period. As such, ensuring regular attendance in instituionalised set up look a bit far fetched.

With respect to background of children enrolled in these centres, it is noticed that they are already exposed to outside world and large number of them having already seen some small economic gains are generally averse to any kind of serious and routinised academic activities. Many of them do not have great academic aspirations. Rather they are interested in acquiring more productive and functional skills. They possess better skills of organising, managing and leading. A few of them also are good at sports, singing, dance and drama and other extracurricular talents. Interestingly, children in these centres seem to be less inhibited and more articulate as compared to their counterparts in mainstream formal schools owing to their exposure to outside world after dropping out from formal schools. Particularly, children who had participated in gainful economic activities are much more outspoken and smarter in their approach. Hence these schools need to focus on tapping and nurturing their respective skills and talents rather than merely focusing on pure academic goals. Ultimately both parents and children are looking for better returns to the time they have invested in these institutions by foregoing the benefits they would have otherwise gained.

In residential programmes, ensuring safe and secured stay for the inmates, particularly for girls is the biggest challenge. Parents need to be convinced about the credibility of these institutions as they are not purely managed by the state government. Secondly, credibility also needs to be established by these institutions with respect to delivering not only good quality education, but also education of great utility value for thees children, worth the time they spend in alternate schools.

Barring the KGBV and NPEGEL, the inputs provided in terms of physical, academic and human resource in other centres under out of school strategies in no way match their regular schools. Owing to small strength, the cost investment in these centres is much lower than that of a regular school. These centres have the barest minimum facilities in terms of physical, material and human resource inputs. As a result, the quality of education that is delivered takes a bigger toll. Yet the expectation for these centres in terms of delivering end outcomes is same as that of a regular school. More importantly, the pedagogical approach followed in these centres does not seem to evoke any fresh breath of air which might inspire these children to fully participate in the curricular activities. They are not only restrictively standardized but also lack seriousness with respect to ensuring attainment of required learning outcomes. It is noticed in general that these children are equipped with very limited vocabulary owing to socio-cultural disadvantage. However, there is no deliberate attempt made in the curriculum to address this issue. Although the residential programmes do make provision for a volunteer support for the inmates, even this person is not suitably oriented to compensate their learning deprivation through proper enrichment activities.

It is also noticed that some of the products prepared by girls in KGBV & NPEGEL do have greater potential for marketing, although in most cases, the training is for traditional feminine occupations. However, no serious effort is made to further strengthen this programme through linking it up with the industry and market. Sustaining these programmes require efforts in this direction.

Mainstreaming all these children being the end goal of the state policy, purpose looks defeated as large majority of them are not ready at all. The state policy with respect to out of school strategies indicates that some of these children are already being mainstreamed in formal schools as per the attainment of required competencies. However, parents demand that their children be admitted in higher grades according to their age rather in lower classes as determined by their learning competencies. Under the circumstance the state is not in a position to resolve this conflict.

Therefore what is needed is a serious relook at the way these strategies have been conceptualised and operationalised so that they become more friendly and acceptable to these usergroups. Most of these children do not even possess basic skills of reading. Being first generation learners in schools, they also do not start on the same level as their other counterparts and are not even equipped with adequate vocabulary even to participate effectively in day to day classroom activities. Hence the first and foremost effort in these centres need to be towards enhancing their vocabulary and reading skills. However instead of addressing these basic learning problems, there appears to be an urgency to finish the remedial/bridge course within the given time and move on to the next for purpose of mainstreaming them.

In fact the very notion of instituionalisation of alternative educational strategies for the marginalized groups seem to be heading nowhere with only a few handful of them using it to their advantage. Even if they all are mainstreamed in the long run, majority of them may end up as functionally illiterate and non productive thus continue to remain in the peripheral margins of the emerging economy which demands sepecialised skills even to become serviceable in the low end occupational spectrum. Hence the state needs to have a rethinking on this policy perspective so that the kind of educational experiences provided in such centers really equip the incumbents to become more functionally productive and enable them to have a better quality of life. Under the circumstances, goals such as empowerment, active citizenry, life skills and vocational skills for sustainable livelihood need to be on the priority agenda in the alternative educational strategies for the marginalized children. Perhaps using more informal pedagogical approaches with the perfect combination of mass media and the information communication technology may delivery better quality educational service than the one which is routinely organized and institutionalized just like a formal school. Of course this requires a total paradigm shift in the planning and development of education. In the light of the argument made by Illich (1973) that institutions such as schools, hospitals have a tendency to end up working in ways that reverse their original purpose, it is concluded that education in whatever form it is offered to the marginalized need to create more informal and life long learning opportunities which can enhance their skills and capabilities to become better equipped to face the future challenges with not only a sense of purpose but also with a sense of responsibility.

REFERENCES

EFA-National Plan of Action India, DEEL, MHRD, GOI, New Delhi, 2006.

India HDR-A Profile of Indian States in the 1990s by Abusale Shariff, NCAER, OUP, 1999.

Economic Survey 2006-07, GOI, Ministry of Finance, Economic Division.

NCERT, 2002, Seventh All India Education Survey, New Delhi.

Illich Ivan, 1973, Deschooling Society, Harmondsworth, Penguin.

CHAPTER-9

LIBERALIZATION AND DEMAND FOR TECHNICAL MANPOWER: CASE OF KERALA

S. Harikumar & T. Remadevi

The modern face of India shows the features of a transforming society where, knowledge and information have made significant changes. Policy measures would be to expand manpower production for a knowledge-driven society through the institutions of higher learning. The requirement of modern industry is for more trainable and trained manpower. The technological changes sweeping the world today are not even in all sectors and its impact on education is notable. The case of Kerala is not different.

Consequent on liberalization some structural changes are observed in the Kerala economy. There is a shift away from agriculture to industry and services. (Prakash 1998). Therefore the quality of education required in the future would be a different one with an emphasis on scientific and technical education. To take advantage of a fast moving global economy the countries cannot afford to limit them to accumulating physical capital. It is necessary to capture the benefits of technological progress (World Development Report 1999).

The waves of globalization have initiated the evolution and development of Kerala as a knowledge society. Knowledge society is a society where creating, sharing and using knowledge are key factors in the prosperity and well being of its people. It is a work in progress requiring significant investment in harnessing skills, technology and learning (Dr. Venkata Subramaniam, 2000). In a knowledge–driven economy the generation and exploitation of knowledge play a predominant part in the creation of wealth. The idea of the knowledge society which has been spreading rapidly around the world, is described as 'Knowledge Revolution'. Knowledge Revolution is leading to knowledge-centred trade and industry (Mashelkar R. A. ,2000). Half of the GDP of the OECD countries is knowledge-based (Altbach, 1993). The research, science and technology investment of the state have to be effectively exploited in order to make Kerala a knowledge society. Knowledge has become an international public good and with the development of IT the transmission of knowledge has become easier and cheaper. Once knowledge is discovered and made public there is zero marginal cost to sharing it with more users. Ideas can be sold without exhausting their source, they do not depreciate in value through their use and their resale value may continue to be high while their reproductive cost remains next to nothing (Varghese 2000). The knowledge economy represents a shift from raw materials and capital to information and knowledge as inputs for production. Liberalisation has opened up the gate way of Indian economy to foreign investment particularly in the IT sector and it has given a chance to our technocrats to prove their capabilities in the knowledge based industry. Interdependence in international trade and economy, cyber networking, technology sharing and globalisation of Research and Development will bring the nation more prosperity and uniquely identify its position in global scenario (Patnaik and Patnaik, 2001).

This new technology greatly facilitates the acquisition and absorption of knowledge offering the state unprecedented opportunities to enhance educational system, improve policy formation and execution and widen the range of opportunities for business and the poor. One challenge for the government, therefore, is to recognize the persistence and universality of knowledge gaps and information problems. For countries in the vanguard of the world economy the balance between the knowledge and resources has shifted so far towards the former that knowledge has become perhaps the most important factor determining the standards of living-more than land, than tools, than labour (World Development Report, 1999). Today's most technologically advanced economies are truly knowledge based. They are creating millions of knowledge-related jobs in an array of disciplines that have emerged overnight–knowledge engineers, knowledge managers, knowledge-coordinators etc.

INFLUENCE OF GLOBALIZATION, KNOWLEDGE REVOLUTION AND INFORMATION TECHNOLOGY ON EDUCATION

The competitive edges of countries especially in the context of globalization are built around the quality of human resources as measured in terms of health condition and level of education. The need for higher education is based on the requirement of the third level manpower which depends essentially on the service activities in research, education and government administration. In the field of education the current trend emphasizes on technical and professional education and newer varieties of lucrative employment opportunities. Wider prospects for the development of skills, efficiency and productivity and possibilities for greater social and economic contacts have come to stay as some of the major dimensions of economic life. Because of this opening of broad social and economic contacts the role of education has been extremely important in the global network. Superior technology is invariably linked up with promotion of higher labour productivity provided they are operated by a highly specialised group of technically skilled persons. This calls for increasingly greater proliferation of training and education especially in the technical and vocational field. Higher education leading to the development of the faculty of mind is visualized as an input for developing superior technologies of production and management which empower the educated persons to dominate the global trade and investment scenario.

A growing economy like Kerala needs people with up to date technical skills to participate in the global economy.

The globalization of the economy has led to a globalization of higher education. The higher education institutions everywhere are subject to global trends, the impact of the new communication technologies, accountability of academic institutions to government, an increasingly international and mobile academic profession, global research network and other phenomena. (Altbach, 2001). There is a virtual invasion of foreign universities into India either hunting for students or indirectly enrolling through associate institutions. The students, without any hesitation, pay the unduly high fees charged by these institutions as the course content and exposure offered by the foreign universities are of a high order. There is no need to feel shy of such association if they serve to enhance academic standards and provide scope for diversifying and exchanging the standards and contents of current programmes. (Kerala Education Commission, 1999). The migration of students to other states is also important. Many students either migrate to other states or opt for an area of study or specialization such as computer education, travel and tourism, hotel management etc. that are offered by private providers because government institutions do not provide these courses. (George and Kumar, 1999).

In Kerala the system of education fails to meet the global challenges. Technology, particularly substantially knowledge based technologies such as IT, will thrive only in the ambiance of excellence in higher learning, and scientific research. Kerala educational system does not appear to be adequate in this regard. The failure to diversify and modernize our system of education, comes at a time when the state's economy is getting integrated with the global economy which is becoming increasingly knowledge-driven. Kerala's educational system seems to be oblivious of both the emerging threats and opportunities provided by a globalizing society driven by science, technology and management. (K.K. George,2000) The social sector development, the legacy of the Kerala Model, has created a necessary condition for growth in the present day world. The knowledge base of the economy has been strengthened in the past and it is the efficiency of the system which can translate this into a sufficient condition for the future growth of the economy. A major opportunity for growth in the Kerala economy lies in orienting production towards more knowledge based products. In the situation of globalization a diversification of programmes for revamping the higher education system will link the economy with the global challenges and will not only help build upon what has already been achieved but also to sustain a high rate of growth of the economy. Globalization has brought about a shift from manufacturing economies to knowledge economies as a result of which the knowledge content of production has grown. In knowledge based production the sale of ideas has a higher premium than goods. Education, no doubt, enhances human capacity and choices to improve the knowledge content of production. Educational systems within many countries are adapting themselves to these changes . The examples of Korea, Indonesia, Japan and many Francophone African countries indicate a move towards expanding higher education (George, 2000). One of the key factors driving 'Knowledge Revolution' is the role of research, science and technology in creating knowledge to solve business, social and environmental problems. The Industrial Research and Development Expenditure indicates the speed at which the economy moves towards the knowledge society.

The growth rate of expenditure on Research and Development in the post reform period shows dynamism in some states and retardation in others. In Kerala the rate of growth registered a slight decline during the post reform period. It declined from 8.65 in 1981-90 to 6.86 in 1991-96. But in states like Gujarat, Madhya Pradesh, Punjab etc. there has been significant boosting up of Industrial Research and Development expenditure consequent on the process of globalization. So it is time for Kerala to recognize the fact that any sophisticated technology will require a highly skilled workforce that may not be readily available. The state has to restructure the educational system to suit the needs of the economy. Developing economies advance by learning from the technology of industrial economies. As a result of globalization the research and development spill over from the industrial countries to the developing economies is substantial (Pissarides 1997).

Table 1
Research and Development Expenditure Across the States

State	*1976-96*	*1981-90*	*1991-96*
Andhra Pradesh	10.11	2.87	10.10
Bihar	7.04	2.28	-16.94
Gujarat	8.44	5.35	14.66
Haryana	10.91	10.15	3.51
Kerala	7.96	8.65	6.86
Karnataka	9.71	11.39	- 9.26
Madhya Pradesh	9.58	3.80	13.26
Maharashtra	14.65	9.23	11.55
Orissa	7.42	0.87	-20.76
Punjab	10.31	17.92	26.86
Rajasthan	16.33	7.11	.11
Tamil Nadu	9.36	9.03	8.53
U P	11.64	5.39	-0.90
West Bengal	5.82	7.56	-4.16

Source: Research and Development in Industry (Various issues) Department of science and Technology, Government of India.

Realising the impact of globalization on higher education the Government of Kerala felt that computer industry which is growing at exponential rates in India need to be supported. Since a serious mismatch is observed between the type of qualified personnel already available in the state it is imperative that a massive planning exercise is undertaken to identify new areas of higher education that will match the needs of the industry and the markets on the one hand and enable the people to reap the benefits of industrialization and globalization. Higher education and technical training are needed to build a labour force that can keep up with a constant stream of technological advances.

As Information Technology industry is one of the emerging industry segments in the country the Govt. of India has drawn up an ambitious programme to make India a software power by 2010. The Department of Electronics has formulated vision document- software industry vision-2010 to achieve this goal. The Government of Kerala announced its IT policy in 1998 and a separate government department was formed for effective coordination and implementation of the programme. The measures taken so far have been based on the recommendation of the Taskforce on IT.

The IT Revolution is making a tremendous impact on industry and trade by relentless technology innovation, massive growth in computer power, world wide networks and ever growing electronic factories. It works like a lubricating oil to make the system work better. Now the role of higher education is much more than that of orienting people towards skill and specialization. These changing trends in education levels of the labour force offer positive opportunities for Kerala.

In the early 1990's there were two major institutional interventions to promote the growth of software industry in the state. The first was the setting up of a software technology park in Trivandrum. Further in accordance with the recommendations of the Eighth Five Year Plan Taskforce on Software Development a Techno park was set up by the Government of Kerala. It aims at providing infra structural support to electronics research, design development and manufacturing as well as for software development units. With the setting up of software technology parks and the techno park Kerala experienced substantial improvement in software development activity in the state (Economic Review, 1999).

DEMAND FOR MANPOWER IN A KNOWLEDGE ECONOMY

There is a general perception that technological change would lead to unemployment. This is unfounded in the case of knowledge-based production catering to global markets. The unemployment rate in all countries that established a lead in knowledge-based production has declined. The USA has the lowest unemployment rate in the past fourty years. Similarly unemployment rate in European countries such as Sweden, UK, France, Germany etc. has declined (Varghese, 2000). Many future jobs will be based on technology which is today in its infancy and these jobs call for undreamed of skills. Nations, enterprises and individual workers who are able to acquire, transform and use Information Technology productively and imaginatively will benefit from the technological advances now set in motion (Kari Tapiola 1999).

The knowledge-based economy is reshaping the job market. Some IT related jobs did not even exist prior to 1994-95. The history of the developed countries indicate a growth path wherein at first there was a shift in the share of GDP and total employment from agricultural to manufacturing sector. When the supremacy of the manufacturing sector gets established and per capita income increases considerably there will be a shift of the major share of incomes and employment to the service sector. But now the situation has changed. Information Technology allows leap frogging, which can help countries skip generation of technology and stages of growth and place them directly in the service-dominated economy (Jeemol Unni and Uma Rani, 2000). It integrates the world into a closer community of interdependent producers and consumers of goods and services. It creates new jobs, destroys a whole lot of traditional middle management jobs and has the potential to reallocate jobs globally.

In the post liberalization period since 1991 the productivity norms and work culture have changed in the industry. But the rate of unemployment is mounting up and this is clearly due to the mismatch of the quality produced by educational institutions and the industry expectations. The demand for IT professionals is bound to grow in geometric proportions and India still produces operators and programmers while upper end jobs like systems design go to non Indians (Sashibhushan Rath, 1998). Globalization has forced us to change our own game rules in economic sector. Job pattern is changing internally also and for a uniform development through out India there is need for creation of trained human power in specialized areas and in basic fields with sound knowledge base in core disciplines with abilities to adopt new demands.

The possibility of generating employment through transnational networking depends on education and training to create requisite skills. The capabilities developed through schooling are the ability to absorb and understand and the ability to apply these skills to daily life and work. Some of the new IT based services may provide opportunities for creation of better jobs especially for the educated work force and provide opportunities for expanding the base for entrepreneurship because of their relatively low capital intensive and highly skill intensive nature. The structure of labour demand shifts as industrial structure and technology change and then the so far successful educational regime may not be adequate to cope with the future demand structure. The major input for the software industry is skilled labour. But in Kerala the colleges and universities are producing conventional science and social science graduates who cannot find adequate job opportunities. On the other hand there is a grave scarcity of computer trained manpower. Among measures to increase competitiveness, growth and employment in a globalising world economy, the critical role of a high quality educated and skilled workforce must gain more prominence (World Employment Report, 1998-99).

The major institutions in the state imparting software training are the Lal Bahadur Shastri Centre for Science and Technology (LBS) and the institute of Human Resource Development for Electronics (IHRDE).

The total intake in various computer courses offered in the state is 18,923. Out of this government institutions account for about 15,393. Apart from this there are some private institutions also which impart training to students in software training. It is estimated that about 60,000 to 70,000 students are being trained each year (Govt. of Kerala, 1997). The structure of the out turn of software manpower in India during 1999 shows that it is only a small share of the world out turn and is highly insufficient to meet global demands.

Our graduates fail to find a job at a time when educated and professionally qualified people are becoming an imperative for further growth in the more developed world. (Varghese, 2000). Some estimates indicate that Europe and the USA alone will need an additional 20 million IT professionals

Table 2
Computer Courses and their Annual Intake

Course	*Total Intake*	*Govt. Institution LBS, IHRDE, CUSAT*
P.G. Degree (M.Tech)	25	25
P.G. Degree (M.C.A)	284	184
P.G. Degree (M.Sc)	45	45
Degree (B. Tech)	840	840
Degree (B.Sc+B.C.A)	1,035	835
Diploma (Tech)	1,140	1,140
P.G. Diploma	4,270	3,640
Diploma	5,100	2,500
Certificate Courses	6,184	6,184
Total	18,923	15,393

by 2002 and Korea requires 50,000 IT professionals. The corresponding estimates for other countries are 17,000 for Hong Kong and 0.8 million for Thailand in the next 15 years. India requires 2.2 million by 2008 and Singapore needs 10,000 IT professionals annually (Chanda,2000). Further it is estimated that nearly 0.24 million Indian IT professionals will be migrating to the USA within a period of three years starting from 2001. Nearly half of the foreign IT workers in Malaysia are from India. The battle is now for the 'best brains' (Varghese, 2000). All these support the view that Indian experts are the backbone of the 'Knowledge Revolution' in the world over (Dr. Arun Nigavekar, 2001).According to the NASSCOM- Mc Kinsey Study (1999) Indian IT sector will require 2.2 million globally competitive professionals to achieve an annual revenue of $ 90 billion by 2008.

The National Taskforce on Information Technology and Software Development (NTITSD) has also projected that the software industry will employ 2.2 million workers by 2008. The industry is creating job opportunities for highly qualified engineering graduates. According to the NASSCOM surveys the software industry employed some 3,40,000 professionals as on march 31, 2000 including software professionals working in software organizations compared with 1,60,000 professionals in 1996. Yet another survey showed that 900,000 IT jobs were available this year, about half of which will remain vacant due to a lack of skilled workers (*source*: *e-commerce times*. 2001).

Table 3
Employment and Revenues through IT-Enabled Services

	1999		2000	
Designation	*Employ-ment*	*Revenue Rs. Crores*	*Can be Emplo-yed*	*Prospective Revenue (Rs. Crores)*
Back office Operators/ Revenue/Accounting/ Data Entry/Data conversion	1400	680	2,60,000	19,000
Remote Maintenance and Support	4100	270	1,80,000	13,500
Medical Transcription/ Insurance claims processing	6100	300	1,60,000	11,000
Call Centres	2800	100	100,000	6000
Date Base services	1400	70	100,000	6500
Content Development	12,600	610	300,000	25000
Total	28,400	2030	11,00,000	81,000

Source: *www.nasscom.org* 1999.

To fulfill the target and an edge in global competitive environment the Indian IT professionals will be in great demand (Yojana, Nov. 2001). After several years of boom there has been a slow down in the economy of the US and a fall in software business (Yojana,2001). This has resulted in a wave of panic in the Indian IT Industry. Though the slow down has not brought any negative revenue growth to the IT sector in our country it has lowered the prospective growth rate and employment of software professionals. But it is stated that the US slow down has provided a great opportunity to the Indian software and service companies (Confederation of Indian Industries, 2000).

Given the boom in the world market the employment of the software sector increases. It has been found that there is a deficit of about 10,000 teachers in software training (Economic Times, Jan. 16.2001). The Task force on Human Resources Development in IT recommended that the intake of students in IT related programmes needs to be doubled in 2001-2002 and tripled by 2003 -04 for doubling info Tech student intake next year (Times of India Jan. 16.2002) While the cost of software manpower in India is much less than that in the developed economies it is much higher compared with the prevailing wage rate in other sectors. The salaries of software personnel have been growing at a rate of 25-30% per annum (Kumar, 2001). Although India has traditionally been surplus in highly qualified engineering and technological manpower, with the rapid growth of the IT Industry over the past decade, demand is outstripping supply. In particular experienced personnel and project managers are becoming highly scarce. (Arora *et.al*, 2002).

The labour cost comparison for different IT personnel will reveal the intensity of the difference in the salaries of IT professionals in India. It brings to light the sharp difference in the salaries of professionals with the same qualification and designation. Perhaps this may be a popular cause for the large-scale exodus of skilled personnel. The data show that for the same profession there is about eight times difference in the US and Switzerland. For example, for systems analysts in India the maximum salary is Rs. 14000 while it is Rs. 74,000 in the US. Also for development programmer the salary in India is Rs. 8000/-, which is at par with the salary of a person in clerical cadre. But in the USA it is Rs. 56000/- This difference in labour cost is the single most significant factor which attracts foreign collaborators to India.

THE TREND IN THE DEMAND FOR TECHNICALLY QUALIFIED PERSONS IN KERALA IN THE PRESENT SITUATION

The current world situation is characterized by a powerful shift from manufacturing economies to knowledge economies. The idea conveyed in the development theories of the 1950's was that capital was the missing link in development and that industrialization was the route to economic growth. During the 90's the development concerns have shifted to human development. Also the conventional wisdom that capital is the prime mover of economic development has now yielded to Sen's thesis that building capabilities is the key to opening opportunities especially in a knowledge based society (Oommen, 2000). Therefore a major challenge for the policy makers is to increase the supply of trained manpower quickly enough to satisfy the growing demand for domestic industry as well as that of other countries. Increasing competition for knowledge workers means that management of human resources is becoming a key to corporate success in the industry (Nagesh Kumar 2000). Info power has become an inescapable phenomenon in every day life.

Education becomes meaningful when the products of education succeed in finding chances of productive employment. If the labour market can adjust itself to changes in demand for different types of manpower and if the educational system could adjust by producing workers with the necessary knowledge there may not be a question of unutilisation or underutilization of manpower. In Kerala in the light of the wide spread unemployment and under-employment there is no doubt that neither the labour market not the educational system satisfies this condition. A balance between manpower of various grades and types produced by the educational system and the demand that the economy generates for different levels and types of manpower is significant in educational planning. No country can afford to set up its target for enrolments on the basis of manpower requirements for economic growth alone. But since the level of employment is the single crucial variable determining the efficacy of the educational system the authorities will have to keep an eye on the employment trends in the changing economic scenario. So decisions regarding the courses to be started and the maximum available seats for different courses have to be guided by the fact that expansion of education for high level manpower should be based on realistic demand and not on wishful anticipations.

In this situation it is imperative to have an idea of the changing trends in the demand for technically qualified persons in Kerala. To some extent, the placement of engineering graduates by campus interviews throws light on the emerging trends in the demand for manpower. It follows from the fact that so long as an inevitable link exists between production sector and education, such placements represent a portion of the society's demand for the type and quality of manpower. The data regarding the campus placements from the four leading engineering institutions in the state, viz, the Government Engineering College, Thiruvananthapuram. T.K.M. College of Engineering, Kollam, Regional Engineering College, Kozhikode and Govt. Engineering College, Kannur for a period of five years from 1994-95 to 1998-99 are used to analyse the trend in the demand for engineering graduates in Kerala in the situation of globalisation and the emergence of the knowledge economy. The courses available in common in these four institutions are considered and comparison is made between the placements from those courses. The comparison, in essence, is between the traditional courses such as Civil Engineering (C.E), Mechanical Engineering (M.E) and Electrical and Electronics and the emerging courses such as Electronics and Communication Engineering (ECE) and Computer Science and Engineering (CSE) which seems to be a sinequanon of the knowledge society.

The placement records in the above mentioned colleges in recent years reached cent per cent for students who have cleared all semester exams in the first appearances. More there are cases students who got placements more than one, the salary received by these students are fairly high and are comparable to that of premier institutions. For the same purpose we collected data from selected engineering colleges by discussing with students and found that on an average only 50 per cent of students got placements during their last semester. There are institutions who managed to provide placements to all students who could cross the cutoff level to attend campus recruitment. The demand for various branches of engineering discipline shows that electronics and computer related subjects have the highest demand, it is due to the fact that major recruiters are IT companies.

Table 4
Campus Placements in the Four Engineering Institutions in the State

Year	*Courses and Branch*				
	CE	*ME*	*EEE*	*ECE*	*CSE*
1994-95	72 (22)	210 (62)	134 (42)	161 (70)	83 (52)
1995-96	61 (18)	238 (70)	202 (63)	172 (75)	112 (70)
1996-97	94 (28)	272 (80)	176 (55)	188 (82)	118 (87)
1997-98	183 (55)	227 (67)	186 (58)	193 (84)	112 (70)
1998-99	121 (36)	250 (73)	224 (70)	161 (70)	140 (88)

Source: Data supplied by the respective institutions.
Note : Figures in parenthesis represents per centages with reference to the total available seats for each course in these four institutions taken together.

The comparisons between placements show a relatively higher and consistent percentage for Electronics and Communication Engineering and Computer Science and Engineering. The analysis of future placements for these different courses by means of linear regression trends is done. The prediction may not scientific or precise owing to a multiplicity of factors like the changing economic conditions of the state, the technology factor, shift in development paradigms and other non economic factors. The trend in the demand for different B.Tech courses, as is done in the foregoing analysis has some significant implications. The trend is positive for all the five branches. But for conventional branches such as civil and mechanical there is no remarkable variation in the demand which in itself is an explanation to the changing trend. Regarding Electrical and electronics also the trend is not decisive. Bus as the regards Electronics and Communication Engineering (ECE) and Computer Science and Engineering (CSE) the positive trend is remarkable. This proves the fact that the emerging perspective for the state is in favour of computers and communication. In the case of computer science and Engineering (CSE) course the demand shows a trend to outstrip the total supply in the coming years which indicates that an increase in the number of seats for the course is called for. The minimum percentage for recruitment by these companies stood at 74% in 1999. Now this criteria has changed and the companies have included many other conditions such as rank in the entrance exams, number of back papers, number attempts to get good rank in the entrance test, age etc. This also brings to light the fact that the new technology requires only the best brains.

The data relating to technical education in Kerala provided by the Nodal centre of CUSAT for the year 2002 reveals that 29 per cent of the diploma holders, 64.6 per cent of Degree holders and 83.1 per cent of postgraduates were employed of which 22 percent of diploma holders, 56 per cent of degree holders and 36 per cent of postgraduates migrated out of the states. Only 2 per cent of this migrated to abroad. The average salary received by them shows that RS 2,827 by the diploma holders, 11,116 by the degree holders and RS 9122 by the post graduates.

The discussions with the placement cells of various engineering colleges and that of arts and science colleges throws some interesting light to the demand for graduates. Most the arts and science colleges operating in the urban area had campus placements during the last two years. But most of the appointments were made in BPOs, Call centres and in new generation banks and Insurance Companies for their operations within the state. The recruitments were made with some common parameters and with similar pay packets. The Average salary was nearly Rs. 7000/ which is three times lower than the salary offered by the same companies outside the sate. In the case of engineering graduates of the 85 colleges only less than 40 colleges have the placement arrangements. Out of which many colleges' claims cent per cent placements but on deeper enquiry we fond that less than 10 colleges could achieve this, the reason for this is in many colleges the percentage of pass is only 50 per cent and for the sate is only 45 per cent. The low pass percentage and the significant increasing the drop out rates of students from these colleges demand for an academic audit. The quality of students passed from the new generation colleges are also questioned due to many reasons. As a result most of them are doubtful to get decent employment and in turn joins with some BPOs with low salary, which is called the structural disequilibrium.

The impact of globalization, knowledge economy and IT Revolution on education and employment lead to the conclusion that the state cannot afford to set up its target for enrolments on the basis of manpower requirement within the state. The products of our educational system are for the global market. There is in essence an internationalization of human capital. In a growth led employment approach the prospects for generating employment depends on the growth rate and composition of the GNP. The experience of Kerala in general, has shown that the output growth in different sectors has not been able to absorb the backlog of the unemployed because of lower and more declining employment output elasticities (Kishore. C. Sanyal 1999) So the state has to find economically feasible alternatives for the productive employment of the products of education. Education that helps to make workers more flexible and adaptable to new technologies is now considered a valuable way of contributing to manpower development just as much as education that prepares them for specific jobs (Psacharapaulos and Wood hall, 1985) The Information Age records one of the master narratives of our times and the market prefers only those graduates who have practical application of knowledge. In that sense the reorientation of the educational system towards the emerging demands of the economy is the need of the hour.

REFERENCES

Arora, Ashish, Arunachalam V. S. (2002), The Indian Software Services Industries-Carnegie-Mellon University-Pitsberg.

Nigavekar, Arun (2000), Convocation Address, Amaravati University, March 2001.

Chanda, Nayan (2000), The Tug of War for Asia's Best Brains. Far Eastern Economic Review, Vol. 163, No. 45.

Economic Review (1999), State Planning Board Govt. Press, TVM.

George K. K. and Kumar, What is Wrong with Kerala Education CSES, Kochi.

Human Development Report (1999), UNDP, ILO, Geneva.

Kerala Education Commission (1999), KSSP, Kochi.

Oommen M. A. (2000), National Conference on Education December, TVM.

Altback, Philp G. (1993), Dilemma of Change in Indian Higher Education in P. G. Altbach (ed) Higher Education in International Perspection.

Prakash B. A (1999), Kerala's Economic Development Issues and Problems, Sage Publications, New Delhi.

Psacharapaulos G. and. Wood hall M. (1995), Education For Development. World Bank. Varghese. N. V. (2000): Learning By Trading–*World Bank Economic Review*, Jan–1997.

Venkata Subramaniam (2000), National Conference on Education, December, TVM.

World Development Report (various years), ILO Geneva.

Rema Devi. T. (2003), The Higher Education System and Structural Disequilibrium in the Job Market for the Educated in Kerala, (Unpublished Ph.D Thesis) Department of Economics, Pondicherry University.

Manoj P. K. (2007), ICT for Governance: The Kerala Experience, Proceedings of the Third National Conference on Innovations in Information and Communication Technology, Department of IT, PSG College of Technology, Coimbatore, Tamil Nadu, September.

Nodal Centre, CUSAT, Annual Technical Manpower Review, Kerala, 2006.

CHAPTER-10

PRICING HIGHER EDUCATION: HOW TO BRIDGE EQUITY AND AFFORDABILITY

Devasia M. D.

THE CONTEXT

Being the basis of wealth, human resource ultimately determines the character and pace of Nation's economic and social development. A country, which is unable to develop and effectively utilize the skills or knowledge of its people, will be hog-tide to build up anything else. The most obvious way by which human resources are ameliorated is the formal education beginning with primary, continuing with various forms of secondary and then higher education including Colleges, Higher Technical Institutes and Universities. According to World Education Report 2003 the share of the developed countries in world's public expenditure on education was 85 per cent. America alone accounted for 31 per cent. With World's 2nd largest population, manpower planning in India especially with respect to education has not yet received the real fillip. As against the targeted 6 per cent[2], the total expenditure on education is currently 3.99 per cent of GDP (2004-05). Yes, India has more than 300 Universities and over 10000 colleges. But, students far outnumber the seats available. Barely 6 per cent of those in the 18–23 age group have access to higher education.

According to the UNESCO World Education Report for 2003, only 6.9 per cent of youth in the age group 17-23 are enrolled for higher education in India. While in US the figure is 80.9 per cent, in UK 52.3 per cent, Australia 79.8 per cent and New Zealand 62.6 per cent. The implication is that there is an overwhelming section of the population is still deprived of higher education in India.

Kerala a tiny State in India has historically been ahead of other states in respect of literacy. However, the students going for higher education of those in higher secondary schools was only 13.8 per cent and Kerala rank 24th among 26 States in the Country.[3] Another estimate have shown that the enrollments in higher education hardly form 3.7 per cent of the relevant age group of population.[4] But, a close examination has proved that actual number of students enrolled at graduate (general) courses of those enrolled in 1st Standard in the State is abysmally low by 12 per cent and the postgraduate (general) enrollment is only 1.2 per cent of those enrolled in the 1st Standard in the relevant year[5].

With costs rising, more students enrolling, universities and colleges lagging behind, there is a growing demand that higher education need to look beyond government money, but how much? The self-financing and cross border institutions is mushrooming all over the country. It is alleged that, the decline in standard of public education has opened the space for such institutions. Kerala has also picked up this thread, forgetting the simple eviction of poor students however meritorious they may be, and much of State's energy and scarce finance has been drained so far on this dispute through arbitration, litigation, campaign, street war and struggle. Is it justifiable to transfer the entire burden upon student? Or government is to bear the cost? Or by private investors themselves bear? Or can government remain without charging the richer sections as they are in govt./aided colleges or 50 per cent quota? Or open the education sector to the free play of the market.

Data and Methodology

The present paper employs mainly the primary data, which is collected from both Aided/Govt. sector students and Self-financing sector students[5] during the period 2003-04. On the whole 348 aided/govt sector students and 86 self-financing students responded promptly to questionnaires, which is distributed at random. For fixing the sample size from the randomly selected colleges in Kerala, the following formula is used.

$$n = \left(\frac{z\sigma}{d}\right)^2$$

To examine the association of variables between both streams of students c^2 test is used.

BRIDGING EQUITY AND AFFORDABILITY/ACCESSIBILITY

Ongoing changes in Global economic structures along with information revolution have produced an environment where knowledge and skills, or to be more specific, education and training are considered increasingly as valued commodities. But, how to price education, especially at its higher levels in a State wherein majority are so poor to afford the educational expenditure of their wards? Thus, the issue of pricing is more pressing to (1) a resource-crunch Govt.[6] (2) lower income groups whose access is restricted by higher net cost of colleges[7] and (3) colleges that are more concerned about quality up-gradation.

Proper utilization of beneficiaries and resources in ensuring maximum benefit to the society is a difficult task for a resource crunch State where most of its educational provision is on subsidized basis. Setting up of Self-financing colleges is suggested as a remedy for cost minimization of govt. But, it is criticized that the cost of education for poor will be unaffordable or inaccessible. But, how can one improve or maintain quality without adding or admitting rising cost? Can one go on compensating the rising cost through subsidies or without raising price and run at loss? In this context, equity, affordability, cost, price and quality conditions must be dealt together to resolve the deadlock in the light of the socio-economic structure of our State.

Ensuring Equity

Indian Constitution provides for equality of opportunity and equal treatment of students in the distribution of education. Since the concept 'equity or equality' is very broad and is very difficult to define in concrete terms, the policies and practices should ensure and promote equality and justice[9]. This can be attained by treating pupil of like circumstances equally (horizontal equity) and of unlike circumstances unequally (vertical equity). Thus, given the provisions of communal quotas, the only remedy to resolve the crisis of inequality in the distribution of educational opportunities is to follow "student's merit"[10] as the demand exceeds the supply of seats. At the same time, there should be a rethinking on the feasibility of the continuation of the said communal quota systems and the options of continuously reducing the quota system to reach the system of "universal merit"[11] for student admission in all types or all levels of education.

In this context, a comparative analysis is carried out with regard to the statuses of students in Aided or Govt. streams and Self-financing streams on the basis of field survey and examined the association with the help of c^2 Test. It is observed that (a) females constituted the major components in enrollment in both streams (b) it is impossible to make a distinction between two streams of students in rural-urban representation with regard to their origin of stay (c) with regard to family size and age composition both streams of students are in equal status (d) there is no significant difference between both streams of students in the occupation status of their family members of 15-55 age group, (e) the mean score of marks obtained in the SSLC Examination is 63.95 per cent and HSS Examination is 63.4 per cent in the case of Aided/Govt. students, and 59.4 per cent and 58 per cent in the case of Self-financing students, respectively for SSLC and HSS Examination, (f) both streams of students are found in the same footing at least on their immediate goals-continue studies and try for jobs later and (g) financing on education of their wards is still the responsibility or considered to be the privilege of parents, in Kerala.

Obviously, students in both streams of education are belonging to the like circumstances at least in the above criterions of comparisons, except a very small fraction of the student community, whose presence could not influence the result of the analysis in a significant way. Thus, students should be treated equally in front of the provision of educational opportunities.

Affordability or Accessibility in Higher Education

The idea embodied in the theory of human capital is that the knowledge and skills found in labour represents valuable resources for the market. Thus, (1) Human capital is an investment for the future, (2) Training can compensate for skill shortages (3) More training and education leads to better work skills, (4) Training enhances employability (5) Reduces overall job queue and (6) Guarantees better future earnings.[12] All these stimulate the demand for higher education.

Studies have shown that, higher education in India is mostly availed by the top 30 per cent of the income groups. They receive full elementary education free of cost and occupy about 70 per cent of the seats in secondary education and 80 per cent of higher education.[13] Similar study done in Kerala has also shown that, high-income groups appropriate majority of engineering seats and economically weak students may not even venture to apply for engineering courses.[14] Thus it is opined that, under such a discriminatory system, high-income groups, which at present get higher education almost free of cost, would be priced appropriately based on their capacity to pay while the low-income groups would be totally or partially exempted.[15]

This has suggested for making a comparison on the financial capabilities of both streams of students. For this purpose, the data pertaining to the annual income of parents were collected and classified under five income slabs. The distribution given in Table 1 shows that there are students in all income brackets in both streams viz; Very Low Income Group; Low Income Group; Middle Income Group; High Income and Very High Income Group.

Obviously, there are affordable and unaffordable students in both streams. For instance, nearly 43 per cent of the students in Self-financing courses/institutions are in unaffordable categories of income group. While, more than 27 per cent of the students in Aided or Govt. stream are in affordable income category. Thus, it is high time to make a revision of the fee structure in the Self-financing as well as Aided/Govt. sector. Taking note of the innumerable benefits[16] that education brings forth, affordable students/parents has to welcome such a revision or hike in price so as to assure quality education to their pupil. At the same time unaffordable students in Self-financing streams must be subsidized. And Self-financing institutions should be ready for a reasonable re-structuring of the fee structure.

Table 1
Income-wise Distribution of Students

(Fig. in per cent)

Income Slab	*Aided/Govt.*	*Self-financing*
Below 50000 (VLIG)	33.6	12.8
50000-100000 (LIG)	20.7	32.6
100000-150000 (MIG)	12.3	24.4
150000-200000 (HIG)	17.4	17.4
Above 200000 (VHIG)	10.2	9.3
Not Responded	5.7	3.5
Total	100.0	100.0

Source: Field Survey.

Accounting Higher Education Cost

The cost of education is of crucial importance to educational planners and policy makers. There are a number of ways of defining and measuring costs.[17] But, one should be extremely careful in discriminating the cost and purpose.[18] Here are some tips. Initially the total cost of education[19]may be divided into Private Cost and Social Cost on the simple logic or backdrop of 'giver and taker'[20]consideration of education process.

The private costs are those amounts, which an individual or his/her family (parents) spends for his/her education in the form of tuition fee, special fee, capitation or donation if any, expenses on study equipments, food, clothing, accommodation and travel, forgone earnings while undergoing studies, forgone benefits if invested those money in alternative purposes, and mental or physical stress and strains of his/her family and himself/herself.

Chart 1
Cost of Higher Education

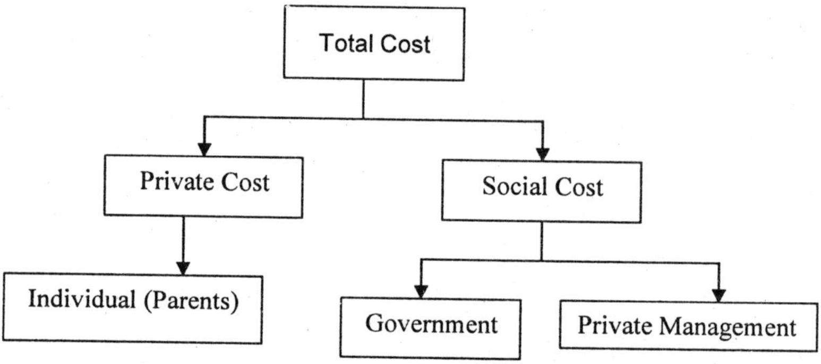

Chart 2
Components of Private Cost

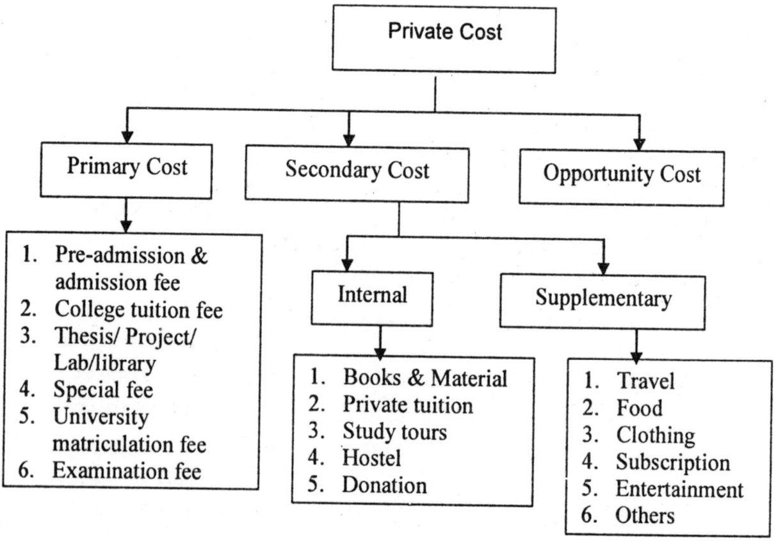

Chart 3
Components of Social Cost

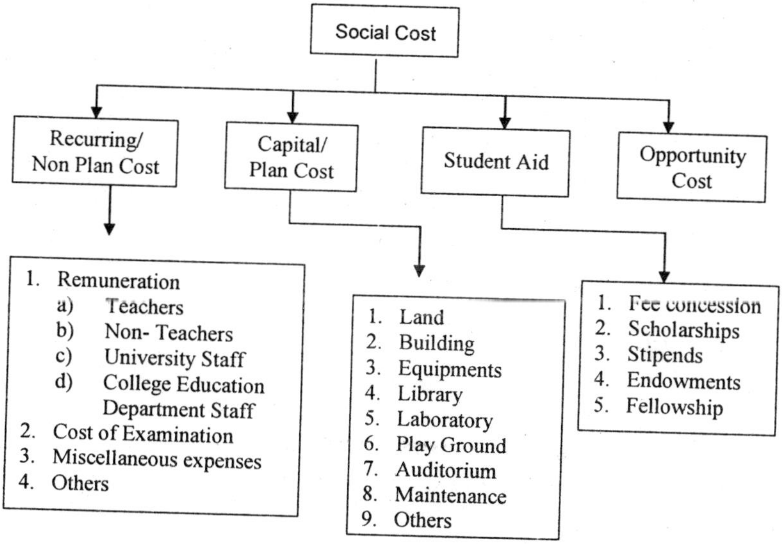

Whereas, social costs are those costs incurred by government and/(private) managements in imparting a certain level of education including expenditure for providing facilities (all sorts of infrastructure, say staff, land, building, books, lab, equipments, materials, etc.), payments for fund procured to invest in education (interest), the foregone benefits to State (economy) while prolonging individuals' education, forgone benefits if invested those funds in alternative projects and the stress and strains of people who are engaged in imparting education.

Analysis was also carried out with regard to the per capita private cost of education of both Aided/Govt. and Self-financing streams of students on the basis of the field survey information. It is seen that there is substantial difference between both streams of students with regard to per unit expenditure incurred. Self-financing students pays an amount 5-6 times higher than what is paid out by govt./aided stream students for the 'purchase' of same level of education. That is, selling of same product at different prices to persons of same denominations, say 'unequal treatment of equals'. Almost 69 per cent of Aided/Govt College students remarked that the fee in their institution is low and welcomed an increase in fee. Contrarily, almost 91 per cent of the self-financing students feel that the fee in their colleges is high and remarked as unaffordable.

Added to this, on distribution of "student aid," self-financing students are nowhere in the scene although they pay high. While, 80 per cent of students in aided/govt stream enjoy some relaxation in their fees either in the form of scholarships or concessions despite a low fee.

Maintain Quality in Higher Education

Kothari Commission even in 1966 had suggested that at least 6 per cent of GNP would need to be earmarked for education in India, which remains elusive even after 45 years. Studies have shown that the level of educational development is low in terms of quantity, quality and opportunity. The break-neck speed at which the higher education system has been expanded over the past four decades has led to a fast deterioration in quality. Academic standards have been relaxed to accommodate more and more students. .... Quality is being traded-off against quantity by spreading scarce financial resources thinly over a large number of students/institutions. Surely, the quality standards have been coming down steeply at all level of education in the State.

Analysis based on field survey data has revealed that the students go for higher education to that of 1st standard enrollment is only less than 15 per cent. This may be accounted more to the dropouts from the education stream at primary level and secondary level. The actual dropouts at primary levels itself is around 50-70 per cent over the last decade. Of which 40-50 per cent go out of the stream without even reaching to 10th Standard and the rest fails in their attempt to clear the final exam. Besides, it is seen that the marks obtained by 55 per cent of students at degree level have decreased when they move from SSLC stage to Higher Secondary stage. In the case of Postgraduate students, marks have decreased for about

57 and 27 per cent respectively, when they move from SSLC stage to Higher Secondary stage and then from Higher Secondary stage to Degree level. On the whole, it could be seen that students could not maintain their test scores when move to higher levels of education, so to say quality deterioration at higher education level.

Most of the Aided/Govt. colleges in the State have started functioning in 1960's and 70's. However, due to severe financial crisis of the govt, the facilities in these colleges have not improved even after 40-45 years. This is often one of the strong arguments for opening up of self-financing colleges in the state. In this context, the study has collected student's opinion on the existing facilities in both categories of colleges under four-point scale viz; Very Poor; Poor; Good; Very Good.

Nearly 68 per cent of aided/govt. college students remarked that the facilities are very poor in their colleges. The situation is quite opposite in self-financing colleges. More than 52 per cent of the self-financing students remarked that the facilities are very good. Of course, technological advances are another important reason that makes education or training a valuable commodity in the present world. Installation of infrastructure embedded by technology for quality maintenance and up-gradation in educational institutions requires huge capital investment. For which the govt. is musing in the darkness.

Pricing or Fixing Fee for Higher Education

As in any other endeavor the basis of pricing in higher education shall be the cost. But, the incidence of such price shall be shared at par with the benefits derived or shared out of it instead of putting it all upon students or parents. Various country studies on costs and benefits of education have shown that both society (social benefit) and private individuals (private benefits) benefit out of education. Whether the private benefit exceed social or otherwise, is one of relative concern and depends on various factors and benefit components chosen for analysis. As for Kerala is concerned however, the social benefit of education is found greater than the private benefit. Thus, the

State/Govt. need to bear a portion of the cost of higher education albeit in which stream the students are studying.

But it, should be noted that "although Colleges and universities sell goods and services (education) for a price (tuition fee), make those goods and services with purchased inputs and hired workers (professors, staff), use a lot of plant and equipment (classrooms, labs, parks and computers) and they compete hard for customers and for faculty inputs, it isn't like a firm. There are half a dozen economic characteristics that differentiate colleges and universities fundamentally and economically from for-profit business firms like, (1) "Non-distribution constraint"–non-profit firms can make profits, but they can't distribute those profits to their owners and, indeed, they don't have any owners. (2) Asymmetric information-customers don't really know what they're buying. (3) There's reduced pressure on management to operate efficiently as they are being motivated by idealistic goals (4) Revenue sources-"Donative nonprofits" rely for revenues on charitable donations, endowment income and gifts, and government appropriations in addition to tuition fees. Thus they cannot charge a price that fully covers their production costs, so to give their customers a subsidy. (5) The way it's produced: "customer-input technology"– students help educate students i.e., "peer effects". (6) "Heterogeneity,"-schools differ very much in quantity, quality (both in input and output), type and price they charge."

METHOD OF DIFFERENTIAL FEE STRUCTURE

Foregoing analysis suggests for implementing a differential fee structure in higher education in Kerala. In doing so, one should clearly remember that (1) the institution is not like firm (2) students will not take away the asset but add value to assets, (3) it emanate a wide rage of social benefits, and so on.

Method 1

If the cost or expenditure of starting/running an education institution is made out purely from the pockets of the private investor and that the society in no way benefit out of this process, then the cost incidence must fall upon students after making a discount on value addition to the assets, with an expectation or discounting for at least 20-25 years. Thus,

$$\text{Price} = \frac{[\text{Recurring Cost} + (\frac{\text{Non-Recurring Cost}}{T})] - \text{Share of Asset}}{\text{Number of Students Admitted}}$$

where T = Number of years, say 20-25 years or so.

In this price system, difference between the estimated price and the price that a 'financially weaker student can afford to pay' must be paid by the government to the education institution. If all the students admitted could meet the estimated price, then govt. need not pay anything. Thus, the 'differential fee' in this case has to be worked-out by taking into account the financial capabilities of the students admitted.

Method 2

If a portion of the cost or expenditure of starting/running education institution is through donation or charitable contribution then that amount has to be deducted. Therefore,

$$\text{Price} = \frac{\left[\text{R.Cost} + \left(\frac{\text{Non-R.Cost}}{T}\right)\right] - [\text{Share of Assets} + \text{Donation}]}{\text{Number of Students Admitted}}$$

In this price system too, difference between the estimated price and the price that a 'financially weaker student can afford to pay' must be paid by the government to the education institution.

However, the entire burden of price thus estimated cannot be shifted to individual student or his/her parent, since the society or govt. also benefits out of his/her education. Thus, at par with the social benefit, govt. or public exchequer has to provide a general subsidy for education, which is applicable to all students. Thus the 'sticker price' or the price that full-pay student has to bear must be estimated after deducting the general subsidy from estimated price through the method 1 or 2, whichever the case may be. Thus,

$$\text{Sticker Price} = \text{Price} - \text{General Subsidy}$$

After estimating the sticker price, "individual subsidy" may be determined on the basis of individual student's capacity to pay. For instance,

If a student can afford to pay the sticker price, then he gets zero govt. subsidy;

If he/she can study only with full concession, then the subsidy will be equal to sticker price (100% subsidy);

If he/she can meet the expenses partially, then the subsidy will be less than sticker price and that may be divided into convenient slabs, say 25 or 50 or 75 per cent of sticker price, depending on his/her capability.

Looking from this angle, there is no need of bifurcating student admission into 50–50 or 25–75. All students get admission on merit basis and they may be free to choose the course or institution (either aided/govt. or self-financing). The difference between sticker price and actual price paid by students shall be met by public exchequer, since the higher education scenario of the State is not yet ripe for free market operation. Otherwise, it may throw out the weaker sections (violation of the social obligation of a democratic govt.) however meritorious they may be.

Obviously, Scholarship is an incentive for education and the purpose of which is to encourage meritorious students. Thus, it should not be clubbed with student aid or subsidy. This may be a grant/award to all (full-pay or partial-pay or no-pay student) depending on their educational merit.

CONCLUSION

To meet the growing demand for higher education, huge fund/investment is required. Inability from the part of govt. to continue funding has opened the higher education market for Self-financing institutions. But, the conditions in the State are not yet ripe for such a free market operation as that may put majority of poor students in disarray. Obviously, a series of criterions (socio-economic and educational) are chosen and analyzed between aided/govt. and self-financing students, on the basis of field survey data. It is observed that, except in the amount of fees charged and in the distribution of student aid, both streams of students are in equal status. This warrants equal treatment of students in front of pricing irrespective of streams or course one is studying. But, the recent policy change has resulted in treating "equals unequally", and hence is unjust. Therefore, the study recommends a systematic strategy–differential fee structure (price system)–notwithstanding in which stream the student is undergoing studies. According to this, the burden must be shared between students, managements and govt., at par with costs (private & social), benefits (private & social) and the financial capabilities of students. Of course, govt. through public funding (subsidy), which is quite meager at present, cannot improve the facilities and maintain quality in higher education. And, since financially better-off students are ready/affordable, govt. should step to implement a differential fee structure, even in government/aided sector institutions, so as to preserve vertical as well as horizontal equity. At, the same time management of the self-financing institution must be ready to provide adequate facilities in accordance with the price they charge and to follow the differential fee structure, leaving the idea of pure profit accumulation at once. Finally, it is the duty of the government to meet the price difference between the sticker price so fixed and the price that financially weaker student can afford along with general subsidy not only in govt/aided stream but also in Self-financing streams. Again, the current financial position of the government is not that in the 80's and 90's. It has substantially improved. So, the government should regain the position of public funding through subsidies and act as a major player as BSNL do in Telecom sector, by investing enormously in higher education sector of the State. Government should set aside the policy of " I CAN'T & YOU DON'T". If this is done, each student will be made accessible to higher education according to one's own merit and equality of opportunity will be preserved in the provision of higher education facilities.

In short,Government should consider public funding as a prime concern not only in primary education but also in higher education and shall formulate a policy of differential fee system as one suggested above.Private investors has to leave the pure profit maximization goal by taking note of the harsh realities of our social and economic structure, source of funding, cost, time value of money, period of return, etc. students/ Parents by realizing the potential higher education as well as being the real benefactors should be ready to pay accordingly in a differential fee system, if they are financially better off.

NOTES

1. Harbison (1973).
2. The Govt. of India appointed an education commission in October 1964, with Dr. D. S. Kothari as its Chairman. The report of the Commission submitted on June 29, 1966 guided the policies, programmes and development of education for many decades.
3. George (1999).
4. Tilak (2001) & Mitra (1999).
5. Devasia (2005).
6. For details regarding the fixation of sample size and sample design, See, Devasia (2005).
7. Mathew E. T. (1991), Thomas (1994) & Salim (1997) At present the financial position of the government is not a constraint for investing in education or higher education. Look at the GDP growth (it has crossed 9 % per annum), budgetary allocation, daily expenditure on consumables by the people, etc. But the question is willingness and capable governance.
8. McPherson & Shapiro (1997).
9. Gafar (2001).
10. student achievement viz, mark or grade in the basic course for the next course or study.
11. all admissions in all courses must be 100 percent merit basis.
12. Bouchard (2002).
13. Balachander (1989).
14. Joy (2002).
15. Salim (1997).
16. Externality, See Devasia (2005).
17. Woodhall (1987) Psachoropaulos (1987); Coombs and Hallack (1972).

18. *Psachoropaulos* (1980).
19. The terms 'cost and expenditure' of education are often synonymously used. For more discussion see, Tialk and Bhatt (1986) & Salim (1997).
20. Instead, some others use the terms producer and consumer. See, Hallack (1969).

REFERENCES

Ashok Mitra (1999), Report of the Kerala Education Commission, Kerala Sasthra Sahithya Parishad.

Balachander, K. K. (1989), Financing of Higher Education; A Public Finance Perspective, Mainstream, March 25.

Balachander, K. K. (1989), Financing of Higher Education; A Public Finance Perspective, Mainstream, March 25.

Bouchard Paul (2002), Training and Work: Some Myths about Human Capital, ch. 10 in Sue Scott and Bruce Spencer, Learning for Life, Canadian Readings in Adult Education.

Carbone J. C. & Lewis E. G. (1998), What's Been Happening to Higher Education, Williams Project on Higher Education, DP 47.

Coombs, H. Phillip and J. Hallack (1972), Managing Educational Costs, Oxford University Press, London.

Devasia M. D. (2005), Economics of Human Resource Planning with special reference to Higher Education in Kerala, Ph.D Thesis, Dept. of Applied Economics, CUSAT.

Gafar John (2001), Some Equity Issues in Education in the English Speaking Caribbean Countries, *Canadian Journal of Development Studies*, Vol. XXII, No. 3.

George K. K. (1999), What is wrong with Kerala's Education System? CSE&ES Working Paper, Kochi, No. 3, December.

Gordon C. Winston (May 1997), Why Can't A College Be More Like A Firm? Discussion Paper No. 4 2, Williams College.

Gordon C. Winston (January 1998), A Guide to Measuring College Costs Discussion Paper No. 46 Williams Project on the Economics of Higher Education.

Hallack, J (1969), The Analysis of Educational Cost and Expenditure, IIEP, UNESCO, Paris, pp. 16.

Harbison Frederick, H. (1973), Human Resources as the Wealth of Nations, Oxford University Press.

Joseph, Thomas A. (1994), Education and Economic Development, Anmol Publications Ltd., New Delhi.

Joy Job K. (2002), Socio-Economic Background of Self-financing Students, School of Social Science, M G University & *The Hindu*, 7th Jan. 2004.

Lewis E. G. and G.C. Winston (1997), Subsidies, Costs, Tuition and Aid in US Higher Education, Williams Project on Higher Education, DP 41, April.

Lyall Sarah (2003), What Price Education? *The Hindu*, December, 27.

Mathew E. T. (1991), Financing Higher Education, Concept Publishing Company, New Delhi.

Michael S. McPherson and Morton Shapiro (June 1997), Financing Undergraduate Education: Designing National Policies, Discussion Paper No. 43, Williams College, University of Southern California.

Padmanabhan, C. B. (2 August, 2001), Human Resource Development in East Asian Countries, *The Hindu*, pp. BS 4.

Panikkar K. N. (2003), Higher Education: Perilous Prospects, *The Hindu*, November 17, Editorial Page.

Psachoropaulos G. (1980), Higher Education in Developing Countries: A Cost- Benefit Analysis, World Bank Staff Working Paper No. 440, The World Bank, Washington, D. C. USA (November).

Psachoropoulos G. (1987), The Cost-Benefit Model; Economics of Education: Research of Studies, Pergamon Press, New York.

Salim Abdul A. (1997), The Cost of Higher Education in India: with Special Reference to Kerala, Anmol Publications Ltd., New Delhi.

Salim. Abdul A. (1997), The Cost of Higher Education in India: with Special Reference to Kerala, Anmol Publications Ltd., New Delhi.

Tialk. J. B. G. and Bhatt, Gopesh, K. (1986), Cost of Supply of Education at Micro Level, NIEPA, New Delhi.

Tilak J. B. G. (2001), Higher Education and Development in Kerala, Working Paper, No. 5, Center for Socio-Economic and Environmental Studies, Kochi, February.

Woodhall, M. (1987), Cost Analysis in Education, ed. in, Psachoropaulos, G, (1987), Economics of Education: Research of Studies, Pergamon Press, New York, pp. 393–98.

CHAPTER-11

TAKING GENERAL HIGHER EDUCATION TO THE POOR AND THE ROLE OF THE STATE

G. V. Joshi

INTRODUCTION

The central goal of the 11th Five Year Plan is to attain faster and more inclusive growth. We believe that the focus on inclusive growth should lead us to well thought out, sustainable and effective strategies to address the problems of poverty and inequality rather than any populist government interventions.

Prevalence of poverty among a large section of the population is a scar on India's development performance that has refused to fade quickly. A recent official estimate places the proportion of population below the poverty line at 28%, implying that over 30 crore people are not able to buy the basic caloric requirements for their subsistence.[1]

The surveys conducted by NSSO suggest three worrisome aspects of the problem of poverty: (1) The goal of eradication of poverty appears quite distant on the basis of current trends. At the rate at which poverty is declining in India at present, it will take over 35 years to eradicate poverty; (2) The absolute number of poor is still large and quite sticky. The number of people below the poverty line was over 32 crores in 1993-94, which came down to around 30 crores in 2004-05. Going by the current rates of population growth and reduction in poverty ratio, India could still have more than 22 crore people below the poverty line in 2020; and (3) If one compares the pre-reforms (1983-84 to 1993-94) and post-reforms (1993-94 to 2004-05) periods, the growth rate clearly accelerated in the latter period but the rate of poverty reduction slowed a bit. It is in this background that we have to consider the task of taking higher general education to the poor.

POOR ACCESS TO HIGHER EDUCATION

India has a well-developed and comprehensive higher education system. Though it has the second largest system of higher education next only to U.S.A, the total number of students represent only about 10% of the relevant age group aged between 18 and 23 years, which is much below the average of developed countries (47%) and less than that in many developing countries which varies between 20 and 25%. There is an overwhelming need to undertake major expansion to increase access to higher education without sacrificing quality. As the 11th Five Year Plan Document states the triple objectives of expansion, inclusion and excellence will require a substantial increase in resources devoted to this sector by the center and the states.[2]

Secondly, inter-state variations in the development of higher education are glaring in India. Some states have expanded their higher education systems fast, but many are lagging behind. For example, the enrolment ratio was as high as 29 percent in Chandigarh, but less than five per cent in Jammu and Kashmir and Nagaland in 2002-03. In as many as 15 out of 31 states/union territories on which estimates are made, the enrolment ratio is below the national average, less than nine per cent.

The World Development Report for 2004 titled "Making Services Work for Poor People" is in a sense an eye opener. It has shown how services are failing poor people. First public spending on health and education is typically enjoyed by the non-poor. Second even reallocation towards the poor does not help the poorest among the poor. Third there are no incentives for effective delivery of services to the poor. The fourth way services fail poor people is lack of demand.[3]

DEMOGRAPHIC DIVIDEND

The quantitative aspect of taking general higher education to the poor is revealed by some recent research studies which indicate that there will be significant changes in national income and per capita income in the new 50 years. The present age structure of the Indian Population is such that India has now certain advantages not available to developed countries and even fast developing countries like China and this is called demographic dividend. The bulge in the population at present is concentrated below the working age (15-60 years) group. Over the coming decades this bulge will move but all these people will be in the working wage bracket contributing to GDP. Even China may experience labour shortage in the next decades because of the belated effect of the strict one-child norm imposed much earlier. So India may be more favourably placed in terms of its age composition of the population. Our dependency rate is falling whereas in industrialized country and even in China it is rising. The presence of a skilled young population in an environment where investment is expanding and the industrial world is aging could be a major advantage. It is important to realize that we can only reap this demographic dividend if we invest on human resource development and skill to provide productive employment for our relatively young working population. If we fail to do so, the demographic dividend will be turned into a demographic nightmare. The state has to play an increasingly important role in formulating plans for human resource development, which should benefit the poor.[4]

EMERGING FINANCIAL SERVICES SECTOR

The knowledge services sector over the last few services has emerged as a significant growth engine. There is a reliable report that in the coming 15 years many job opportunities will emerge in financial services consequent upon Full-scale financial liberalization. The Chairman, Oxford International Group reported on May 1st 2007, that many global financial firms were mulling shifting of jobs to India.[5] This would be followed by the arrival of Internationally known financial services. Further, increasingly, the financial services are being out sourced to India and this would call for steps to develop financial services sector as different from BPO or IT services, he added. Research has shown that so far, only a tenth of the global addressable market for these services has been tapped. With its early lead and strong fundamentals India is positioned to take advantages of this opportunity. According to the 11th Five Year Plan Document these fundamentals are demographics, economics and expertise. If the country is to capitalize on the huge opportunity in this and other areas of knowledge services, what is needed is a major thrust at all levels of education. The general higher education is obviously included. Clearly substantial expansion and radical reform of the education sector are called for to help the poor. This would necessitate unflinching support of the state.

SEMINAR IN HELSINKI IN FINLAND ON 30-31, AUGUST 2001

There was a Seminar on the financing of higher education in the Han Holmen Conference Centre, Helsinki, Finland on 30-31, August 2001. The Seminar was organized by the OECD Programme on Institutional Management in Higher Education (IMHE) in collaboration with the Association of Nordic University Rectors' Conferences (NUS) and the Nordic Association of University Administrators (NUAs) University representatives and higher education policy makers from more than 20 different countries participated and there were representatives of leading developed countries. There were some excellent presentations including the one by Prof.Nicholas Barr of the London School of Economics on paying for higher education and the lessons to be learned from economic theory. Common to all these presentations, was a feeling that overall funding especially public funding, for higher education was increasingly inadequate for the achievement of diverse objectives set by Universities themselves.[6]

Prof. Gudmund Hernes, Director of the International Institute of Educational Planning in Paris. He noted that Universities are probably victims of their success. Hernes invited participants to consider the main funding issues affecting higher education institutions today including.

- Achieving ever wider and more equitable/socially inclusive access;
- Maintaining institutional support for teaching and research in the face of a declining unit of resources;
- Responding to demands for transparency and greater accountability for institutional effectiveness and quality assurance;
- Responding appropriately to student-based funding;
- Managing institutional performance in relation to performance related funding models;
- Meeting the challenges presented by private and commercial providers;
- Developing funding formulae that facilitate life-long learning.

FOCUS ON PUBLIC FUNDING SQUEEZE

In the Seminar there was a focus on public funding squeeze. This was keenly felt in developed countries. Pressures to "do more with less", improve efficiency and reduce dependence on public funding were very real, as were concerns about maintaining standards in the face of declining units of resource. Similarly, less developed and emerging economies are facing the challenge of finding or devising alternatives to increased public funding (which is simply not available) to meet expanding demand and need for higher education.

In the Seminar concern was expressed for the consequences of changed funding regime. Increased autonomy was superficially attractive and there was the possibility of such autonomous institutions becoming economically bankrupt. Prof Sheldon Rothblatt, University of California at Berklay noted that Vs experience with more market-oriented higher education systems was that there could be no guarantee of institutional continuity. He recalled for example, that some 250 colleges had disappeared across the U.S.A. during the 19th century.

DANGERS OF UNIVERSITIES GOING TO MARKET

There are some instances and events in India, which vividly indicate the dangers associated with the withdrawal of state from higher education. The Bombay University is thinking in terms of getting listed on stock exchanges. This sets us on thinking about the objectives of educational institutions, their finances and the purpose of stock exchanges. The first petition to set up Bombay University was sent in 1852 to the British Parliament by the Bombay Association. The petition stated that the purpose of setting up the University was to impart education to the citizens to become knowledgeable and thereby wealth creators. The University was destined to become a facilitator and not necessarily a wealth creator itself. The reason no University has gone public to raise funds is that the institution is regarded a provider of great social service and not as a profit-making avenue. A day may come when the Vice-Chancellor of Bombay University would be seen quarter after quarter defending the profit numbers and not talking about the merits of good education. On the flip side, the courses would be priced to the market. Hence all the "inefficiencies" of the University would be built into the pricing of the courses. There are all possibilities of poverty of money and knowledge. Considering all such possibilities, Deena Mehta writes that a regulator or an authority, a University included cannot and should not be held by a few shareholders seeking profits. Instead it must continue to be held by public at large via structure of the government.[7]

THE FATE OF GENERAL HIGHER EDUCATION

When certain stark realities are considered, we may be justified in developing the impression that the fate of higher education is almost doomed. One of the prestigious Colleges of Delhi will have 40% seats reserved for its own community. Granted by the Supreme Court, it enjoys the status of a 'minority institution'. Though its expenses are borne by the UGC upto 95%, neither the University nor the UGC has any self. In admissions, appointments and expenditures, it frequently violates the rules as it suits its governing body. There are as many as 75 other colleges in Delhi, which are notorious for violating rules. With FDI flowing into higher education, foreign colleges are mushrooming in Bangalore. Thousands of degree holders that these colleges turn out are unemployable. A Bangalore based Foreign University charges very high fees but employs only part-time faculty. Deemed Universities, Foreign Universities, autonomous colleges, fully self-financed colleges, fully self-financed courses and minority colleges-all of these have discriminatory standards that nullify our dreams of general higher education. Any withdrawal of the state from this field would amount to denying general higher education to the poor. Only the state funded and the state controlled colleges and Universities could at least provide avenues of general higher education to the poor.

It must be noted that despite massive growth in numbers of colleges and universities, quality and equity dimensions of higher education need serious attention. Inter-regional variations in quality, quantity and equity dimensions of higher education are marked. 'Empowerment of higher education', as Dr. A.P.J. Abdul Kalam, the former President of India observed, is the critical need of the hour. Higher education needs to be empowered, as it, and it alone, helps in sustainable social, economic and political development of the society and some assurance of equity.

NEED FOR INCREASED STATE FUNDING IN INDIA

Higher education determines its (India's) economic and technological progress. Government funding must continue to be an essential and mandatory requirement for support to higher education. The Government/State must continue to accept the major responsibility for funding. Report of Justice

Dr. K. Punnayya Committee on UGC funding of Institutions of Higher Education (1993).

Empowerment of higher education requires liberal funding by the government. But the funding pattern has been far from satisfactory. As the Government of India has admitted in the Tenth Five Year Plan, "part of the problem facing universities is the inadequate provision of budgetary resources from the Government". In a sense, higher education in India is in a deep financial crisis, with escalating costs and increasing needs of the system on the one hand, and shrinking provisions of the public budgetary resources on the other. As a result, several universities and institutions of higher education are in continuous deficit. The unveiling of economic reform policies in the early 1990 also contributed to the accentuation of financial hardships of the institutions of higher education. Some of the recommendations of the UGC committee on UGC Funding of Institutions of Higher Education (under the chairmanship of Justice Dr. K. Punnayya, 1992-93), and the AICTE Committee on Mobilization of Resources for Technical Education (under the chairmanship of Dr.D.Swaminadhan, 1994) have been implemented and same not. All those that were implemented have not necessarily produced desirable results, while some which have not been implemented may still be relevant.[8]

Thus we need a serious rethinking on policies relating to financing higher education, including specifically financial reforms that have been introduced during the last decade and a half. In this context, it may be noted that the UNESCO World Conference on Higher Education held in 1998, the International Task Force on Higher Education and Society that consisted of members of the World Bank, UNESCO and the present Prime Minister of India among others (Higher Education in Developing Countries: Peril and Promise 2000) and the World Bank (Constructing Knowledge Societies, 2002), have highlighted: (a) the importance of higher education, including the importance of liberal higher education in development, and (b) the importance of State funding of higher education and have argued for almost a U-turn in the policies on higher education in developing countries. It is time for us now to reexamine our recent policies and to have a fresh look at the problems of financing higher and technical education in the country.

The strong wave of globalization and trends of internationalization of higher education further reinforce the need to develop a strong and vibrant higher education system for two reasons: (a) our institutions of higher education have to become centers of excellence and be internationally competitive. Global competition in higher education put additional emphasis on the need for serious efforts to improve the quality of higher education. After all, only those societies could reap gains of globalization that have strong and widespread higher education systems, while the countries that have not made much progress in higher education suffered severely. Strengthening of our higher education institutions, even on a selective basis, may help in facilitating our institutions to compete with foreign institutions that are coming into the country and even to force them to exit from India, if necessary. After all, many foreign universities are coming to India and other developing countries, where higher education systems are weak. Hence, given the wave of globalization, increasing international competition, building of knowledge society, and also increasing rates of international outflow of human capital, the need for according a higher priority to higher education arises in countries like ours. (b) Secondly, as inequity-enhancing aspects of globalization are very strong, leading to progressive reduction in social opportunities, it becomes imperative to pay serious attention to improvement of access and equity in higher education. Otherwise, a large number of our young population may get increasingly marginalized during the phases of globalization.

It is increasingly felt that the emergence of knowledge-economy has brought into focus the interesting linkages between higher education, knowledge, and wealth creation. Knowledge is a driving force for enhancing economic strength of a nation, and that this can be realized only if education and research in liberal as well as in professional disciplines is of sound quality. While technical education produced technical manpower, it is humanities social sciences, languages and natural and physical sciences that help in producing all-rounded citizenry. Given all this, higher education cannot be a 'non-priority area' anymore, and higher education institutions cannot be treated as if they are a part of a non-essential sector with the attendant vulnerability to the vagaries of fluctuations in public funding. Higher education thus needs sustained funding form public exchequer.[9]

THE REPORT OF CABE COMMITTEE ON FINANCING OF HIGHER EDUCATION

The report of the Central Advisory Board of Education (CABE) Committee on Financing of Higher and Technical Education in its report submitted in June 2005 has made the following observation:

"Thus, given (a) the current level and status of higher education in the country, (b) the highly iniquitous system in general and in higher education in particular, (c) the relationship between higher education and development, (d) the rising aspirations of the people, and (e) development goals of the country such as creation of a 'knowledge society' and transforming itself into a developed economy, some of which are stressed in the Tenth Five Year Plan, the need for according a high priority to higher education and specifically the need for substantial increase in allocation of public resources for quantitative expansion, for promotion of equity in the system, and for improvement of quality in higher education is obvious".

VENKATASUBRAMANIAN'S SUGGESTIONS

Dr. K.Venkatasubramanian,[10] Former Member of Union Planning Commission delivered Silver Jubilee Foundation Day Lecture at Mangalore University on 10.09.2004 on the topic "Financing of Higher Education". He has made some useful suggestions:

(1) The colleges and Universities must reduce their non-teaching staff drastically. There will have to be a massive outsourcing of various activities like security,

sanitation, messenger services, transportation, data entry, maintenance of buildings, gardens and facilities. This is likely to promote efficiency as well as reduce staff expenses.

(2) In view of the resource crunch, to optimize cost effectiveness, it may be necessary to have assessment of performance in relation to the set objectives. Financial assistance to universities should be based on vigorous assessment of their performance.

(3) Internal Resources may be generated through donations and differential fee structures.

(4) The Universities could also resort to innovative methods of saving the money by optimum utilization of space, centralized purchase system, centralized admission and time-table process, development of a network of higher education institution and sharing of physical and faculty resources, and

(5) In order to avoid deprivation of poor but deserving person, to avail of such education, provision of scholarship, freeship and loan funds may be made. Schemes such as "Earn while learning", under which students work in Labs, Libraries etc and earn money, could also be launched. The cross-subsidization of education will, thus, ensure equitable access to higher education.

To conclude the task of taking Higher Education to the doorsteps of the poor calls for greater involvement of the state which in term would necessitate greater financial commitment of the Central and State Government's. This financial commitment may have to be periodically monitored and reviewed to ensure the optimum utilization of financial resources as also to guarantee quality of higher education in the interest of the poor in India.

NOTES AND REFERENCES

1. The implications of various estimates of poverty in India are discussed in G. V. Joshi, "Removal of Poverty in India: Can

Microfinance Alone Do It?", *Nitte Management Review*, Vol. I, Issue No. 2, November 2007.

2. Government of India, Planning Commission, Towards Faster and More Inclusive Growth: An Approach to the 11th Five Year Plan (2007-2012) December, 2006.
3. The World Development Report, 2004, Making Services Work for the Poor People, Oxford University Press, Washington, 2004.
4. The Demographic Dividend can Either be a fortuitous Economic Opportunity or a missed chance, depending on how the Government deploys the huge emerging workforce into productive streams of economic activity. For details see his paper "India must leverage the 'demographic dividend', *The Hindu Business Line*, March 28, 2007.
5. The Hindu Business Line dated May 2, 2007 reported that Financial Services will be bigger than IT sector volume. It further reports that with the employability of graduates at a low, the best way to create talent for financial services would be to forget collaborations with reputed financial institutions and business schools.
6. The necessary information regarding Financing of Higher Education and the Issues raised in the Conferences cited in this paper may be obtained in *NigelFrench_.doc*, dated 21.12.2001
7. S.D. Naik examines the need for improving the quality of Higher Education and expanding the supply of top institutions in his paper "Taking Education to a Higher Plane" published in *The Hindu Business Line* dated 22.12.2006. The Dangers of Universities going to the Market are explained by Deena Mehta in his article "Why a University must not got to the Market" published in *The Hindu Business Line*, dated March 12, 2007.
8. See for details the report of the Central Advisory Board of Education (CABE), National Institute of Educational Planning and Administration, New Delhi.
9. The implications of W.T.O and GATS including Higher Education are discussed in Gurpreet Kaur, Changing role of Educational Take Holders under GATs., published in *The Management Accountant*, Vol. 42, No. 1, January 2007.
10. Dr. K. Venkatasubramanian delivered Silver Jubilee Foundation Lecture at Mangalore University on 10.09.2004. The theme of his lecture was Financing of Higher Education.

CHAPTER-12

RIDDLES OF HIGHER EDUCATION POLICY-A REMINDER

K. Mallikarjuna Reddy

THE RIDDLES OF POLICY

The dialogue on higher education in India, waxing eloquent on the philosophical foundation of knowledge, observes a tacit silence on its Eurocentric emphasis in the conception and dissemination of academic knowledge. This dialogue is a typical case of transcendental categories overshadowing the ground realities. Various policy statements on higher education bear testimony to this romanticized view of the scene. From the day of independence to the present times, this discourse has always shown a remarkable bias for a grand vision and a spectacular formulation by all the policy makers cutting across political affiliations and ideologies. While this unity augers well for our official educationists, it does not necessarily indicate a healthy trend for a critical and free debate on what is good for higher education in India.

The UNESCO world conference on 'Higher Education' in the 21st Century held at Paris in the year 1998 had India as one of its major participants and the policy statements that emanated from India on this important occasion gives us a fair idea of how the Indians view the activity of higher education and what objectives they envisage for the same. 'The vision and action country paper' prepared for this conference states, "Pursuit of integral knowledge and liberation, which has been a constant endeavour of Indian culture, is also the central objective of education. Education is also visualized as an evolutionary force so that each individual is enabled to evolve from purely material consciousness towards superior planes of intellectual and spiritual consciousness. Education is also perceived as a bridge between the past, present and the future and as a means by which the best of the heritage is transmitted to the new generations for its further progression."

While this formulation is most laudable in its intentions, the concept of integral knowledge and liberation remains hazy unless both these ideas make some sense to the recipient of higher education. No one disputes the holistic claims of knowledge, the problem, however, emerges when this whole comprises in itself, a large segment of borrowed knowledge. The idea of liberation too remains in the domain of spirituality unless interpreted in the concrete socio-political reality of India. Any idea of liberation would necessarily include the question of liberation from the colonization of our academic knowledge. The current review of a few policy statements on higher education in India hardly finds any echo of this liberating sentiment.

THE POLICY OF HIGHER EDUCATION IN A CHANGING WORLD

Minister of India, said It is interesting to see how the policy formulations on Indian higher education have retained its commitments to the higher values even as the world around us has been changing fast towards value-neutrality. This commitment has been a running theme ever since India became independent from its British colonizers. Addressing the graduates of the Allahabad University in 1947. Jawaharlal Nehru, the first Prime Minister of India, said:

"A university stands for humanism, for tolerance, for reason, for the adventure of ideas and for the search for truth. It stands for the onwards march of the human race toward higher objectives. Universities are places of ideals and idealism.

If the universities discharge their duties adequately, then, it is well with the nation and the people."

The above statement sums up the essence of university education in independent India and makes hundreds of Indian universities harbingers of higher education in the country. If we take the year 1947 as the cut off point for our purpose of assessing the status of higher education in India, then we have more than fifty years of higher education activity for our scrutiny.

THE PRESENT NOTE SEEKS TO HIGHLIGHT THE SALIENT FEATURES OF THE SAME

Education has been an abiding concern in India from the time immemorial and has been an integral part of India's culture. The idea of 'higher education', however, is the construct of colonial regime and can be traced to the infamous Macauley's minutes wherein the colonial rulers foisted an alien culture, through its language on the native Indians. It can be said that in Macauley's audacious expectations, India had its first formal policy statement on higher education. It would be an interesting exercise to see whether India has successfully fought back this colonial onslaught or is still reeling under its spell ever since it was cast more than a hundred and forty years ago. It would also be quite instructive to know the steps, independent India took to formulate and consolidate the process of higher education in the years that followed 1947.

The Ministry of Education took the first step in this matter when it appointed a Commission on University Education under the Chairmanship of Dr. S. Radhakrishnan.

The report, it appears, tried to strike the balance between the practical and the visionary aspects of Indian higher education when it said, "Democracy depends for its very life on a high standard of general, vocational and professional education. Dissemination of learning, incessant search for new knowledge, unceasing effort to plumb the meaning of life, provision for professional education to satisfy the occupational needs of our society are the vital tasks of higher education." The report further quoted the great seer of India, Sri Aurobindo, on education: "The past is our foundation, the present our material, the future our aim and summit. Each must have its due and natural place in a national system of education". These and many such highfalutin sentiments form the carnal of India's higher education policy. The Commission also tried to concretize this abstract vision by delineating certain aims of university education in the following terms:

- Higher education policies and programmes should be in line with the social purposes which we profess to serve;
- There should be a sufficient unity of purpose in the diversity to produce a community of values and ideas among educated men and women;
- Institutional forms may vary as time and circumstances require, but there should be a steadfast loyalty to the abiding elements of respect for human personality, freedom of belief and expression for all citizens, a deep obligation to promote human wellbeing, faith in reason and humanity;
- Mere vocational and technical education, important though they are, does not necessarily serve the spirit. We might have a number of scientists without conscience and technicians without taste who would find a void, a moral vacuum, within themselves;
- We should preserve the values of democracy, justice and liberty, equality and fraternity, Universities must stand for these ideals which can never be lost so long as men seek wisdom and follow righteousness;
- The Indian Constitution lays down the general purposes of the State. The universities should educate people on right lines to make the understanding and vision of the framers of the Constitution, the common possession of all the Indian people.

One can not, but, agree with these aims as they sound pan-Indian and grapple with our social reality of pluralism, poverty, unemployment and newly acquired democratic polity. These aims, laudable in their vision, however, do not tell us exactly what are the socio-political components of higher education in the country and what is its emphasis? It appears to be the case of 'intents substituting contents'. Where there is a mention of democracy and freedom, the factor depriving India of its freedom and the insidious agenda of the colonizer by which Eurocentric education was paddled as 'liberal education' in our university campuses does not find any mention in the report.

In the absence of clear expectations, the idea of higher education appears either too universal or too philosophical. It does not seem to be anchored in the native Indian tradition of education. The present note proposes that this age old Indian tradition is equally liberal, in the case of Upanishadic knowledge, rigorous in the case of six systems of Indian philosophy, pragmatic in the case of ancient Indian classics, comprehensive as it addresses both material as well as spiritual concerns of man and above all, accessible in the mother-tongue to the recipient.

A cursory reading of different policy statements on higher education emanating from various Government and Semi Government bodies like Education Commissions and UGC etc., some of the details of which figure in the current note, makes one wonders whether policy formulations on higher education in India has produced more sound bites than light!

The Government of India later appointed Education Commission in 1966 and the commission in its report said, "While the fundamental values to which the universities owe their allegiance are largely unrelated to time and circumstances, their functions change from time to time. Their tasks are no longer confined to the two traditional functions of teaching and advancement of knowledge. They are assuming new functions and the older ones are increasing in range, depth and complexity." In a single breath the policymakers summed up the idea of education as something permanent and timeless and at the same time changing and dynamic. In this dialectical formulation, the cleavage between the ideal and the practical comes to haunt our policy makers.

Can one call this a typical manifestation of Indian psyche?

The said Commission further set out the following functions of the universities in the modern world:

- To seek and cultivate new knowledge, to engage vigorously and fearlessly in the pursuit of truth and to interpret old knowledge and beliefs in the light of new needs and discoveries;
- To provide the right kind of leadership in all walks of life by helping the individuals develop their potential;
- To provide society with competent men and women trained in all professions who, as cultivated individuals, are inclined with a sense of social purpose;
- To strive to promote equality and social justice and to reduce social and cultural differences through diffusion of education;
- To foster in the teachers and students, and through them in the society generally, the attitudes and values needed for developing the 'good life' in individuals and society;
- To bring the universities closer to the community through extension of knowledge and its applications for problem-solving.

After these pretentious formulations, the country did not have any significant review of educational scene for the next two decades. What happened to this vision? No assessment of this vision is available for the current note and an average person is left with a question whether our universities fulfilled at least one, if not all the functions listed above.

NATIONAL EDUCATION POLICY (NEP) 1986

The review of our educational policies, belated as it may have been, came in the year 1986, with this new formulation: "Education is a unique investment in the present and the future. This cardinal principle is the key to the National Policy on Education".

Higher education, said the 1986 Policy, "provides people with an opportunity to reflect on the critical social, economic, cultural, moral and spiritual issues facing humanity. It contributes to national development through dissemination of specialized knowledge and skills. It is, therefore, a crucial factor for survival. Being at the apex of the educational pyramid, it has also a key role in producing teachers for the education system".

Once again the echoes of cultural, moral and spiritual concerns are heard in the policy formulations but this time these concerns are laced with national development, specialized knowledge and appropriate human resource development necessary to strengthen the idea of higher education in the country.

However, the most important policy statement that came out of the 1986 review is the idea of Open University system in Indian context. It "called for launching the Open University system as an instrument of democratizing education and to develop a new pattern of the Rural Universities to take up the challenges of micro-planning at grass-root levels for the transformation of the rural areas".

Open Universities, it appears, aimed at tilting the balance in favour of rural population and restore the privilege of education to the underprivileged class. And who can find fault with this aim?

OPEN UNIVERSITY SYSTEM

In view of this policy, the Indira Gandhi National Open University (IGNOU) was set up with a nation-wide jurisdiction in the field of distance education. A Distance Education Council too has been established as a statutory authority under the IGNOU Act, which provides development funds to various Open Universities and distance education institutions of the county. The Central Government makes these funds available to the Council.

The idea of Open University, with all its claims to encourage rural population in the field of higher education, provide an alternative frame work of higher education and "check the proliferation of formal sector in the field of education" has not lived up to its promise and the benefits of

Distance Education has been appropriated by educated elites of urban India. It appears that the facilities of Open Universities are exploited more by the educationally entrenched to hone their existing skills and acquire new ones, something which was not possible in the erstwhile closed system of higher education. The aim of Distance Education was also to 'encompass rural areas attracting more girls, especially from small towns and rural centers to participate' in the venture of higher education. But a close look at the IGNOU's achievement tells us that just about 10% of the rural based girls have been benefited by the idea of Distance Education.

It would be an interesting exercise to know how much the idealized and romanticized venture of higher education in India has deviated from its stated policy objectives and how many times in the last sixty five years, it changed its course to adjust itself to the global reality. The ever trickling policy statements on higher education make one wonder whether everything is well in this field. While our policy makers re constantly busy coining new idioms and developing a series of new emphasis, the higher education scene in India remains as confusing as ever and its Eurocentric obsession gets even more legitimized under the current wave of globalized market economy. The growing popularity of Management Studies and I.T. courses bear testimony to this trend.

The above observations do make an average person, a little skeptical about the policy makers' stated and real intentions. But this again will be a popular mistake. To know exactly where we have gone wrong, it would not suffice to pin point a proverbial gap between words and deeds, but to prove with empirical data, that our very conception of higher education was flawed from the beginning. It is not so much the intents but the contents of our higher education which needs to be examined and here, our policy makers.

Deserves a left handed compliment for not implementing what was, any way not worth implementing!

This brings us to the core value of our much hyped idea of higher education. This value, it should be remembered, is largely determined by the Anglo-Saxon conception of knowledge and enquiry into the natural world. While it is suitable for Anglo-Saxon population, it is highly unsuitable for the Indian population.

HIGHER EDUCATION IN ANCIENT INDIA

The glaring mistake of our policy makers while drafting policies on higher education was to overlook the fact that India too has a n old tradition of knowledge and learning. Infact, a well-established system of higher education functioned in India as early as 1000 B.C. "In that system, the construction of knowledge, the beliefs on which knowledge is based, basic concepts and the organization of learning are very different from the European tradition. The Indian system of education is validated by the fact that it sustained Indian civilization for centuries". This means that the Indian idea of education established a symbiotic link between the learner and his/her civilization world-view.

Learning during those days did not mean alienating the learner from his own cultural identity but the learner affirmed it, rather quietly, as part of his learning process. The components of this learning included various skills for survival (handicrafts) and variety of knowledge which exposed the learner to the knowledge of his choice. The system also had a distinctly native institution of education called Gurukul. The system, as is well known today, was suppressed by the colonizers to advance their own interests. But hardly any current policy statement wishes to recounts the contribution of this civilization model of Indian education.

THE ORIGIN OF SERVITUDE

The European system of higher education was introduced to India by the British in 1857 with the establishment of universities for European education in Bombay. Calcutta and Madras. Although modeled after the University of London, these universities were not meant to be institutions for the advancement of knowledge, or full-fledged centers of higher learning. The British government had established them with two limited objectives:

- To introduce the Indian elite to European culture, and thus, to colonize the country culturally;
- To produce a cadre of Indians equipped to serve the British administration India and to practice the professions of law, medicine and teaching, as required by the British.

These twin aims set the tone of Indian higher education in the later half of nineteenth century. Today the colonizers' agenda seems very shocking but more shocking is its insidious impact on our currently held view of higher education. Although higher education project in India began with the echoes of most inspiring sentiments, it was essential anchored in the exclusionist, elitist idea of education of the colonial rulers.

As a consequence, this idea ended up in splitting our country into two radically different worlds, one that is India in which the urban elites got themselves entrenched and enjoyed all the privileges of modern state and the other, that is Bharat, consisted largely of rural population, was kept away from any benefits that are associated with higher education in India. English as a medium of instruction for higher learning brought about this spilt. The mastery of English language is implicit in the current discourse of higher education in the country and an authentic alternative model of higher education in the country can not but, subscribe to the breaking of the English language monopoly at the centers of our higher learning and replace English with the major vernacular languages of the country.

This brief overview of India's higher education policy rigmaroles drives home the point that are interpretation of the idea of higher education must be done immediately.

WRONG POLICIES, WRONG FINANCERS

In addition to these 'off the mark' policy orientations, the current thinking on higher education also raises an important issue of financing the same. "Autonomy and sustainability' have become watch words in the current discourse on higher education. Higher education, today, is linked with market economy which is determined by the various multinational corporations operating globally with a sole of aim of making profits. In this environment higher education is being used as a passport to enlist oneself in the corporate world. This desire has produced a scramble among our educated elites to grab managerial posts in various multinationals. This mad rush leaves higher education devoid of any higher value. The present note also proposes that such a model of higher education runs counter to the civilizational model, so necessary for the country.

Financing the venture of higher education in the country is an important issue because it will decide who will control the reigns of this enterprise and to what end? Today this control is sleeping in to the hands of private institutions and corporate sectors. The trend seems to have become a norm after the Supreme Court of India upheld the need to privatize our higher education. This privatization drive seems more worrisome on the background of Central Government's ever reducing budgetary allocation for the country's higher education.

CHALLENGES BEFORE MULTIVERSITY

Multiversity with its commitment to the idea of genuine alternative to the prevailing idea of higher education can not just acquiesce with these official policy formulations. The real challenge before Multiversity would be to deconstruct the policy edifice on higher education and show how it has misconstrued and forged the idea of higher education in the country. This will call for a detailed analysis of the emphasis, course components, the socio-political aims and lastly the source of finance of the country's higher education.

REFERENCES

A.I.U., Excellence Achieving and Relevance in Higher Education.

A.I.U., Policies of Higher Education.

A.I.U., Higher Education in India, Retrospect and Prospect

Arrora, D. S. (1976), History of Education in India.

Biswas and Agarwal (1971), India Education Document Since Independence.

G. Ram Reddy (1975), Open Universities, the Ivory Towers Thrown open, Sterling Publishers Pvt. Ltd.

Government of India, Annual Review of Education in India for 1953-54.

Iqbal Narain, 'Visiting Lecturer', G.U. Room 1, on Higher Education its dilemma and Problems.

Kothari, D. S. (1964-66), Education Commission Report.

Raj, N. R. Crisis of Higher Education.

Siquira, N. B. Modern Indian Education.

U.G.C., Annual Report, 1988-89.

U.G.C., Annual Report, 1974-75.

U.G.C., *Bulletin of Higher Education*, Vol. 1, No. 1, April 1975.

U.G.C., *Bulletin of Higher Education*, Vol. 5, No. 1-2, September.

U.G.C., Report of University Grants Commission, 1981-82.

Chapter-13

EDUCATION- AN 'INVISIBLE CAPITAL': EVIDENCES FROM MIGRATED CULTIVATORS IN MALABAR

T. K. Sebastian

INTRODUCTION

Economic progress expands the material base of the people, which is the means for fulfilling the human needs. The extend of the material progress, in the long run, is determined by the quantity of education[1] attained by the society as well as the efficiency with which they utilize the educational gains for material progress. The first section of the paper focuses on the material status and the composition of the human capital of the workforce of the migrant cultivators. The pace of mobility to an upper ladder fastens with education and the tradition of learning influence the social maturity of the weaker sections (Awasti, 1987 and Agnihotri, 1991). On the contrary, exclusion from minimum schooling leads to lifetime exclusion from other basic entitlements, from employment, from social acceptance and dignity and above all from the rights of citizenship. In other words, basic education is a precondition for overcoming many forms of exclusion. Hence the second section looks into the intergenerational mobility of the migrant community in terms of education and occupation. The specific objective of the study is to see; how far the educational achievements of the parental generation are capitalized by the subsequent generations in terms of both education and occupation.

DATA AND METHODOLOGY

The data for the study is collected through a field investigation in the following way. The representative localities of migrated centers of Malabar were selected as the study area. Stratification of the entire migrated belt of the region is made into two: (a) leading centers, with accessibility to road, educational institutions, electricity, telephone, postal service etc. (b) backward centers, which are generally lagging behind the leading centers in almost all the facilities mentioned above and further handicapped with hostile climatic conditions and proximity to forest and wild life. The settlers of these backward centers have to travel several kilometers to reach even an LP school. The sample is selected in such a way that 50 per cent is shared by each categories. The households are randomly selected from the list of migrants provided by the earlier migrants of each locality. A questionnaire based field survey of 263 households is conducted during Oct-Dec of 2005[2].

The analysis is based on the components of education measured in relative terms. This valuation is important for many reasons. For example, in order to know the relative position of the household in terms of its total human capital stock, aggregation has to be done on the basis of each component of the human capital. In order to assess the collective influence of the human capital stocks on the level of development, the components would have to be aggregated, which necessitates valuation.

The value of the education to the economic development can be evaluated mainly through three ways: (a) returns to education method, (b) years of education method, and c) the expenditure method. There is no reliable estimation of educational returns available, which can be readily applied in the present study. The next method is years of education approach. But the problem faced is that of accounting the value differences due to different specializations in graduations. The method for the valuation of different components of the human capital stock, in the present study is based on the approaches of Mathur (1990) and Mathur and Mamgain (2004) This work drew upon resemblance of the educational system to an input-output system in which each stage of education is treated as a process in which the basic inputs are students of a lower stage, teachers who themselves are output of some higher stage of education, and other material inputs obtained from various sectors of the economy engaged in productive activities. Outputs of educational process are students, who get qualified to one stage higher and hence become a part of the human capital. The values of the human capital at each stage of education is calculated as:

$$P[\sum_{i=1}^{i=n} a_{ij}.(\pi_i) + \sum_{i=1}^{k=m} g_{kj}.(\pi_k)$$

$$=[\sum_{i=1}^{i=n} b_{ij}.(\pi_i) + \sum_{i=1}^{k=m} h_{kj}.(\pi_k)]$$

where, a_{ij} & b_{ij} indicate input and output coefficients respectively of technology matrix of the productive sector; g_{kj} & h_{kj} indicate input and output coefficients respectively of technology matrix of the education system;

i = 1,2.....n are material inputs.
k = 1,2.....n are human capital inputs.
j = 1,2.....n are material inputs.
j= (n+1), (n+2),......, (n+m) are educational processes.
π are prices of material inputs.
π^i_k are prices of human capital inputs.
P is the uniform profit factor for each j.

The value of forgone earnings, which forms an important component of the value of human capital in the rate of return studies, does not figure in this approach[3]. They derived the values using the data pertaining to the nineteen sixties. Since these prices depict only relative levels, it has been assumed that the relative structure would not have changed markedly since then.

Table 1
Relative Value of the Human Capital Components

Category	*Human capital content*	*Value per unit*
I	Primary and middle levels	1
II	Secondary and higher secondary level	1.8
III	Non- technical graduates	4.3
IV	Technical graduates	6.1
V	Technical diploma holders	2.5

Source: Mathur and Mamgain (2004).

The Value of Human Capital Stock at the Household Level

The valuation of the household human capital is made for all members and workforce of the households as follows:

(a) Total human capital content of the household $= (n_a{*}v_a)+(n_b{*}v_b)+\ldots+(nv{*}2.5)$

Where,

n_a = the number of persons with educational level a.
v_a = the value of educational level at a

The average human capital content of the household is obtained by dividing the total human capital content with the total members (both working and non working, who crossed 18 years of age) in the family.

(b) Human capital content of the workforce $= (n_a{*}v_a)+(n_b{*}v_b)+\ldots+ (nv{*}2.5)$

Where, n represents only the working members of the household. Aged and economically unproductive are not accounted in this case. The average human capital content of the workforce is obtained by dividing the total human capital content of the workforce with the total workforce in the house.

SECTION–I
EDUCATIONAL ATTAINMENTS AND ECONOMIC PROGRESS

EDUCATIONAL ATTAINMENTS

Dis-aggregated Examination

A study of the current human capital status is attempted in this sub section. The pie diagram given below (Figure 1) presents the compos:tion of the workforce with different educational attainments. The largest portion (40 per cent) of the workforce is high school or PDC educated, primary educated comprise of 37 per cent and general graduates constitute 12 per cent. Technical diploma holders form 7 per cent of the workforce and another 3 per cent is technical graduates. Illiterates comprise one per cent of the workforce.

Figure 1
HD Levels of the Work Force

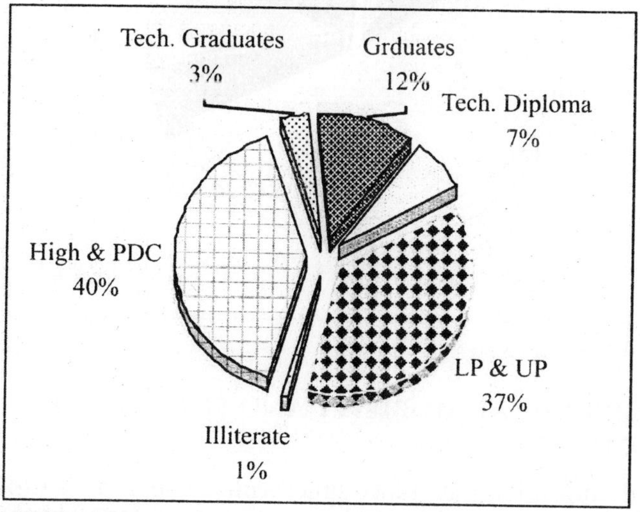

Source: Field survey.

The non-working members constitute students, aged, permanently sick and retired hands. Their human capital role is relevant, because, they also exert influence over the economic and education decisions of the households. Therefore, an examination of the human capital composition in the total population is attempted. The share of illiterates in the total population is 4 per cent and that of technical graduates is 10 per cent. The share of primary educated is 54 per cent and that of high school or PDC educated is 20 per cent. The differences in the educational content of the work force from that of the entire population is due to the inclusion of the students and non-workers in the second category (Figure 2).

Figure 2
The HD Levels of the Entire Population

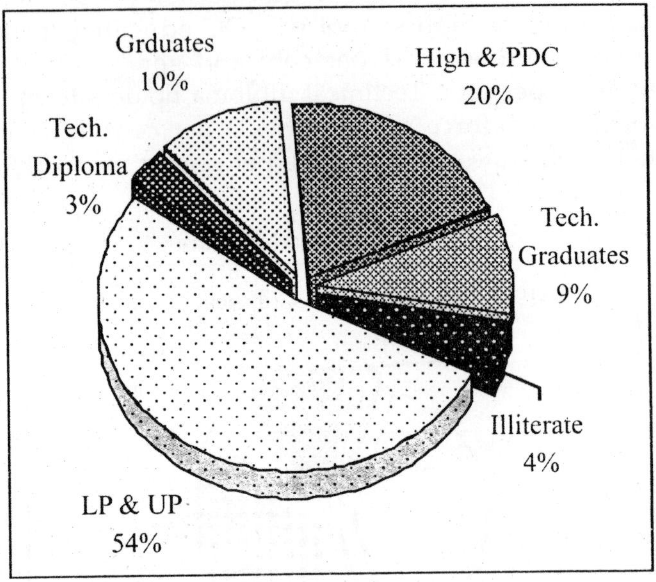

Source: Field survey

GEOGRAPHICAL MOBILITY AND SOURCES OF INCOME

Though migration took place specifically in search of cultivable land, the current origins of income are widely diversified. The geographical spread points towards the mobility of labour and exploitation of the career opportunities offered. Of the present workforce, 84 per cent are deriving the income either from own land or working as labourer-in agriculture or non-agriculture sphere. The remaining 16 per cent are staying away from home. Of the total, 9 per cent are employed within the country, i.e., 6 per cent outside the state and 3 per cent within the state. The third region of occupational importance is Middle East; 5 per cent bring home income from this region. One per cent each receives their income from Europe and America respectively, (Figure 3). The diversity in the locations from which the 16 per cent receive their income for livelihood can be viewed a continuation of their tendency for geographical mobility.

Figure 3
Present Income-Points of Origin

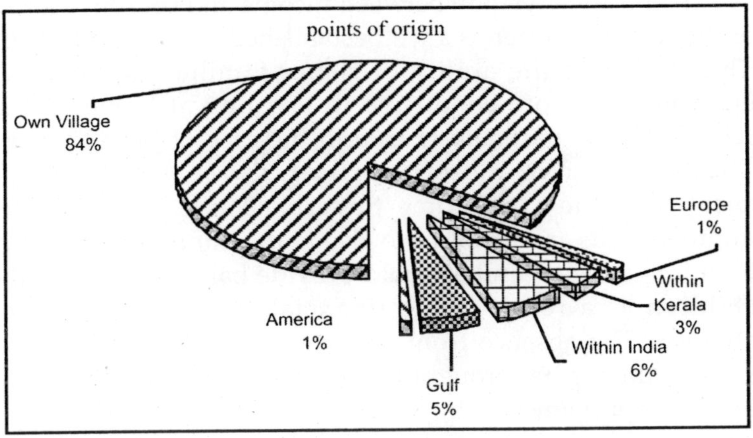

Source: Field survey.

THE HOUSEHOLD LEVEL FUNCTIONING OF THE HD-EG CHAINS

In the literature, studies like Wheeler, 1980; Wha-Lee, 2005; Ranis, 2004; UNDP, 1996 and Ranis, Stewart and Ramirez (2000) brought out the channels through which both HD and EG interact at national and unit level. In the following discussions, we are examining the farmer specific links and the connection strength between the two variables among the migrant cultivators.

Link I–Economic Improvement Leading to HD

The economic improvement of the households and society contributes towards their education via individual household allocation of scarce resources and collectively by social efforts and allocations. The allocation of household financial resources towards improving education is a function of total expenditure, of how much of this flows to education sectors and of the way in which it is allocated within these sectors.[4] In Brazil, a ten per cent increase in income has resulted in 5.8 per cent improvement in educational attainments. As families' income rise, they can spend more on school materials and they are in a better position to socially contribute for better educational facilities.

The positive relation between income and cognitive levels of the school children is a well-established fact (UNDP, 1996). This is due to the ability of richer families to create an environment more conducive to learning at home and at school. This is particularly true in the case of poor farmers. They could give more priority-*resource wise and time wise*-when they overcome poverty. The cognitive level improvements are attributable also to the improved quality of food intake. The families could provide balanced food to the children as a result of the financial status improvement attained. The absence from the school due to ill health and malfunctioning are brought to the minimum as a result of the health improvements. In short, the increased income of the household contributes to the HD by ensuring food security, medicine, meeting the direct and indirect expenses of education etc.

The subsequent, but equally important linkage is through the *'resource time'*. The household allocation of time has got an influence over HD. How much of the time of the children at school going age is freed from other household responsibilities and how intensively they could make use of it. The freeing of women from the field to managing household, raising children, assisting the children in their home works, clarifying doubts, better care for the academic development etc., provide much strong HD outputs. The participation of women in voluntary organizations, credit unions, social activities, attending classes, etc. improves the financial security of the household and enlarges the social and cultural capital base of it.

A closely related issue is how much of the above resources are consumed out due to ill health of the family members[5]. The underlying determinants of these allocations are the economic standard of the household, the degree of altruism followed and general health standard of the family members. Health and nutrition is potentially important HD component contributing to household productivity. And its opposite is also true–the household economic position affects the health attainments via health promoting consumption at different income levels. Both these factors are undoubtedly charecterised by thresholds beyond which their effects on output are negligible. The provision for health and nutrition is influenced by the accumulation parameters of the household. Education through its response role influences the maintenance of health and nutritional standards[6]. Therefore, it is consistent to take education as a proxy for HD[7].

The social capital and association among migrants are other strong pillars leading to the infrastructure for HD. The school buildings, libraries, roads, culverts etc. were built and maintained on a voluntary basis. The informal arrangement of 'labour exchange' has been applied at the social level also. The feeling of togetherness and need for social action led towards developing these social capital. This is nothing but the practice of sharing their incremental income and leisure time (due to reduced subsistence value of time) for the common good and other members of the society. All these productive involvements contributed to the education of the children. The experiences of the migrants are comparable with that of the Republic of Korea, which over the past three decades has had the largest increase in mean years of schooling in the world, achieved much of this through private spending (UNDP, 1996). The share of private expenditure in the case of migrants came mainly in the form of infrastructure. A narration of one migrant belonging to the second generation, who is a retired teacher, is worth quoting at this point.

".....The committee decided to apply for an aided school in our locality. We have to complete the construction before the official visit for it next month. My father who was a member of the committee offered all the materials, bricks and wood kept for the construction of our house as the seed capital, many others also did the same. Though we have had to wait long for a decent house, we all got chances to study...." (Interview with John Vattakkuzhy, Palathinkadavu on 6th December 2005).

The third generation compared to their parental generation is freed from the role of baby sitters due to the increased application of the family planning methods by the second generation. There are examples from the field to support the arguments that the parents discontinued their education due to unfavorable family pressures and maintained the urge to compensate the missed opportunity by providing the best to the younger generations. This inspirational factor prompted the parents to send their children to school, even if the family is facing financial difficulties. Of the sample150 couples adopted permanent family planning methods, among them 18.6 per cent considered the education of the children as the first priority, 52.6 per cent perceived the economic condition as the important motivation to do so, the remaining 28.8 per cent see other reasons (health, general norm, civic consciousness etc.) as the primary concern. A mother from the second generation explained her life example in the following way.

"...Being the eldest, I had the responsibility of looking after my younger siblings. When I was in the fourth standard my mother gave birth to the fifth child, since my mother had to work in the field I was asked to look after kids at home. My younger brother also stopped schooling after IVth standard to help my father... But I kept the thirst for education; we have adopted family planning and limited the number of our children to three. None of them had to discontinue education for taking care of the youngsters...I tried my best to give them what I could not gain from the school...." (Interview with Smt. Mariakkutty Chempakasserry, Plathinkadavu on 30th November 2005).

Link II-HD Leading to Economic Progress

Higher levels of HD itself enhance the productivity of the farm household production unit. The educated households must be more scientific in their utilization of land and resources. In the purchase and use of farm-related inputs their education supports more prudent, economic and scientific approaches. In the case of migrant farm cultivators, the HD along with enhancing the farm output and income influenced the overall economic performance through other means. Very concrete examples from the field are pointed out below.

(a) *Entrepreneurship*: Instead of depending directly on the income from the farm, entrepreneurial initiatives from the farm households are observed. There is no regular pattern or systematic enterprises but opening up of printing press, ornamental fish cultivation and sale on a large scale, bio-fertiliser processing and distribution, production of ayurvedic medicines, taxi operations, poultry farm, cattle farm, beekeeping etc. are the different types of supplementary income generating projects noticed. The initiatives and management of these units are from the educated hands and not by external professionals. Hence the HD levels have a bearing on the entrepreneurship of the group under study.

(b) *Non-farm income*: Another string connecting the HD to levels of household income is the source and amount of non-farm income. Earlier it was noted that 16 per cent of the current workforce is employed away from the native locality. The income earning power of this group is a direct function of their education, training and skill base. The foreign remittances brought home by the nurses and other skilled personnel are further examples to substantiate the argument.

(c) *Social actions:* The upper hand enjoyed by the educated in social actions, assimilating knowledge, dealing with government officials etc. are the specific areas where the less educated perceived themselves as their handicaps, which had a crippling effect on their economic functioning. There is a specific example where the student could not avail the subsidy just because the parents are illiterate and socially introvert, and unaware of the means to attain it.

(d) *Health effects*: The impact of education on family planning and spacing of children have bearing on health and productivity of the household members. This role of education further influences the per capita income/expenditure via the denominator.

These specific linkages discussed above are not exhaustive, and there are some catalytic factors, which can fasten the interactive process between the two variables at household level. A simplified model of above linkages is presented in Figure 3.7.

In the long run EG and HD generally move together and tend to be mutually reinforcing. Cross-country studies found that economic growth has a positive impact on several HD indicators[8]. But it doesn't mean that, EG will invariably and automatically get translated into HD, if other important factors are not in place. The way in which growth translates in to poverty reduction and HD depends on the expenditure pattern of the households–in particular on the egalitarian allocation of the time and other resources; whether it is guided by future vision or temporary gains. If the expenditure and allocation mix is HD-oriented rather than lopsided, then the household is more likely to improve than if the increased disposable income is expended on consumption of alcohol, tobacco etc.

Figure 4
A General Model of HD-EG Linkages in Farm Household Production Unit

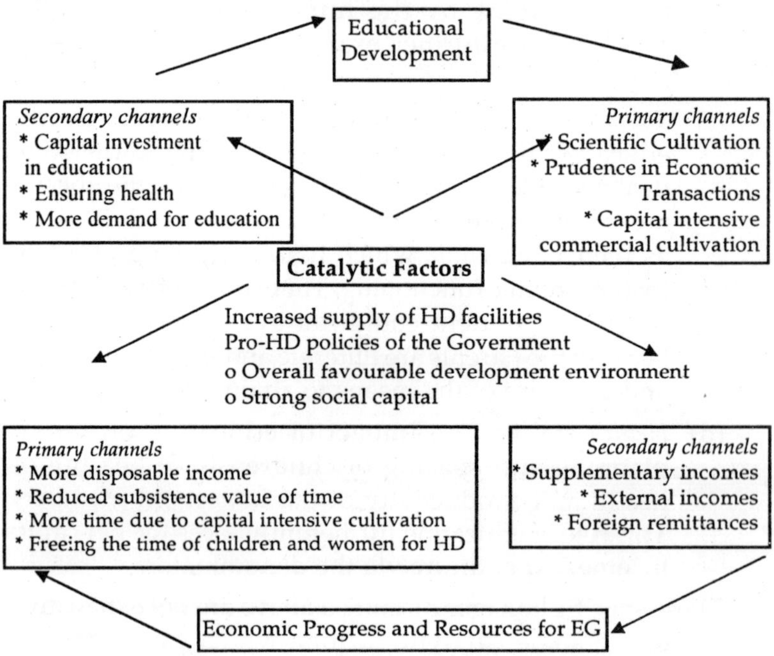

Catalytic Factors

The HD-EG rapport at household level could explain the process partially. There are exogenous variables also which are conducive to facilitate the process. These variables are kept outside the purview of the present study because except locational factors, others are equally applicable to the entire community. Differences are there only in the dynamism in assimilating and capitalizing the opportunities. The differences in economic progress across households are not only due to the level of inputs but also by how effectively they are used and for what purpose. The difference derives from people's choice and behaviour pattern. Therefore, an examination of the expenditure pattern and significance attached to availing HD opportunities could explain the differences in attainments to a great degree.

The parental motivation along with infrastructure facilities played a significant role in attaining a relatively better educational level by the third generation. The observations of a father, who could not continue after 10th standard and being the eldest in charge of the land, points towards the risk of depending on agriculture by the younger generation.

"The world of my children is of education and knowledge, they shall not be blocked by engaging their time in the field. The agriculture, which was the source of subsistence for my parents and me, is no more going to help in building up the life and career of my children. Therefore, I always insist them to study well and earn a living out of it." (Interview with Mani Nellimala, Kalanky on 16th November 2005).

The overall societal environment is a significant exogenous factor, which varied from region to region. An example to it is provided by a social activist that:

"when our Parish General Body (Palli Pothuyogam-in Malayalam) faced the question, whether to construct the high school or church immediately, the general body decision was for high school, which helped the overall educational development of the locality." (Interview with Kunjunj Vattamala, Karikkottakkari on 18th December 2005).

Another factor is the social leadership and social capital of the group. The church leadership, during the early decades of migration, has helped in forming the feeling of diaspora and social psyche among the migrants. Had it not been for the openness of the migrants to the opportunities offered by the state, the development attained would not have been possible to the fullest. The pro-HD and Economic progress policy followed by the governments, social actions and the democratic set up are other vital catalytic variables.

The Combined Picture of the HD and Economic Standard

This section goes deep into the role of HD as a "source of economic progress". We entertain the hypothesis that HD variables have an impact on the productivity of the households. The increased disposable income allows families to purchase more HD enhancing goods and services.

To evaluate the hypothesis concerning the impact of HD on economic improvement one has to take simultaneity into account; because economic well being depends on other non-HD variables, and many of them are exogenous to the family production unit also. The EG-HD linkages may be indirect through the effect of HD on investment behaviour. Therefore, role of human capital variable has to be studied in two contexts, (a) accumulation and (b) response role.

Within the productive period of a generation, the income, housing conditions, expenditure standards, assets, and the human resources possessed change in response to market conditions (both labour and goods), human development infrastructure, government policies and macro developments. These rates are, in turn, influenced by the full set of induced changes. All the non-human capital variables, which are indicative of the development levels of the household, are fixed in the short run and therefore conveniently be referred as 'accumulation parameter'. Similarly human capital measures induce and join the different living standard variables and hence can be treated as 'response variable' (Wheeler, 1980).

The existence of two chains linking HD and economic growth at micro and macro levels are already established theoretically and empirically by various studies. The present study also established the mutually reinforcing interaction of both the variables at farm household economy level. This means that a household economy may be on a mutually reinforcing upward spiral, with high levels of HD leading to high living standards and high living standard in turn further promoting HD. Conversely, weak HD may result in low growth and consequently poor progress towards HD improvement. The strength of the links in the two chains influences the extent of mutual reinforcement between HD and EG, in either direction (Ranis, Stewart and Ramirez, 2000).

Household performances can therefore be usefully classified into four categories as did in the case of countries, virtuous, vicious and two types of lop-sidedness, i.e., lopsided with strong human development and weak economic basement–called HD-lopsided and lopsided with strong economic standard and weak HD - called EG-lopsided. In the virtuous cycle case, good HD enhances economic standard, which in turn promotes HD, and so on. In the vicious cycle case, poor performance on the HD tends to lead to poor economic performance, which in turn depresses HD achievements, and so on. The strength of the linkages in the two chains decides the interaction between the two variables either in positive or dampening direction. Where linkages are weak, cases of lopsided development may occur. On the one hand, good economic standard may not bring about good HD, if, for example, there are weak linkages such as high expenditure ratio on demerit goods like alcohol, internal disturbances in the family fabrics, locational disadvantages etc. On the other hand, good HD performance may not generate good economic performance if there is a dearth of complementary resources like income, mobility in search of job opportunities, physical health etc. Such cases of lopsided development are unlikely to persist. Either the weak partner in the cycle eventually acts as a brake on the other partner, leading to a vicious cycle case or, if linkages are strengthened a virtuous cycle case results (Ranis, Stewart and Ramirez, 2000).

MAPPING THE DEVELOPMENT ATTAINMENTS

In the developmental process what a society accumulated as capital in terms of both physical as well as human capital is reflective of its inner urge to move forward in the developmental track. The first generation started with an average education of 2.2 years of schooling and an average landed property of 14 acres per household. The current status of the development attainments in both these aspects of the 263 households is depicted in Figure 3.8. One way of classifying the households into four categories is to compare their attainments in HD and Economic basements. Figure 3.8 presents this classification based on current status. The horizontal grids line at 10.7 represent the average of the index of the economic standard of all the 263 the households and the vertical line passing through 1.9 represent the average of human development values of the 263 households.

Figure 5
Avarage HD Value and Economic Standard

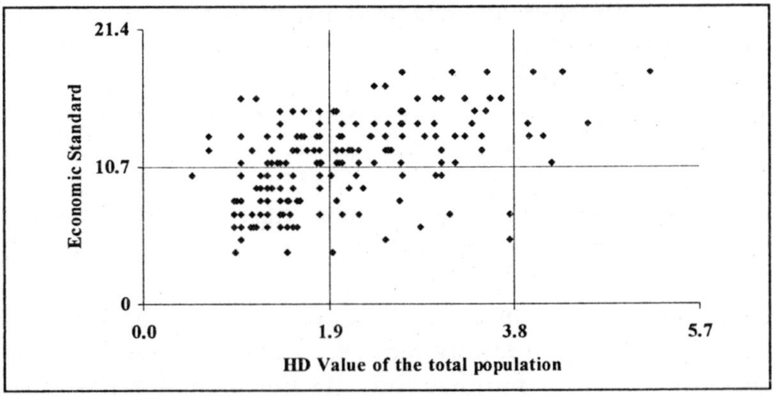

Source: Field survey

The largest portion of 96 households (36.5 per cent) falls in the third category. These households have both HD and physical economic potentials less than that of the societal household average. In this case the two variables are not in a position to contribute for further betterment of the other. The household property, assets and expenditure are not sufficient enough to attain an average HD. With the relatively poor HD the family is further lagging behind in the labour market and hence the income earning potentials remain sub optimally utilized, hence the household is further forced to be in the vicious cycle.

The virtuous quadrant occupies 86 households (32.69 per cent). Their main features are the strong positive linkages between HD and economic performance. The high HD standards lead them to attain corresponding economic standards. The higher standards in HD have been attained also through the higher economic footings, which they enjoyed. Hence it can logically be concluded that the virtuous status attained by these households are through a process of simultaneous interaction of the two variables among themselves. Therefore, this quadrant may rightly have the nomenclature 'the ideal zone'.

Households having lopsided economic standard is the third category in terms of size, which comprise of 59 (22.4 per cent). In terms of assets and other indicators of living standards they are above average, but in terms of HD, their attainments need further uplifting, at least to reach the average of the societal standard. The sustainability of the high standards in the economic front requires a corresponding HD progress in future. The diagonally opposite quadrant is charecterised by an above average performance in HD but less than average levels in economic indicators. This segment constitutes 22 (8.4 per cent) households. These households, though attained high HD levels, face shortfalls in economic front. The continuation of the HD for long requires an economic base sufficient to support it in future.

The above discussion is based on taking the average HD of the entire household. A question reasonably be raised is against the inclusion of unproductive members in the analysis. But the assumption is that those who are not directly engaged in the productive activity, but as an active member may positively contribute his/her experiences and HD attainments towards the productivity of the active members[9].

Figure 6
Per head HD Value of the Workforce and Economic Standard

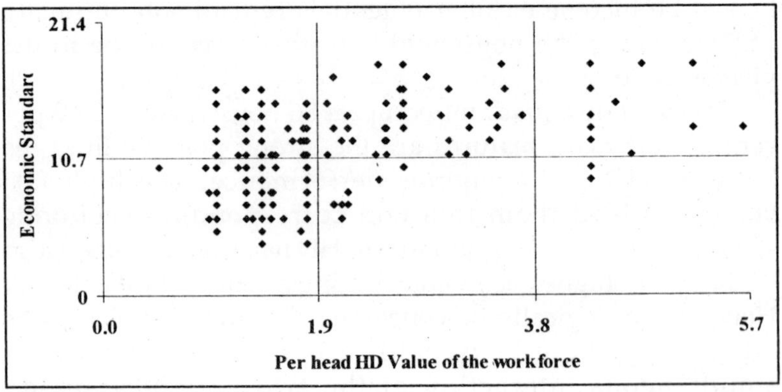

Source: Field survey.

A further disaggregated examination taking the HD aspect of the workforce alone is presented for comparing the human capital content of the present workforce with the household living standard. There is a general movement from the virtuous and HD lopsided quadrant to the other two segments. But the average HD remains the same. This is because the more educated student community and less educated aged members are exempted from the calculation. The average educational standard of the workforce is the same as that of the entire community.

The correlation between average HD of labour power and ER of the household is derived as 0.447363, while that of the ER and HD per member is 0.500874. Both are statistically significant at the level of 5%. The results support the hypothesis of mutually reinforcing interaction between HD and economic standard. The trend lines in both cases are positively slopped and indicative of the togetherness of the two variables.

SECTION–II
THE INTERGENERATIONAL EDUCATIONAL AND OCCUPATIONAL MOBILITY

The major assumption of the present analysis is that the influence of a man's ancestors in determining his education/

occupation is transmitted entirely through his father. Similarly, the influence of a woman's ancestors in determining her education/occupation is transmitted entirely through her mother (Prais, 1955).

EDUCATIONAL MOBILITY OF THE SONS

First to Second Generation

Of 875 sons of II generation, 18 per cent have illiterate fathers, 13 per cent have primary educated, 5 per cent have high school educated and 1 per cent have secondary educated fathers. Compared to their fathers, the sons improved their schooling levels. Primary educated and high school educated together constituted above two third of the total sons in the second generation. High school educated constituted the highest category of second-generation sons, ie, 34 per cent followed by primary educated 33 per cent. Secondary educated sons were 6 per cent, graduates 5 per cent and professionally qualified 4 per cent of the total. The illiterate category came down considerably to 5 per cent. The just literate second generation sons constituted only 15 per cent.

The highest mobility took place from primary educated fathers to high school educated sons, i.e., 54 per cent. The second highest mobility had taken place from illiterate fathers to primary educated sons, i.e., 38 per cent. Of the sons of literate fathers, 32 per cent moved to high school education.

Of the 40 second generation illiterates, fathers of 55 per cent were illiterates, means this proportion were not mobile educationally. The remaining 45 per cent were forced to remain in illiteracy through a process of downward mobility, whose fathers were either literate or primary educated. This rare phenomenon is due to the supply side constraints in the educational facilities and poverty of the households, which prevented the households from sending their children to schools. The graduates in the second generation is 40 (5 per cent), 75 per cent of them have literate fathers and 15 per cent have primary educated fathers. The mobility towards professional education is observed relatively high among the sons of educated fathers. As a corollary to it, none form second generation whose fathers are illiterate could catch up with professional education.

The pleasant observation of this group is the upward educational mobility of the sons of second generation. The migrants started with very little HD in terms of education. More than 95 per cent of the male working force was with primary education or less than that. But they could hand over to the youngsters an amplified human capital. More than 45 percentage of the second generation could avail education, higher than the primary level. Only 5 per cent of the fathers were educated high school or above, but 49 per cent of their sons had been educated high school or above.

Second to Third Generation

The movement from second to third generation, educationally, is considerably positive. Only two sons remained illiterate, that too due to physical handicaps. The sons with secondary or above education increased to 43 per cent, while only 6 per cent of their fathers were having the same educational attainments. The high school educated sons constituted the highest share in third generation, i.e., 37 per cent, where as one third of the total sons have primary educated fathers.

In mobility terms, of the 68 sons of illiterate fathers, 54 per cent received high school education. This is the biggest educational shell breaking over the generations. The second highest mobility is among the sons of just literate fathers, 47 per cent of them received high school education. Compared to the educational mobility of the second generation, the third generation spread out more in education above high school. All the professionally qualified sons are from literate or more educated fathers, 65 per cent of them have fathers either high school or secondary school educated. This is the continuation of the same educational phenomenon of the fathers of professionally qualified sons of second generation.

Of the 18 just literate sons of third generation, 44 per cent have fathers with same level of education, means educational immobility over the generations. Of these 18 just literates, 17 per cent reached this category through a downward educational mobility over the generations. A further probe into the reasons for this downward mobility showed the biased expenditure pattern of the head of the household and the locational disadvantages of the settlement area. Compared to the second generation (Table 5.1) the concentration in primary level education is reduced from 33 per cent to 13 per cent. At the same time, the concentration is shifted towards high school education from 34 per cent to 37 per cent. The share of secondary educated increased from 6 per cent to 21 per cent. The point is that the distribution of the second generation was highly skewed towards high school education or less than that, but for the third generation, this concentration became thin and widely spread towards education above high school.

EDUCATIONAL MOBILITY OF THE DAUGHTERS

First to Second Generation

The mothers of second-generation daughters are educationally concentrated at just literacy or less than that. Of the 677 daughters, 94 per cent have either illiterate or just literate mothers. But daughters improved their educational levels and only 27 per cent belongs to either of these categories. Of the second-generation daughters, 44 per cent have education higher than high school. Compared to the 15 per cent of sons, 20 per cent of the daughters stopped schooling at the just literacy level. At the secondary stage, the daughters' per centages exceeded that of sons i.e., 7 per cent compared to 6 per cent for sons. But at the graduate level, the percentage of sons is greater than that of the daughters.

Of the 30 professionally qualified daughters (including nursing), mothers of 30 per cent are illiterate and of 63 per cent are just literate. The mobility among daughters towards nursing and other job oriented courses is high compared to traditional graduate courses, which were more attractive for sons. This points towards the struggle among the female to find a space in the job market, even sidelining the male counterparts.

The biggest educational mobility took place among the daughters of primary educated mothers, with a movement of 36 per cent towards high school level education. Comparable upward educational mobility is observed in the case of daughters of literate mothers, with a movement of 29 per cent and 30 per cent respectively to the primary and high school level education.

Of the 45 illiterate daughters of the second generation, 58 per cent has illiterate mothers, which is indicative of the relative educational rigidity among the daughters of less educated mothers. Within this category, 38 per cent has literate mothers, which shows educational descending over generations. This phenomenon can be looked from the supply side constraints in the educational services available to the second generation, while their mothers got the literacy from the place of their origin. Similar trend is observed with the education of the male counterparts of the same generation.

Second to Third Generation

The general educational level of the third generation went up in the ladder. The share of the illiterates, just literates and primary educated came down in percentage terms to 1, 2 and 8 respectively. At the same time, the percentage of high school educated increased to 39, which was only 30 per cent for the previous generation. The share of the secondary educated and graduate groups also increased to 17 and 12 per cent respectively, which was only 8 per cent and 2 per cent for second generation. The professionally qualified along with qualifications above graduation constituted 20 per cent, which is remarkable improvement over the educational attainment of the second generation, where these two groups together constituted only 4 per cent.

The biggest leap of 75 per cent is noticed among the daughters of illiterate mothers to high school education. The second biggest mobility is among the daughters of primary educated mothers towards high school education, i.e., 42 per cent. The movement towards graduation and higher educational levels were observed high among the daughters of secondary educated mothers. The highest concentration of the third generation daughters was at the high school level, i.e., 39 per cent, while 42 per cent of the daughters were having mothers with primary levels of education.

The above examinations brought out some important features of the educational mobility of the migrant cultivators, which are closely linked to their HD trajectory: (a) Compared to the second, the third generation is more widely spread out in different levels of education. (b) There are no substantial evidences to support the hypothesis that female population has been educationally discriminated. (c) There are instances to argue that daughters are encouraged to opt professional courses like nursing, which ensure direct entry into the job market and are suitable for the feminine characters. (d) There is a general tendency among the parents for providing higher education for their children, which, in turn, resulted in an upward educational mobility; this is particularly true of the third generation. (e) There were prevalence of illiteracy and just literacy among the second generation of sons and daughters, due to supply factors. But towards the third generation, this social handicap is brought down to a considerable low level. (f) Though the society is mobile upward, still there are instances of downward mobility even in the third generation, which must be a concern for policy makers.

OCCUPATIONAL MOBILITY

Inter generational occupational mobility tells us how far the HD achievements are translated into occupational standards of the generation. The observed occupations of the study group comprises of nine categories.

(1) Agriculturists-those who depend on cultivation as major source of income, (i.e., cultivation in the own land or leased land).

(2) Casual labourers (CL)-daily income earners, either from agriculture or non-agricultural sectors.[10]

(3) Teachers-up to high school level.

(4) Government servants and bank employees.

(5) Businessmen-merchants and those who are running small business firms.

(6) Religious-fully devoted for religious activities, and earn for them through religion-based activities.

(7) Professionals-qualified professionals and teachers above high school level.

(8) Shop keepers-working on other's shops and business institutions as shop keepers and sales man/woman

(9) Technicians-doing jobs, which require technical expertise and skill.

Occupational mobility of the Sons-First to Second Generation

The main income generating engagement of the migrated generation was agriculture or agricultural labour. None migrated during 1940s or 1950s to exploit other labour market opportunities or to conduct business. Therefore, there is no inconsistency in the observation that 80 per cent of them are engaged in cultivation and remaining 20 per cent in the category of CL. Towards the second generation, the mobility was so wide spread that occupationally 14 per cent of the sons moved on to other fields; 3 per cent opted teaching, 3 per cent government service and banking, 2 per cent business, 3 per cent technical and skilled category as their source of income. Another 3 per cent turned themselves as religious and a nominal 1 per cent as shopkeepers. The mobility in occupation is mirroring the educational levels and the nature of the dwelling localities. Since geographical mobility is very limited, only 33 per centages could find out occupations other than that of their fathers'.

The row totals tell that 53 per cent of the second-generation sons turned back to agriculture for survival, while 80 per cent of their fathers depended on agriculture. The percentage of casual labour increased from 20 to 33 percent from first to second generation. Of the 27 percent of second generation who moved from agriculture, 13 percent became casual labourers. The remaining segment got disbursed in other occupations.

The greatest flow was towards two categories (a) professionals and (b) government service.

Of the 178 sons of CL only 9 per cent could move towards agriculture as their main occupation, while 62 per cent remained on their fathers' occupation. At the same time, of the 701 sons of agriculturists, 25 per cent have weakened asset-wise and turned CL and 60 per cent of them remained within the fathers' occupation.

Second to Third Generation

The occupational mobility from second to third generation is more diverse and the proportion of sons continued their fathers' occupation came down considerably. This dynamism in reaching non-traditional occupations has economic as well as HD implications on the next generation. The flexibility observed within the occupation of the second generation is attributable to the establishment of educational institutions through out the migrant belt.

The greatest mobility was towards technical and skilled sector, i.e., 16 per cent. It is interesting to note that the flow towards this category is high among shopkeepers and businesspersons' sons. A further examination of this behaviour showed that traditional agricultural opportunities have been almost nil for them, and the businesses conducted in the migrant centers were not lucrative to attract their sons in to this field. Professional courses remained financially out of their reach, and hence, the search for survival of their upcoming generation ended up in the skilled and technical category as the easy option. There is movement of as much as 7 per cent towards religious way of life. The second biggest non-traditional occupational opportunity observed is teaching, which can be explained in terms of the demand for teachers due to the rise in the schooling facilities through out the agricultural belt. The greatest mobility among the sons of agriculturists and CLs also noticed, after the traditional sector, towards this category. Sons of CLs showed the lowest mobility, with 51 per cent of them turning back to their fathers' occupation. This is due to the poor financial situation of their fathers, which blocked their opening towards higher HD and job market entries.

OCCUPATIONAL MOBILITY OF THE DAUGHTERS

First to Second Generation

All the able bodied women of the first generation were treated either as agricultural labour or cultivator, because invariably all of them did the same and none remained within the household chores. During the initial years of migration, the stress for survival on the peasant households had been very heavy that the mothers had to work in the field to maintain the food security of the households. Hence in the analysis of family behaviour one has to account for the works of the female members in the land. The comments of one lady are translated here, which is self-explanatory.

"The household was poor and have few assets; small hut to protect ourselves; the crops were always under the threat from wild animals; no treatment facilities were available anywhere; ...from dawn to dusk all of us worked in the field, except the very young, the very old, the disabled and those who were seriously sick; women worked long hours at domestic tasks and outside the home; there were no paid jobs, we helped others to complete their work in exchange for their labour to complete our work ... Mainly annual crops like tapioca, rice, lemon grass, banana, sweet potato, vegetables, etc. were cultivated to overcome poverty." (Interview with Theyyamma Kandankary, Peratta on 17th December 2005).

It is reasonably assumed that the movement from agriculture or casual labour to housewife (HW) is due to improvements in the financial positions of the family. The female members were getting more time for looking after the children, their education, feeding the cattle and doing other household activities. This movement was made possible by the economic freedom enjoyed by the family, whereby more time was freed from subsistence cultivation to leisure activities and HD related engagements. Therefore, the greatest movement, i.e., 69 per cent towards HWs shows the economic improvement of the second-generation over the previous generation. This doesn't mean that they had totally withdrawn from the land and restricted themselves to the household chores. Their major role had shifted from the workforce in the field to HWs, who devoted more time to the children, their education and other HD requirements of the family as a whole. This was facilitated further by the change in cropping pattern towards commercial crops and resultant availability of cash balance, which made possible to avail the services of the CL for meeting the labour requirements of the land. The shift in the cropping pattern from labour intensive annual crops like, paddy, tapioca, sweet potato, lemon grass, ginger etc., towards capital intensive crops like rubber, coconut areacnut, cashew, pepper etc., also reduced the labour requirements for cultivation.

Of the 81 daughters of CLs, 58 per cent moved to the category of HWs, 4 per cent to nurses, 9 per cent to teaching 5 per cent to CL and 7 per cent to technical/skilled category. Of the total 693 daughters of the second generation, the greatest portion, 69 per cent became HWs. And 13 per cent remained as CL, which is more or less constant for both first and second generations, 12 per cent of their mothers were also casual labourers. The proportion of the second-generation daughters who did cultivation declined to 8 per cent. The three occupations, HW, cultivation and CL together encompassed 89 per cent of the second-generation daughters. Others engaged in all other occupations constituted only 11 per cent. Hence it may be reasonably concluded that occupationally the second-generation daughters were less mobile towards the non-traditional sectors, and greatest concentration occurred towards HWs.

Second to Third Generation

The third generation was relatively mobile as compared to the second generation. The agriculturists, casual labourers and HWs together constituted 80 per cent of the third generation as compared to 89 per cent for the previous generation. Of the third generation daughters 58 per cent have mothers engaged in household activities alone, i.e., HWs, 31 per cent of the mothers were CL, 10 per cent were agriculturists and a nominal 1 per cent was teachers. In the third generation share of cultivators came down to 4 percentage and CLs to 10 percentages, while that of HWs crossed the 50 percentages. The second highest concentration is towards teaching followed by nursing. The girls choosing religious life was 8 per cent for third generation, where as it was 3 per cent for he second generation. The probability for a CLs daughter becoming HW is greatest, i.e., 62 per cent, where as the probability for the HW's daughter following mother's occupation is 46 per cent.

The general features of the occupational mobility can be summarized that the female folk of the migrated generation started with agriculture as the main occupation or as CL. As a corollary to the improvement in economic well being, their involvement in these two occupations came down and restricted themselves in to the household activities. Of the 509 third generation daughters, 36 per cent are working outside the traditional productive engagements like cultivation, CL and HWs. In the case of third generation sons, just fifty per cent have opted non-traditional occupations as means of livelihood. A non-negligible 8 percentage of third generation women are leading religious way of life.

CONCLUSION

The study has shown the achievements of the study group in terms of economic development potentials-physical and human capital assets. The present human capital status of the sample is: 54 per cent are primary educated, 20 per cent high school/secondary educated, 10 per cent are general graduates, 9 per cent technical graduates, 4 per cent illiterate and 3 per cent technical diploma holders. The human capital composition of the economically active work force consists of 37 per cent primary educated, 40 per cent high/secondary School educated, 12 per cent graduates, 7 per cent technical diploma holders, 3 per cent technical graduates and 1 per cent illiterates. Sixteen per cent of the Malabar migrant workforce is currently earning their income away from the region of settlement. Gulf region provides income for the largest group who work abroad.

The two way relationship between the economic standard and education suggests that, as in the case of nations, families may enter either into virtuous cycle of high economic standard and large gains in education, or a vicious cycle of low economic standards and low rates of education. In the first case, the level of economic standard and education are mutually reinforcing each other leading towards an upward spiral of development. In the second case, if persists long, the households may fall into a poverty trap. The existence and persistence of these cycles depend on the strength of the linkages between the two variables. Households may also find themselves into a lopsided state, with relatively good economic potentials in physical terms but poor education or vice versa.

Compared to other traditional social groups, the study group is upward mobile in educational and occupational ladder. The migrated group started with very low educational standards, but their third generation is spread out widely in different branches of education. There is no remarkable gender wise differences in the attainments of the above two upward motilities of the third generation. The economic improvement of the migrants resulted in the withdrawal of active women workforce from the land related subsistence involvement to household management and educational activities.

Occupationally, in the third generation, only 50 per cent of the male work force banks up on traditional occupations. There are strong linkages between the education attainments of the family and their economic performance. Financially weak could not afford to avail the modern job oriented education, which, in turn, block the economic attainments. The relative educational immobility observed among the sons/ daughters of low educated ancestors support the above hypothesis. Another supporting evidence is the sons/ daughters of CL are facing the problem of relative immobility in occupation. These education -economic standard linkages are connected to the household inability to free the children at school going age to go to school, due to the high subsistence value of the time for the household concerned.

The occupational mobility attained by the third generation, irrespective of gender, is high compared to what attained by the second generation. This flexibility in mobility can be looked in close conjuncture with the shift in cropping pattern from labour intensive annual subsistence crops to capital-intensive long run commercial crops. Households could devote the economic times of its members for productive consumption like education. Not only that the above shift in cultivation to commercial crops made cash balances available within the household, which worked as the capital for obtaining education services. Simultaneously, education supply constraints came down considerably and third generation extensively benefited out of it. Along with it, the realization of the households in the economic risk of dependence on agriculture by their upcoming generation for subsistence pushed them out of the land in search of other employment avenues.

The role of invisible capital of education in the economic progress of the households can reasonably be summed up in the words of Schultz, (1988): "A final dimension of the adaptive response of the more educated farmer is his supply of family labour off-farm. In other words, the occupational mobility that education facilitates is also linked to dual employments, on and off-farm."

NOTES

1. Education is recognized as a fundamental entitlement. It can improve the freedom of individuals in many ways. Being educated itself is an achievement. Other than just being educated, it helps in getting jobs and making use of economic opportunities. Greater literacy and education can facilitate public discussion of social needs and encourage informal collective demands. The processes of schooling can have benefits even outside its explicitly aimed objectives, like reducing the incidence of child labour. Greater literacy and educational achievements have empowerment and distributive roles, since disadvantaged groups can increase their ability to resist oppression, to organize politically and to get fairer deal (Dreze and Sen, 1995). In this sense, access to basic education is a matter of basic right, universal life claim, which constitutes the very basis of decent living.

2. At present, there are about 40000 migrant families in the district of Kannur, from which it is calculated that during 1950s there may be around 4500 migrant households in the district, who constitute the population of our study.
3. For other points of difference between the two approaches see Mathur (1990).
4. The significance of expenditure choices for improving HD at macro level comparing Kenya and Malaysia is presented in Ranis, Stewart and Ramirez (2000).
5. Mayer's (2001) argument on the health of the grand parents give us further insight into the inter-linkages between family economics and HD. "healthier grand parents may also contribute to strengthening the economy of younger families, burdening young adults less at the time when they most need to invest in children."
6. See e.g., Rosenzweig and Schultz (1982); Wolfe and Behrman (1987): Barrera (1990) for further discussion on the health and education interaction.
7. In households whose members endure ill health and nutritional deficiency, it is plausible to suppose that productivity is below its potential level with existing stocks of capital and effective labour. The evidence doesn't suggest a rejection of the hypothesis that these factors can make a difference. (Also see, Wheeler, 1980 for a macro level analysis of the issue).
8. The importance of economic growth for raising resources to promote HD at macro level is illustrated by Ranis, Stewart and Ramirez (2000) comparing Botswana and Sudan.
9. See Mathur and Mamgain (2004) for the reasons for considering the HD attainments of the non-working members in the calculation of human capital content of an economy.
10. The terms casual labour and agricultural labour are used synonymously to mean the people whose major source of income is from their daily work either in the agricultural or non-agricultural sector. If an individual is simultaneously an agriculturist and also a CL, then his/her major source of income is accounted for deciding his occupation.

REFERENCES

Agnihotri C. S. (1991), "A Cross Cultural Comparative Study Between Tribals and Non-Tribals of First Generation of Traditional Learners in Relation to their Social Maturity and Educational Adjustment," Ph.D., Edu. Agra University.

Awasti, B. P. (1987), "A Study of Interrelationship Between Education of the ST and Their Socio-Economic Mobility," Independent Study, New Delhi, National Council of Educational Research and Training.

Barrera, A. (1990), "The Role of Maternal Schooling and its Interaction with Public Health Programmes in Child Health Production," *Journal of Development Economics*, 32 (1), 69-91.

Bhalla, S. (2002), "Imagine there is no Country: Poverty, Inequality and Growth in an Era of Globalisation,"Washington, DC: Institute for International Economics.

Chambers, Robert (1983), "Rural Development: Putting the Last First," Longman, 109-111.

Chen, S. and Ravallion, M. (2001), "How did the World's Poorest Fare in the 1990s?" *Review of Income and Wealth*, 47(3), 283-300.

Dollar, D. and Kraay, A. (2002), "Growth is Good for the Poor," *Journal of Economic Growth*, 7, 195-225.

Dreze, Jean and Sen, A. K. (1995), "Indian Economic Development and Social Opportunity," Oxford University Press, Delhi.

Krishna, Anirudh (2006), "Pathways Out of and into Poverty in 36 Villages of Andhra Pradesh, India", *World Development*, Vol. 34, No. 2, 271-288.

Mathur, Ashok (1990), "Human Capital, Spatial Disparities and Economic Development in India", *Manpower Journal*, Vol. XXVI, No. 3, Oct-December, 1-37.

Mathur, Asok and Mamgain, P. Rajendra (2004), "Human Capital Stocks, Their Level of Utilisation and Economic Development in India," *The Indian Journal of Labour Economics*, Vol. 47, No. 4, 655-676.

Mayer, David (2001), "The Long Term Impact of Health on Economic Growth in Latin America," *World Development*, Vol. 29, No. 6, 1025-1033.

Prais, S. J. (1955), "Measuring Social Mobility," *Journal of Royal Statistical Society*, Series A (General), Vol. 118, 56-66.

Ranis, Gustav (2004), "Human Development and Economic Growth," Center Discussion Paper, No.887, Economic Growth Center, Yale University, *http://www.econ.yale www. Edu/_egcenter / reseach.htm.*

Ranis, G; Stewart, F and Ramirez, A. (2000), "Economic Growth and Human Development," *World Development*, Vol. 28, No. 2, 197-219.

Rosenzweig, M. R. and Schultz, T. P. (1982), "Child Mortality and Fertility in Columbia: Individual and Community Effects," *Health Policy and Education*, 2, 305-318.

Saleena, N. J. (2005), "Small Scale Farmers in Kannur District in the 1990s: Socio-Economic Characteristics and Development Problems," in Mathew, K. S. Singh, Mahavir and Varkey, Joy, eds., *Migration in South India*, IRISH and MAKIAS, Shipra, Delhi, 159-165.

Schultz, Paul. T. (1988), "Education Investment and Returns," in Chenery, Hollis and Srinivasan, T. N., eds., *Handbook of Development Economics*, North Holland, Oxford, 542-632.

Timmer, C. P. (1997), "How well do the Poor Connect to the Growth Process?" CAER Discussion Paper No. 17, Harvard Institute for International Development, Cambridge, MA.

UNDP (1990), "Human Development Report 1990," New York University Press.

UNDP (1996), *Human Development Report*, New York University Press.

Wade R. H. (2004), "Is Globalisation Reducing Poverty and Inequality?" *World Development*, 32, 4, 567-589.

Wha Lee-Jong, 2005, "Economic Growth and Human Development in the Republic of Korea, 1945-1992," Occasional Paper 24, *http://hdr.undp.org/doc/publications/occasional_papers/ oc24aa.htm.*

Wheeler (1980), "Human Resource Development and Economic Growth in Developing Countries: A Simultaneous Model," World Bank Staff Working Paper, 407.

Wolfe, B. L. and Behrman, J. R. (1987), "Determinants of Women's Health Status and Health Care Utilization in a Developing Country: a Latent Variable Approach," *Review of Economics and Statistics*, 56.

Chapter-14

DALIT EDUCATION FOR THE UPLIFTMENT OF SOCIETY

M. C. Rosa

Education is a man making process. We have to equip our children to live in this century by enabling them to compete with their counter parts globally. So education is a strong instrument to uplift the society. The capability to deliver productive input to Society can best be developed by instilling knowledge, skills and literacy through education. The actualization of one's abilities helps, individuals not only in attaining gainful employment which help to ensure a sustainable means of lively hood, but also provides a continues flow of services to the society at large. The resultant reduction of deprivation assists considerably in empowerment and the process of human development.

The dynamic and responsive systems of education are in continuous process to assimilate the emerging expectations and aspirations of the people and society. The drastic changes occurring both domestically and internationally lead to educational reforms. Looking into the future, the government of India devoted itself to the educational mission as follows.

- To provide equal opportunity of education for all citizens.

- To provide resources and assistance necessary for unprivileged sections.

Education is a Continuous project for construction and reconstruction of society. It includes nation's industrialized activities, transport, mechanization of agriculture, communication system, information technology etc. It enables citizens to be on journey from learning to be to learning to become by organized and diversified interactions, it is an ascending process involving materialism and spiritualism.

On 26 January 1950, in the words of Dr. B.R. Ambedkar, we entered into a world of contradictions between our democratic politics and our feudal economic and social structure. Today, those same contradictions to which Ambedkar referred almost 60 years ago continue unabated. Instead of repudiating the outdated law of varnashram Dharma, 57years of democracy have only served to prove that caste hierarchy is still the law of the land, and not the democratic and socialistic principles enshrined in our constitution.

Our constitution stands for the ideals of equality and justice. Still every Society has its inequalities and disparities in one form or other. In India the scheduled castes are a stigmatized lot and on this account they suffer from a number of disabilities. Some of their disabilities are untouchability, low economic status, politically less powerful, low level of education and little chances of mobilization. Though legally or constitutionally they are no longer untouchables, in practice, many of them still bear that stigma. Education is the strong instrument for eradicating all these inequalities. For the proper development of the Society the downtrodden should be brought to the mainstream of the Society. Herein lies the significance of Dalit education.

The term dalit has been used to include all those people of different communities among the scheduled caste who were traditionally subjected to invidious discriminations on grounds of 'untouchablity' and categorized as untouchables, downtrodden, exterior cast, depressed classes or dalits.

If education is the key, then Dalits are lockedout, the Indian constitution mandates the state to Provide within ten years

(1950-1959) free, compulsory and universal education for all children up to 14 years, with special care and consideration given to promote the educational progress of SCs. Sixty years later illiteracy still plagues almost two thirds of dalits as compared to about one half of the general population.

Dalits are backward in general, in all areas and they are backward in the field of education in particular. There are two important points that need to be remembered in the context of the education of Dalit children. One is they have been traditionally denied opportunities for education. The lack of exposure of generations to skills of literacy, numeracy literature and other forms of knowledge considered desirable is likely to put them at a disadvantage. This would imply that such children are likely to require specific pedagogic support from the school system. This is integral to their right of education. The other point is that Dalit communities have been denied learning in the past specifically because of the caste to which they belong. There is hence need for special vigilance to see, that they do not continue to face Social discrimination within the school.

Article 46 of the constitution directs the states to promote educational and economic interestes of Dalits and other weaker sections. But it is a matter of concern that Dalits remained economically and educationally vulnerable even by the turn of the century. Along with the right to equality, the constitution of India provides separate and special provisions for the advancement of backward classes. It is often called compensatory discriminations, protective discrimination and discrimination in reverse. These provisions permit the govt to undertake special steps for the upliftment of backward classes. Article 15 (4), which was incorporated into the Indian constitution under the constitution act, 1951 declares: Nothing in Article 15 or in Clause (2) of Article 29 shall prevent the state from making any special provision for the advancement of any socially and educationally backward classes of citizen or for the scheduled cast and the scheduled tribes. For a long time it had been regarded that Article 15 (4) and 16 (4) are exceptions to Article 15 (1) and 16 (1). According to this view, the claims of the backward classes could be projected only through exceptional Clauses and not outside them.

Inspite of the welfare measures and special efforts taken by the govt, the progress of the educational development of untouchable was very low and slow. Not withstanding, special measures of the growth of Dalit education was very low in comparison with the literacy level of general population. The economic backwardness, social disabilities and consequent fear of oppression by the cast Hindus were major hurdles in the progress of Dalit education. So education is a very powerful instrument for emancipation. Educaiton helps to bridge wide disparity in social status, political acceptance and income distribution. This also plays a significant role in transforming the existing social order.

Education is a means through which one inculcates knowledge, values, skills and atitudes. It is a major tool for socio economic improvement of an individual and it also reduces social inequalities. So Education for All is the slogan for us.

Hence a study was conducted to analyze the drop out reasons of Dalit children.

OBJECTIVES OF THE STUDY

(1) To find out the reasons for the dropout of Dalit children.

(2) To determine the parental role in Dalit children's education.

(3) To offer suggestions to minimize dropouts of Dalit children.

METHODOLOGY IN BRIEF

The present study was intended to find out the reasons for the dropout of Dalit children. So survey method was adopted. Sample for the study was 50 drop out children, 20 teachers and 25 dalit parents from Iritty sub educational district. In the present investigation the method of sampling used was simple random sampling. Tools used for the study was questionnaire and interview schedule.

The selection of sample was made from Aralam tribal colony, Veerpad and Iritty.

PROCEDURE FOR DATA COLLECTION

In order to collect data for the present study, the investigator personally approached the colonies and schools. Precaution was taken to obtain best possible responses from the subjects. The purpose of the study was made clear to the respondents and necessary support was established to get true and valid information from the respondents.

ANALYSIS AND INTERPRETATION OF DATA

The data collected showed that the rate of dropouts in kannur district is numerically significant. The girls dropout rate is more than the boys dropout rate. The rate of dropouts is more in government schools than in private ones.

The reasons given by the dropout children, teachers and parents are the following.

- Financial Problem.
- Domestic work including in the care of infants.
- Prolonged illness of the child.
- Continuous failure in the same class.
- Unhealthy School Experience.
- Influence of mass media, Cinema.
- Negative attitude of teachers.
- New revised curriculum, lack of books, uniform etc.
- Lack of interest in studies.
- Inability of Parents to meet the educational needs of the childe.
- Alcoholism and drug addiction.

The most significant variable relating to drop out is financial problem and incapacity of parents to meet the educational needs of the child, such as expenses for books, pencils, pen etc. It was noticed that the Dalit welfare office was supplying financial aid at irregular intervals. Other variables causing school dropout was continuous failure in the same class.

Another major reason cited for drop-out is the lack of child's interest in studies. The child became less and less punctual in his school attendance and home assignments, grew careless about examination and felt more comfortable at home than in School. It was found that parents of Dalit children had low motivation, which was evident from their low educational aspirations.

It was interesting to observe that the School teachers came to know about the drop-out decision of the child at a later stage in most of the cases.

In India, Dalits are among the educationally most deprived sections. A survey conducted by the National council of Applied economic Research reveals that in the mid 1990's only 41.5 per cent of Dalit in rural India were literate and 63.5 per cent of children in the 6-14 age group had been enrolled in Schools at a certain point of time. Compared to the general population, the progress of Schooling among Dalit children has also been slow.

POVERTY AS DETERRENT

The 1986 National policy on education envisaged Universal enrolment of all Dalit children in the 6-11 age group and 75 per cent enrolment in the 11-14 age group by 1990. The District Primary Education Programme in the 1993 stressed the need for access, participation and achievement of children from marginalized groups. The sarva Shiksha Abhiyan, which came into effect in 2000, emphasized involvement of Daliits in the ownership of school committees, setting up of alternative schooling facilities and monitoring attendance and retention of Dalit children. However, according to the National Commission for SC and ST, the most important cause for non-development of SC/STS is non allocation of resources for their development on a priority. It may be recalled that until the Sixth plan only 0.52 per cent of the plan out lay was allocated as special central assistance for the uplift of Dalits, tribes and other backward classes.

The censes data of 2001 clearly indicates that some states require special attention because their literacy status is below that of the state average and the female literacy rate is also very low. A clear problem area is the education of girls in the age group 11 upwards, who have never enrolled in schools. They need specially designed and planned education programs to enable them to enlist and complete their education. Non-grade, group based, pedagogic practices, bridge –materials in a self learning mode allowing transition and completion at learner pace would enormously increase the chances of these children who tend to form the bulk of the vulnerable category of dropout or never enrolled.

From the above study it was found that economic backwardness of Dalits is a dominant factor underlying drop-out incidence. Other factors of varying significance can be listed as uncongenial School atmosphere, domestic exigencies, absence of involvement on the part of parents as well as children in the School activities and unfavorable influences of caste and community.

All these factors singly or in combination, seem to generate an atmosphere in which the schooling of the Dalit Child becomes virtually impossible. Apathy of parents or vagrancy of the child may be the result of poverty conditions. Keeping this in view it was considered necessary to perceive the situation in its totality.

WEST BENGAL'S CASE

Pratichi's Survey report on West Bengal's Primary Education has also mentioned that "75 per cent of teachers belonging to higher and middle class believe that children of ST & SC communities are less intelligence and motivated than their upper cast counter part". The report has also exposed the class character of the villages in the state.

At a time when the gap between commitment to "Education for all" and participation of dalits in the fulfillment of the programme remains large, the role of the state and the political will should be strengthened.

As per general perception, the schooling system offers the Dalit children an opportunity, an equal terms with others, to gain knowledge, and enable them to rise in socio economic status. It allows them to learn and develop along with other caste children, to see and imbibe values of higher communities, the experience of and exposure to which was not available to their parents and grand parents. In short, therefore, education can be defined as a great human experiment in community interaction, a process of constant learning's. Therefore dropping out underscores an end of a potentially fruitful adventure, school drop-out indicates a withdrawal from a system which could eventually render a most valuable support to one's development. So the authorities and teachers should give great care for the education of Dailt children.

SUGGESTIONS

- Considering the low level of literacy of Dailt parents, Adult education programmes should be properly planned and implemented.
- The study shows that poor financial condition of the parents which needed children's help in household and agricultural work is an important factor keeping children away from education. In order to encourage the Dalit children to attend the school some attractive schemes, such as earn and learn scheme, for the Dalit children should be introduced in the school.
- The parents and Dalit students are not much aware about higher and professional education. There is a need to start the career guidance and counseling centers in every school.
- Specialized teacher education programmers directed towards the preparation of teachers and administrations are needed for Dalit education.
- More hostel facilities need to be provided to enable the students coming from long distance for better utilization of the educational opportunities.
- A national charter of children ensuring that no child remains illiterate, hungry or lacks medical care should be instituted.
- Girls education should be viewed as a major intervention for breaking the vicious inter-generational cycle of gender and socioeconomic disadvantages.

- Steps should be taken to widen the scope and the spectrum of child development services with necessary interventions related to empowerment of women and children, families and communities through effective convergence and coordination of various sectoral efforts and services.

CONCLUSION

The study was made as an attempt to explore the reasons of dropouts of Dalit Children. Many of the Dalit Children are found to discontinue education. Hence steps may be taken to make aware of the importance of education among Dalit children. Financial difficulty is found to be a major reason for dropout. So government and voluntary organizations should take initiative to organize programmes for the improvements of the financial status of Dalit. Educational practices should be made interesting and attractive. Awareness Programmes may be organized for parents.

The ideal of Dalit education has sound basis from the legal and humanitarian angles. No Society can afford to do without the investment of its capital in every one of its members. Real Social, economic and political progress cannot take place without it. The kothari commission rightly points out, "Society that values Social Justice and is anxious to improve the lot of the common man and cultivates all available talent must ensure progressive equality to all sections of the population. This is the only guarantee for building up of an egalitarian and human society in which the exploitation of the weak will be minimized." The children of a county should be given right knowledge, essential skills, desirable attitudes, individual and social values on which the progress of the nation depends. Disciplined conduct, Social co-operation, and good citizen ship are essential for the development of society. At this Juncture a dynamic government and creative educational system is needed to strengthen the Dalit education for the upliftment of Society.

REFERENCES

Teacher policies in a new context (Paris Organisation for Economic Corporation and Development).

Digest of Education Statistics (1982), Washington, D.C. National Center for Education Statistics.

Good. V carter (2006), How to do Research in Education, New Delhi, Indigo Books.

Seshadri C. (2003), Equality of Educational Opportunity Some Issues in Indian Education.

Aggrawal, J. C. (2006), Teacher Education in a Developing Society, New Delhi, Vikas Publishing House Pvt. Ltd.

Aggrawal, D. D. (2005), Problems of Quality and Excellence in Education, Sarup & Sons, New Delhi.